Neal Whitten's
No-Nonsense Advice
for Successful Projects

Neal Whitten's No-Nonsense Advice for Successful Projects

Neal Whitten, PMP

///
MANAGEMENTCONCEPTS
Vienna, Virginia

ʃʃʃ
MANAGEMENTCONCEPTS
8230 Leesburg Pike, Suite 800
Vienna, VA 22182
(703) 790-9595
Fax: (703) 790-1371
www.managementconcepts.com

Printed in the United States of America

Library of Congress Cataloging-in-Publication Data

Whitten, Neal.
  Neal Whitten's no-nonsense advice for successful projects /
Neal Whitten.
    p. cm.
  Includes index.
  ISBN 1-56726-155-8 (pbk.)
    1. Project management. 1. Title: No-nonsense advice for
  successful projects. II. Title.

HD69.P75W494 2004
658.4'04—dc22

2004054698

About the Author

Neal Whitten is a popular speaker, mentor, trainer, consultant, and author in the areas of project management and employee development. He has more than 30 years of front-line project management, software engineering, and human resource experience.

In his 23 years at IBM, Neal held both project leader and management positions. He managed the development of numerous software products, including operating systems, business and telecommunications applications, and special-purpose programs and tools. For three years, he also managed and was responsible for providing independent assessments on dozens of software projects for an assurance group. Neal is president of The Neal Whitten Group, which he founded shortly after leaving IBM in 1993.

Neal is the author of five books, including: *The Enter*Prize *Organization: Organizing Software Projects for Accountability and Success* (Project Management Institute); *Managing Software Development Projects: Formula for Success, Second Edition* (John Wiley & Sons); and *Becoming an Indispensable Employee in a Disposable World* (Prentice Hall).

Neal is a frequent presenter and keynote speaker at conferences, seminars, workshops, and special events. He has developed and instructed dozens of project management, software development, and personal development classes, and presented to thousands of people from across hundreds of companies, institutions, and public organizations. He has written more than 50 articles for professional magazines and is a contributing editor of PMI®'s *PM Network* magazine.

The services of The Neal Whitten Group include trouble-shooting projects, performing project reviews, training organizations in the practical application of project management principles, and training all members of a project in the adoption of an effective, productive work culture. Popular workshops include *The Essentials of Software/IT Project Management: Best Practices*; *Leadership, Accountability . . . and YOU*; *Project Review Mentoring Workshop*; *Role Clarification Workshop*; and a workshop based on this book.

Neal is a member of PMI® and has been a certified Project Management Professional (PMP) since 1992. He can be reached through his website: *www.nealwhittengroup.com*.

Dedication

As John Donne, English poet and clergyman, fittingly stated, "No man is an island, entire of itself; every man is a piece of the continent." We are all interconnected and interdependent. I dedicate this book to all peoples of the world who—with boldness and courage—*think for themselves and question their actions* . . . and move humanity toward mutual respect, dignity, and peace. When we leave, we all owe to one another—to humankind—to leave the woodpile higher than when we arrived.

I also dedicate this book to Matt, Katie, and Logan; Jen, Stephanie; Kiara, Talon; Martin, Caroline; Ashley, Kent, and George; Sean, Jesse, and Emily . . . humanity's hope. And especially to Barbara.

Table of Contents

Preface

Successful projects don't just happen—they are made to happen. This book goes beyond the basics of project management and reveals the best practices that make the difference between leading consistently successful projects and playing the victim with troubled projects.

There are plenty of books on the market that do commendable jobs of presenting the basics of project management. As Paul Harvey, popular American radio personality, would say, this book offers "the rest of the story."

What makes this book different? I have written this book in response to being asked questions like this many, many times over the years:

> *Neal, can you help me? I know you have been in the business of project management for over 30 years. I know you have captured a wealth of information on what to do and what not to do. I need the wisdom you have acquired, but don't want the personal scars you have picked up along the way. Can you help me leverage your knowledge, experience, and skills into leading consistently successful projects?*

This is the book that I wish I'd had when I was a rookie project manager—or a seasoned project manager. It shares my favorite best practices for many different situations that fall into the general categories of:

- Leadership
- Soft skills
- Roles and responsibilities
- Project initiation
- Project planning
- Project execution and control
- Project closeout
- Promoting the advancement of project management beyond your projects.

This book is not about theories or history. Rather, it is my best shot at giving project managers the answers they want and need. It is a how-to, real-world, no-nonsense, no-fluff or beating-around-the-bush practical guide to leading consistently successful projects.

Some of the ideas and actions presented go against conventional wisdom, but may become mainstream over the coming years. Many ideas will appear to be common sense—once you understand them. But certainly many are not commonly practiced, although they should be.

This book is specifically targeted to project managers, but can be invaluable to anyone in a leadership position, from the troops on the ground to senior managers and executives. It is for newbies as well as old-timers in the project management profession.

This book offers you insights from a veteran project management practitioner, mentor, author, speaker, and instructor. It collects the experiences and wisdom of thousands of people from across hundreds of companies and projects. The lessons learned are reduced to a simple format for ease in learning and applying them to your projects. The lessons will give you a decisive competitive edge in leading projects and working with stakeholders.

Many people who attend my workshops, which revolve around these leading-edge best practices, remark that the workshops are like a gate. Once you open the gate and pass through—that is, once you are acquainted with the lessons and learn how to apply them—you cannot go back to your old ways. You cannot plead ignorance of what to do or what caused your project to suffer. You will know better.

It is my hope that this book will likewise serve as a gate. Once you have studied the collection of best practices in this book—and taken a personal position within your belief system on each—your behavior, decisions, and actions will become more deliberate, effortless, and natural as you lead your project team.

If you are already a highly effective project manager, this book can serve as a reminder—*a great booster shot*—that encourages you to continue to make a difference. If you are among the majority of project managers who are striving to become more effective, this book can help you reach your goals. I wish you the best.

Now, go make a difference!

Neal Whitten

Acknowledgments

I have been most fortunate to work alongside many talented, skilled, and seasoned professionals over the years. As a work in progress, I continue to acquire valuable skills and knowledge from the thousands of people and dozens of companies, conferences, and organizations with whom and which I work with each year. No one becomes proficient at their craft without help. I am most grateful.

I especially would like to thank the following people for their dedicated, candid, and significant feedback and support through their reviews of the manuscript: Bill Arcudi, Tim Arthur, Judy Maus, Don Norton, and Gary Sutton.

I also would like to thank the following people for their comments, suggestions, and support as the manuscript evolved into the book: JoAnn DeWick, Anthony Gaiter, Julie Griffin, Daun Hugi, Sandy Jenkins, Klint Kneuppel, Mark LaLomia, Dan Lynes, Mike Martin, Janiene Pape, Jim Wooten, and Bob Berry and his staff.

And finally I am grateful to the highly professional staff at Management Concepts for their invaluable support and guidance during the manuscript development, editing, and production. I would especially like to acknowledge the special contributions of Myra Strauss and Jack Knowles.

Thank you all!

Introduction

Successful projects don't just happen—they are made to happen. You make them happen: Your leadership, your behavior, your expectations, and your guidance set the foundation and pace of what occurs. Of course, you and your project cannot be successful without the contributions of your team, but it is your leadership that sets the course and ensures that the final destination is reached.

Have you ever seen a project made up of members that, individually, have impressive résumés of talent, knowledge, and experience? Most of us have been on such a team. Collectively, a team this seasoned and talented should be able to pull off just about any project. You can't help but think how, with a crackerjack team like this, the project is bound to be successful. Then the project fails. Schedules slide, budgets overrun, quality suffers, morale plummets, and the client relationship sours.

What happened? Most likely, the leader of the project—the project manager—failed to demonstrate the leadership attributes required to bring the team together and direct it to operate as a deliberate, cohesive unit.

Many of us are quick to blame our ineffectiveness—our failures—on others. Don't go there. It's not about the ability of those around you to lead. It's about *your* ability to lead, despite what is happening around you.

Let's look a bit closer at this notion of leadership. Leadership is so important to a project or company that I would argue that a company's most important asset is its leaders. It's not its people, profit, products and services, clients, intellectual property, brand, marketing, cash flow, productivity, quality, creativity, or genius. It's its leadership.

> **Leadership, simply stated, is the art of getting things done through people.**

If a company has mediocre leaders and the best employees, it will be a mediocre force in its industry. In contrast, a company with the best leaders and mediocre employees will be a formidable force in its industry. Yes, formidable. It's all about leadership. Interestingly, companies with the best leaders don't have mediocre employees. It's natural for employees to rise to the occasion and become the best while supporting the leaders they believe in.

How does a project manager become an effective leader? The following two steps sound trivial, but, of course, they aren't:

- Know how to behave.
- Behave that way.

Know How to Behave

To date, how have you learned how to behave? On the job? Trial and error? Classroom training? Magazines and books? Professional conferences? All of these are valuable ways to learn, but they can be tedious and often unfulfilling investments in gaining the experience and mental tool set necessary for proficiency. What is often lacking in learning venues is twofold: (1) a genuine foundation in the psychology of leadership, and (2) the direct application of this behavior by the great teachers of any craft—the mentors.

What makes a mentor so valuable? A mentor has been there, done that, messed up, learned from the experience, and moved on. A mentor is expected to be an expert in the area that he or she is mentoring. This person should have a broad base of experience in the subject field to be able to promote the most effective techniques. A mentor can save the mentee hours, days, even years in learning lessons that can make all the difference with project success. There is simply no better way to learn the application of a profession—a craft—than with a mentor by your side.

My objective is to offer you mentoring guidance in achieving consistently successful projects. Because I am not able to reach you in person, I am using this book as a means to help mentor you, the reader—to be there with you when you are faced with a problem but are not sure of the next step to take. For those of you reading this who are already highly effective project managers, this book will serve as reinforcement of what you have already learned and practiced. I welcome all of you and trust that the messages will help you achieve your goals.

Many hundreds of people have asked me over the years for the "golden nuggets" of knowledge that lead to successful projects. I have included in this book a plethora of these nuggets that have served me and countless others exceptionally well. Within these pages is a treasure chest of best practices that show you *how* to behave.

Behave That Way

A project manager becomes an effective leader not just by knowing *how* to behave, but also by actually *behaving* that way. What makes a project manager behave a certain way? The answer comes mostly from within each of us. In this book, I attempt to show you that you choose how to think, what to believe, and how to behave. No one chooses for you. This "sense of self" is difficult for some people to accept. But I will remind you throughout this book that it is your choice—and that your choice will make a difference in your success and in your team's success.

You can play victim and list all the reasons why you are unable to consistently lead successful projects. Although occasionally there are reasons beyond your control, they are so few and far between that it is not a path I want us to take. I want you to focus on what you have influence and control over—which is most things, most times. Look at the people around you that you admire most, people who seem to be able to make things happen. It is not luck or genetics. It's choice.

Insights

I have been associated with many hundreds of projects over the past 30-plus years. My association has been through directly managing those projects, mentoring others who are managing them, and performing project reviews on them. The projects have varied in size from involving a handful of stakeholders to involving thousands of stakeholders. They have varied in duration from weeks to months to years. Through these projects and the many people I have worked alongside, I have had tremendous numbers of opportunities to experiment, learn, and grow in the project management profession.

I have a big "secret" to share. I have messed up many times over the years, more so in the beginning of my career. I am a work in progress—as we all are. I almost always have an answer, but sometimes there may be a better one. I have a lot of scars. I also have had a lot of successes. I believe the scars have been more valuable to my effectiveness and career than the successes. (My bosses and clients might not agree.)

This book offers you insights and best practices from a veteran project management practitioner, mentor, author, speaker, and instructor. It collects the experiences and wisdom of thousands of people from across hundreds of companies and projects. The lessons will give you a decisive competitive edge in leading projects and working with stakeholders.

What do I mean by *best practices*? I will reveal the best way to perform in many different situations. A best practice is simply the best way I know based on my many journeys and contacts. I may know other practices that are just as effective as what I promote, but I am not going to give you 10 ways to do something; I'm going to give you my preferred way. Although I do not expect many of these best practices to change significantly, I reserve the right to change my mind next year—and beyond—as I continue to learn and grow and seek out best practices.

Who Will Benefit from This Book

This book is geared primarily toward project managers, and is written as much for seasoned veterans as for rookies. However, the book also targets project leaders, program managers, project sponsors, product managers, resource managers, functional managers, senior managers and executives, quality control personnel, and anyone and everyone else who aspires to become a consistently effective project manager or leader. In fact, the book has a wealth of information—including life skills—for all members of a project or organization that will help them become more valuable employees.

Helpful Information to Know
before You Read This Book

The book was designed so that it does not need to be read from beginning to end. Many people will read the chapters of the book that they have the most immediate interest in and will briefly acquaint themselves with what's available in the remaining portions. As the need arises, the book can be revisited as a reference as well as for personal reinforcement and encouragement. If you wish that you had a mentor readily available and could walk down the hallway or pick up a phone for advice and support whenever needed, then my objective is for this book to help you through many of those moments. Even if you have a mentor, it can be useful to reference the book *before* a discussion with your mentor.

Many lessons are revealed throughout each chapter, with the key lessons highlighted by a shaded box. This technique allows you to focus quickly on the most notable points being made.

Chapters end with a question-and-answer section. The questions are those commonly asked of me by members of workshops, during consulting engagements, and when mentoring about these concepts and how to apply them. These questions are not already answered in the main body of the text.

This book brings together some of my previous writings and articles in addition to presenting new areas of information. For example, some topics discussed in this book have been excerpted from one or more of my other books in an abridged format. Moreover, I sometimes refer you to those books if they offer more detail on a topic. Those books and publishers are:

- *The EnterPrize Organization: Organizing Software Projects for Accountability and Success,* by Neal Whitten. Copyright © 2000 by Project Management Institute, Inc. Copyright and all rights reserved. Material from this publication has been reproduced with the permission of PMI®.

- *Managing Software Development Projects: Formula for Success, Second Edition*, by Neal Whitten. Copyright © 1995 by Wiley Publishing, Inc. This material is used by permission of John Wiley & Sons, Inc.

To gain the most benefit from this book, I ask that you read it with an open mind. I believe in the worthiness and benefit of every concept, behavior, action, and technique that I have included. These ideas have worked for me and for hundreds of others that I have worked closely with or mentored. However, some of my ideas go against today's conventional wisdoms; moreover, some people may not easily accept some of the ideas because they may feel that their circumstances are unique. In rare cases, that may be true. However, these ideas can work almost all the time—if you maintain an open mind and apply them appropriately.

How This Book Is Organized

The book is presented in eight parts consisting of multiple chapters, each of which is relatively short for easy reading and quick reference. The Project Management Institute's (PMI®) five process groups (initiating, planning, executing, controlling, and closing) are represented by Parts Three through Six.

Part One: Leadership, Soft Skills, and You. The effectiveness of a project manager—a leader—is about the mastery of both hard and soft skills. Hard skills are mostly process- and procedure-oriented, such as the mechanics of planning, tracking, and risk assessment. Hard skills are easier for most people to learn and apply than soft skills.

Soft skills are more people- and behavior-oriented, such as leading, directing, nurturing, enabling, communicating, negotiating, mitigating—in other words, *making things happen*. It is the soft skills that are so critical for a leader in getting things done through people. They are the skills that will motivate a team to succeed, that will inspire dedication and drive. Fittingly, this book begins by focusing on the very valuable and necessary soft side of leadership.

Part Two: Roles and Responsibilities. The roles and responsibilities of the project manager, resource manager, and project sponsor—three huge power players on the project scene—are defined. Also, an age-old question is answered: "How technical must a project manager be?"

Part Three: Project Initiation. Part Three shows you how to learn from past project mistakes and apply those lessons going forward. It also describes how culture training classes are key in promoting an effective project culture.

Part Four: Project Planning. Part Four reveals several best practices for the planning phase of a project, including the importance of providing clients what they *need* rather than what they *want*, the effect of multitasking on productivity, the application of the contingency buffer, and the truth about scope creep.

Part Five: Project Execution and Control. Part Five offers best practices for the execution and control phases of a project. Key topics include: how to set control points, monitor project performance/variance, and manage problems that are heading out of control; how to manage to a project's top three problems; how to treat project members who have different perspectives and points of view; how to determine what you expect from others; how to escalate issues to closure; and how to capitalize on the value of planning with the "S-shape curve 50/70 rule."

Part Six: Project Closeout. Part Six discusses how to perform post-project reviews—an activity of enormous benefit but one that is frequently overlooked or weakly conducted.

Part Seven: Promoting the Advancement of Project Management beyond Your Projects. Up to this point, this book focuses on how project managers—and related leaders—can be far more effective in their day-to-day activities. Part Seven shows project managers what they can do outside of their primary domains of responsibility to promote the advancement of project management across their organizations.

Part Eight: Some Final Thoughts. I believe that everyone has the capacity to be a consistently successful project manager. All the attributes of a successful project manager can be learned and practiced if you choose to do so. Believe you can make a difference . . . and you will!

Glossary. A glossary of terms defines key concepts.

As Henry Ford said, "Whether you think you can or you think you can't, either way you are right." I can open the gate for you, but I cannot pass through it for you. I can share thoughts and ideas, but I cannot receive and process them for you. You—and only you—have control over your belief system and whether and how you choose to modify it. This book has been written for you. I hope it serves you well!

PART ONE

Leadership, Soft Skills, and You

We are always on the lookout for that *silver bullet* in project management—that one thing that will magically ensure success in our efforts. The closest thing I've found is the power to apply passion, boldness, and focus to your duties. It's not about the ability of those around you to lead—it's about your ability to lead despite what is happening around you.

CHAPTER 1

Mind
Your Own
Business

When you start work each day, do *not* focus on moving your company forward. If possible, do *not* focus on your company at all. Yes, you read correctly.

Instead, channel your energies toward successfully completing your assignments—your *domain of responsibility*. If everyone in your company focused on his or her domain of responsibility, the company would do just fine. In fact, your company would probably be more successful than it is today.

> *Do what's best for your domain of responsibility, because that is ultimately what's best for your company.*

Your domain of responsibility includes all responsibilities and commitments that fall within the scope of your assignment. In short, it is the area for which you are accountable. Whether you are a one-person project, a member of a 10-person project, or a member of a 1,000-person project, your project's success—and, therefore, your company's success—is directly related to how well you perform within your domain of responsibility.

> *There is a direct relationship between the success of the parts and the success of the whole.*

If you reach outside your domain of responsibility and attempt to fix or improve something there, I view this as *extra credit* in terms of your actions and your performance. I am not a proponent of pursuing extra credit if it is at the sacrifice of successfully completing your commitments within your domain of responsibility. It has been my experience that if you focus superbly within your domain of responsibility, your contributions and overall career will shine brightly—even without the extra credit.

> *It usually is ill-advised to pursue extra credit at the sacrifice of your own responsibilities and commitments within your domain of responsibility.*

It is important to understand the difference between your domain of responsibility and extra credit. Let's look at an example:

> *You are a project manager of a new project. You also are a member of an organization that has many projects managed concurrently. The organization does not have well-defined project management best practices that you can adopt for your project. Therefore, you (or others at your direction) must define practices to be followed on your project. The pursuit of these tasks is not extra credit because you need well-defined practices to support the success of your project.*

However, the project management practices you define should be created only for your project. They should not be designed and documented to become institutionalized for other projects to use. If they are prepared in a manner to be used beyond your project, then these actions are examples of extra credit. Performing the extra credit would require that much more time be invested, at the expense of your project.

In the course of performing your commitments, any action that you feel you must perform to complete your commitments successfully becomes part of your domain of responsibility. It is often easy to shrug off being accountable for actions that you require from others, but if these actions are required to complete your commitments successfully, it becomes your duty to ensure that they occur.

Your domain of responsibility includes any activities and actions that are necessary to support the success of your commitments.

Examples of items that are in a project manager's domain of responsibility, but often are weakly pursued, include:

- Seeking out a project sponsor and establishing an effective relationship
- Adopting/defining project management best practices for your project
- Ensuring client participation
- Obtaining commitments from others and then holding them accountable
- Escalating project-related issues to achieve their timely closure
- Enforcing effective change control to manage scope creep
- Defending the *right* project plan to the project sponsor, executives, or client
- Boldly driving your project to a successful completion, not waiting for someone else to do it for you.

Focusing on your domain of responsibility doesn't mean that you don't care about your company. Your actions demonstrate the opposite. The success of your assignments strengthens the success of your company. If you care about the success of your company, then care about the success of your domain of responsibility. Focus on you and your team members being accountable for your respective domains of responsibility and the rest will follow.

If you want to turn a company around, then turn around the thinking of the members of that company.

Let's Talk: Questions & Answers

Q1.1   *As project manager of a project with 10 members, are you saying that my domain of responsibility includes the performance of those 10 members?*

A1.1   Yes, for starters. As the project manager, your domain of responsibility not only includes the performance of the 10 members *as it relates to your project*, but it includes perhaps dozens of other people as well. For example, if the successful launch, execution, and delivery of your project includes working with many other people, departments, divisions, companies, vendors, and contractors, then all of these people and the relationships you have with them are included in your domain of responsibility. Anything that can impact the success of your project is within your domain of responsibility.

Q1.2   *As a project manager, does my domain of responsibility include other projects on which my project members may also be working?*

A1.2   No, not directly, because you are not responsible or accountable for the success of those projects. Your focus must be on your project. You do, of course, care that your project members meet their commitments on your project. Your objective is to do whatever is necessary to help them be successful on your project. That could include working with the project managers of other projects that your project members also work on so that you can more carefully balance the workload of your members to help ensure their success on your project.

> *A project manager's domain of responsibility is almost always far broader than first assumed.*

Q1.3   *What if another project is in trouble and its project manager seeks help from me and from members of my project? Should I help?*

A1.3   If anyone ever asks for two hours of your time or two hours of time from any of your project members, you say "yes." Why? Because as a mature professional you should almost always be able to find two hours to help someone. However, if the request for help would cause your project to miss its external commitments, then you must say "no." A project manager does not have the authority to change externally committed dates; only the project sponsor or client has that authority.

However, as a good companywide team player, after saying "no," you can then suggest, if appropriate, that the two of you go to a person or committee that has the authority to prioritize projects. Then, whatever the outcome, you willingly comply because it's in the best interests of the business. The person or committee that makes the decision has the power of authority over the two projects; in other words, that committee's domain of responsibility may include managing the portfolio of projects in which these two projects are included.

Q1.4   *Isn't it good for my career to go after "extra credit," as you call it?*

A1.4   The first best thing that you can do for your career is to focus on your domain of responsibility and perform well in that arena. If everyone in a company focused on consistently performing successfully within their domains of responsibility, the company would benefit greatly. If you choose to go after extra credit, be careful that you do not sacrifice the successful completion of commitments that fall within your domain of responsibility. So, yes, extra credit can be a good thing for your career—but only if your domain of responsibility is well serviced.

By the way, if the "extra credit" becomes part of your overall duties, it no longer is extra credit. It now falls within your domain of responsibility.

CHAPTER 2

Are You
a Benevolent Dictator?
You Should Be!

 Nothing strengthens the judgment or quickens the conscience like independent responsibility."

—Elizabeth Cady Stanton,
American 19th century women's rights leader

In running a country, democracy (more specifically, a republic) appears to be the best thing going to date. However, in running a business or project, my experience has shown that the *benevolent dictator* style is the most effective.

Micromanaging, consensus management, and democratic rule all can be highly ineffective leadership styles.

A benevolent dictator leads by actively soliciting information and opinions from project members and others—listens, then demonstrates the leadership, courage, and boldness to personally make the right decision and stand accountable for that decision.

A benevolent dictator also holds his or her subordinates accountable for their decisions; they, in turn, hold their subordinates accountable for their decisions; and so on. In other words, everyone is encouraged and expected to make the decisions that affect their own domain of responsibility—and to stand by them.

When defining a benevolent dictator, I am not talking about *micromanaging*. Micromanaging occurs when a leader chooses to make decisions for anyone and everyone within the leader's influence. The micromanaging "leadership" style is highly offensive; it neither teaches the importance nor capitalizes on the promise of accountability. It should only be used in rare instances, for very short periods of time, and in cases where the reason for doing so is clearly understood.

Those who are micromanaged lose their deepest passion and sense of accountability.

Many organizations and projects attempt to operate on either consensus or democratic rule. Consensus, which has been overhyped for years, can be an ineffective tool in managing teams and projects. Consensus is obtaining buy-in from a team by adjusting the final decision to a position with which everyone can live. For other than the most highly trained teams, consensus often causes the most important decisions to be compromised, i.e., watered down. In an attempt to satisfy all team members so that they buy into the team's decision, the solution is often non-optimal and, frankly, is often without vision and personal commitment. Consensus can drive mediocrity.

What's that? You say there *is* personal commitment in a consensus-driven team because everyone had a say in the decision? Yes, everyone had an *opportunity* to speak their mind, but my experience shows that many don't speak up or they are quick to compromise or live with someone else's proposal—even if they feel it is weak. It is not unusual for the most reserved and shy members of a consensus-forming team—often those not heard from—to be among those who have the best ideas. Moreover, many members of a group consensus don't feel personally committed. They hide behind the facade of the team.

> *Good business is not about everyone agreeing on an outcome; it's about achieving the best outcome.*

What do I mean by *personal commitment*? Personal commitment is when *you*, personally, are charged with making a decision and then *you*, personally, are held accountable for the outcome of that decision. Teams cannot feel this level of accountability; only individuals can.

> *Individuals, not teams, are charged with accountability.*

What about using the democratic voting process? Projects or organizations that consistently reach decisions by democratic rule frequently can be more ineffective than those reaching decisions through consensus. Why? Because the majority vote is usually enough to lock in a decision. Unfortunately for the bigger picture—say a project—everyone with a vote to cast is looking out after his or her own personal interests or the personal interests of the team he or she represents. Consequently, the right business decision for the *project* can easily be overlooked or dismissed.

> *Reaching a project-related decision through a democratic process often leads to a solution that may not be in the best interest of the project.*

You might be asking about now, "If the benevolent dictator concept is so effective, then why don't more leaders adopt this style of leading?" The biggest reason is that to be a benevolent dictator we have to make decisions that will, at times, be unpopular. Many of us have a hard time making decisions that are criticized by others. In fact, the primary reason project managers fail is because they are too soft and have difficulty making the tougher decisions. (See Chapter 8, Are You Too Soft?)

I often hear project managers and resource managers say they cannot adopt the benevolent dictator approach because they have a serious shortage of project members and employees with the good business sense—the leadership skills—to make the tough decisions expected of a benevolent dictator. I strongly disagree! For most of us, I believe we do have the

> *The No. 1 reason why leaders fail is that they repeatedly demonstrate behavior that is too soft to be consistently effective.*

people we need; they just haven't been trained properly. After all, they watch how we manage and imitate our styles.

All of us need to be trained, coached, and mentored in the skills and behaviors that make for the most effective leaders. Nearly everyone will rise to the expectations that we set for them, provided that we constructively nurture them along the way. If you want your project to be run like a business where decisions are made based on what's best for the business, and you want your project members to consistently take accountability for their own actions, then teach and encourage the powerful benevolent dictator concept at all levels of a project and organization. It's good leadership and it's good business!

Let's Talk: Questions & Answers

Q2.1   *Why do you say that everyone on a project should behave as a benevolent dictator? Doesn't this role belong exclusively to the project manager?*

A2.1   Let's look at a project of 15 members. There is one project manager, say four team leaders, and 10 team members. The project manager and the team leaders operate as benevolent dictators within their domains of responsibility. They have project members assigned to work under their direction. They are held accountable for the performance of their teams and the quality and timeliness of their deliverables. However, the 10 team members, although not leaders of other people, find themselves working with many people from across the core team or from outlying areas such as the human resources department, contractors, vendors, procurement, and IT. The team members are accountable for their own performance and for the plethora of decisions that they must make on a day-to-day basis. They, too, are benevolent dictators within their own domains of responsibility. When this technique is in place and is working well, it complements teamwork, not distracts from it.

> *The benevolent dictator is not an elitist position. Everyone on a project must think and behave as a benevolent dictator within their own domain of responsibility.*

Q2.2   *You say that micromanaging should only be used in rare instances, for very short periods of time. When is it okay to micromanage?*

A2.2   Say a project is in deep trouble. It has no project manager or had a highly ineffective project manager who has been relieved of his or her duties. The newly assigned project manager may need to direct activities on a day-to-day basis until the project can be replanned, roles and responsibilities are clearly understood across the project team, and key processes such as change control and routine tracking meetings are underway.

Another example is when a person is weak at performing his or her duties and another person must specifically and closely direct and oversee the actions of the ineffective performer.

Q2.3 *Are you saying that consensus should never be used and should always yield to the benevolent dictator approach?*

A2.3 If a team can reach consensus and the decision is truly the best business decision, then the outcome is fine. However, the project manager should not be satisfied with a solution that everyone can live with if that solution is not the best business solution. The project manager should have the goal of the team reaching consensus, even if that means planting "seeds" throughout a team discussion and allowing others credit for the seeded ideas. However, as a general rule, if consensus cannot be reached, the project manager should not hesitate to ensure that the best business decision is chosen, even if that means not everyone is happy with the outcome.

There is no limit to what a man can do or where he can go if he doesn't mind who gets the credit."
—Ronald Reagan, 40th President of the United States

Q2.4 *Won't a team reaching consensus more likely come up with a better solution than any one person can, including the project manager?*

A2.4 Go back to the definition of a benevolent dictator. The benevolent dictator "actively solicits information and opinions from . . . others." This means that a project manager recognizes that, more times than not, the collective knowledge/experience/ skills of the team surpass that of the project manager. The project manager needs to tap into that knowledge base in search of the best outcome. If the project manager will be held personally accountable for the final decision, then he or she will not yield easily to the group's consensus. Instead, he or she will actively participate and ask thoughtful and probing questions to help ensure that the very best solution is derived.

This is an example of how the benevolent dictatorship concept helps drive personal accountability instead of deferring decisions to a body of people. If you, as project manager, have to defend the team's consensus-derived decision, you will take a far more serious and active role in ensuring that the consensus is, indeed, defendable.

Q2.5   *If a project manager is trapped in a micromanagement style or consensus-style organization, what can he or she do?*

A2.5   In many cases, those who micromanage do not want to micromanage. They do so out of what they believe to be necessity. If you are being micromanaged, look first at your own actions to see if they are causing the negative attention to be spotlighted on you. Some examples: Are you consistently missing commitments? Are you failing to take the lead on resolving key issues? Are you failing to seek help when needed? Are you failing to keep your project sponsor, client, or resource manager informed of key news?

If you suspect that you may be the cause of the problem, then seek help from a mentor, your resource manager, or your project sponsor. Whether or not you feel that you deserve the micromanaging, professionally confront the micromanager and discuss what you can do to break free of the current level of micromanaging. Learn what actions and behaviors he or she needs you to exhibit to back off. Set small, short-term, very specific, and measurable goals so that it will be apparent whether or not you have reached them. Incrementally improve your credibility with the person micromanaging: maintain rapport in an attempt to read—and meet—his or her needs better.

If you are a project manager trapped in a consensus-style organization, you have control over whether or not that style is used on your project. When working outside your immediate project, if you are the lead person on an issue, assert the benevolent dictator style. If you are not the lead person, then you have the opportunity to influence the consensus-run group of which you are a member.

CHAPTER 3

Ask for Help— or Become Part of the Problem

 *He who asks is a fool for five minutes, but he who does not ask remains a fool forever."*

—Chinese proverb

It's not only okay to ask for help, but you must do so if needed. Moreover, you must communicate this message to your team members. Does this scenario sound familiar?

You are a member of a project. You might be the project manager or another project member. You have made commitments to completing project tasks. The overall success of the project is, in part, tied to you meeting your commitments. Your commitments are in jeopardy. What do you do? Do you continue on your current path, where you know you are not likely to meet your commitments of time, cost, or quality? Or do you ask for help?

If you are like the vast majority of project members, either you don't ask for help or you wait too long to ask for help. You allow your missed commitments to damage the overall integrity of the project plan and the project itself.

You say you would never do that intentionally? Most of us have, by our past behavior and record, brought harm to one or more projects and not asked for help. Instead, we waited for help to descend upon us—and often resented the attention and direction of that help.

We are all guilty of not asking for help at some time or another. To learn from our mistakes and mature professionally, we must understand the importance of asking for help as *articulately* and as *early* as possible.

Most project members either do not ask for help or wait too long to ask for help.

It's not easy to ask for help. Remnants of what I call the "John Wayne mentality"—asking for help is a sign of weakness, while going it alone is a sign of strength and virtue—remain strong in many cultures. Perhaps this mentality was sometimes required for survival. But today, as people come together as a team to pool their talents and skills to create achievements far more complex and remarkable than any one person could

> *Asking for and obtaining help is a sign of professional maturity, not weakness.*

hope to accomplish, asking for help is a sign of strength. *Not* asking for help is a sign of weakness and can undermine the success of the project.

Projects and organizations need to create a work environment where asking for help is encouraged rather than frowned upon. The best leaders and organizations do not create an environment of punishment and discomfort for those seeking needed help—such behavior only discourages project members from seeking the help they need and can add to the attrition many organizations experience. Instead, today's best leaders and organizations encourage teaming and teamwork, and they recognize that a project's success correlates directly with the success of each of its contributors. A great benefit of teams is that they are made up of people with a wide range of skills and experiences, all of which enhance the potential for sharing and helping one another on a project.

When you find yourself in trouble and at risk of not meeting your commitments, seek help. However, there is a preferred approach to seeking help, especially if you need to go up the corporate hierarchy to ask for it:

1. ***Clearly define the problem you need help on.*** A problem that is incompletely or vaguely defined wastes valuable time, energy, and funds. Don't expect someone else to read your mind and do your job.
2. ***Describe the proposed solution.*** If more than one plausible solution exists, you can list them, but be accountable and take a position on the solution you favor. Don't deflect decisions to someone else unless you truly are at an impasse.
3. ***Be specific about what you are asking for.*** A vague request may get a vague response. Telling an executive, for example, exactly what you need, as clearly and precisely as possible, increases the likelihood that the executive will satisfy that request. Being specific has the added benefit of helping the executive feel that he or she is really helping.

> *If you think like an entrepreneur, you quickly grasp the value of asking for help compared to harming a project.*

If you question whether or not asking for help is the right thing to do, ask yourself this: If this were your own business and one of your employees was faced with the same situation as you are today, would you want your employee to ask for help or to continue on a destructive project path? This becomes easy to answer when you think of it in terms of owning the business.

When you ask for help, you show your human side and also send the signal that you take pride in your work and care about the success of the project. This creates an interesting side effect: The respect others have for you typically increases. Asking for help has the additional benefit of building rapport with the person you are asking for help.

The respect a project member receives from peers typically increases when needed help is sought, especially if it is sought as soon as reasonably possible.

Of course, *not* asking for help and endangering the success of a portion or the entire project is a sure way to lose the respect and trust of others.

Don't risk becoming part of the problem because of misplaced pride and an out-of-date "John Wayne mentality." Do what you know is right, not what you might observe happening around you or what you might be accustomed to. We all need help from time to time. And in today's highly competitive, fast-changing climate it is more essential than ever for project members to be honest and to ask for help when it is needed.

Everyone helping helps everyone win—it's a team!

Let's Talk: Questions & Answers

Q3.1   *Aren't you concerned that project members may abuse asking others for help?*

A3.1   Almost all people want to do the right thing and will use good judgment in asking for help. In the infrequent cases where someone has performance issues, is in the wrong job, or is a slacker looking for others to carry them, those are issues that need to be addressed with his or her resource manager.

Q3.2   *A project member can ask for help from a peer, team leader, project manager, or resource manager, but who should a project manager ask for help?*

A3.2   A project manager should ask help from whoever can help. That may be a peer, project member, program manager, project sponsor, resource manager, or perhaps a mentor. It doesn't matter so much where the help comes from; it matters that help is sought—and sought reasonably early.

Q3.3   *Why are people often reluctant to ask for help?*

A3.3   There are many reasons, of course. It could be pride. It could be the assumption that they will look bad, perhaps incompetent. It could be that a person must ask for help from someone younger in age or lower in job level. It could be bashfulness. It could be a cultural thing. *None is an acceptable excuse for not asking for* *help!* A mature professional will ask for help rather than harm the team or project.

Q3.4 *Don't you believe that a project member will ask for help if she says she will?*

A3.4 Not necessarily. Picture this:

> *During the hiring process, a candidate is asked what she would do if she is a member of a project and she is falling behind in her work commitments; would she ask for help? "Yes," she replies. She's then hired and immediately placed on a project. A few months later, she is having problems meeting her commitments, but she's not asking for help.*

What happened? This scenario is not as unusual as it may seem. Many people think and behave differently when in a group setting than when they are working alone or with only one other person. Even though they know the correct behavior when singled out and asked, they are reluctant to demonstrate that behavior in a group unless they feel reasonably certain that it will be viewed as acceptable behavior. The professionally mature response is to always exhibit integrity and do the right thing—to think for yourself—regardless of what's happening around you.

Q3.5 *In Chapter 1, Mind Your Own Business, you caution project members about performing outside their domain of responsibility—"extra credit" as you call it. Who will help a project member when that help may be viewed as "extra credit"?*

A3.5 I typically don't view providing help to others as "extra credit." If a coworker needs a few minutes of our time, we need to make the time to help out. If a coworker requests help that would consume a significant amount of our time and the request will result in us missing our commitments, then we must say "no" professionally. Helping coworkers—up to a point—is what we all do when we function as a team. Being accountable for managing our own commitments is a duty that falls on each and every one of us; no one can manage those commitments for us.

CHAPTER 4

What Good
Is a PM Mentor?

A mentor is a trusted counselor whose primary objective is to help a mentee (one who is being mentored) be more effective in a specific area of interest—to help develop the mentee's potential.

There is no better way to learn the application of a profession—a craft—than with a mentor by your side when needed. *There is no better way!* Not classes, workshops, articles, or books; even on-the-job training is not as effective. Many of us have learned and practiced bad habits for years, not realizing that there are better practices out there. A mentor can help you discover your possibilities.

> *We can learn far more and far faster when we can draw strength from those who have gone before us.*

 We know what we are, but not what we may be."
—William Shakespeare, English dramatist and poet

The best mentors of project managers are seasoned project managers who often have learned the hard way—by making mistakes and learning and growing from those painful experiences as well as from their successes. Mentors are expected to know the best practices available and, at least occasionally, to add to their craft by creating some best practices of their own. Mentors often give you a different perspective, fresh eyes, new ideas; they enable you to see the forest, not just the knots in the trees.

If possible, seek out mentors who can be accessible when you need them most. For example, when performing basic tasks of planning, tracking, and problem management, a mentor can be of great help in ensuring that the tasks get off to a good start. But what about when there is a crisis? A crisis can evoke an urgent need to confer with a trusted third party.

If you question the benefit of having a readily accessible mentor, then picture this. For those of you with years of project management experience, think back to how much a project management mentor—the *right* mentor under the *right* circumstances—would have helped you accelerate your learning of both hard and soft project management skills, avoid some hefty mistakes, and, as a side benefit, move your career ahead sooner. For those of you with limited project management experience, how often have you wished you could have access to someone with the *right* answers the *first* time?

The project manager can have a profound impact on the outcome of a project. Projects can consume enormous resources and funds from an organization or company, often with price tags of thousands, millions, and sometimes more. Moreover, the revenue or operations impact of these projects can be many times that amount. With project managers being in such critical positions within organizations and companies, doesn't it make good business sense for organizations to provide them with appropriate mentoring help? Mentors help nurture company investments by helping set up the project managers—and their projects—for success.

> *A mentor's advice can greatly benefit your career and help protect your projects from "crash and burn."*

Three Key Areas of Mentorship

Three key areas (see Figure 4-1) that both the mentor and mentee focus on in helping develop the mentee's potential are:

- Mentorship relationship
- Ongoing performance
- Goal development.

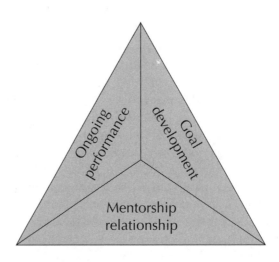

Figure 4-1   Three Key Areas of Mentorship

Mentorship Relationship

The mentee and the mentor must know that they share a penalty-free relationship. The atmosphere they share should be relaxed and conducive to open and candid discussions. There are no dumb questions and all discussions remain confidential. This framework of trust allows the full potential of the mentorship to be reached. The goal is to find a mentor where the chemistry between the two parties enhances the relationship.

The confidential discussions between mentor and mentee should not find their way into a performance evaluation. For this reason, the best mentor typically is someone who is not the mentee's resource manager or anywhere in the mentee's direct chain of management.

Communications between the mentor and the mentee must be strictly confidential for the mentee to gain the most benefit from the mentor.

Ongoing Performance

One of the mentor's objectives is to help the mentee improve his or her ongoing performance. The goal is to help the mentee be a more effective leader in day-to-day activities—to focus on achieving results. "Just-in-time" performance feedback is given to the mentee in the form of praise for noteworthy achievements and actions; immediate feedback is also offered for areas of improvement. The ongoing fine-tuning is, by far, the best method for helping a mentee develop particular skills.

A mentor can help a mentee learn almost immediately from mistakes or potential mistakes, rather than hope a person learns after months or years of making the mistakes.

Goal Development

The mentor works with the mentee in creating a "mentorship development plan" (MDP). This plan maps out the mentee's journey in the pursuit of the stated career goals. For example, the plan needs to profile (1) where the mentee is now in terms of knowledge, skills, and duties, (2) where the mentee aspires to be, and (3) what actions can close the gap.

More specifically, the plan needs to identify the mentee's current relevant skills and the level of proficiency of each skill. The plan should also identify the level of proficiency that must be reached with each skill. The steps for reaching the proficiency must then be identified. For example, classes, workshops, articles/books, conferences, and other learning tools can be identified. The sequence of specific jobs with selected levels of complexity also can be listed. Timeframes are targeted to help the mentee pace progress toward the goals.

Planning your goals greatly increases the likelihood of achieving them.

As the mentee's leadership skills are being developed, some of the activities for the mentee to seek out can include developing and presenting track sessions and workshops within the organization or at conferences, writing articles for relevant publications or for use in-house, and creating and documenting improved processes for use on projects.

The Initiative Is in Your Court

If you do not already have a mentor, I urge you to seriously consider the benefits to both your ongoing performance and your career. The time and cost invested in acquiring a mentor are small compared to the benefits that can be gained. Don't wait for a mentorship program to come to your organization. Take the initiative to seek mentorship in the areas that will affect your projects and your career most significantly.

A mentor can help you become a far better project manager in far less time than otherwise is likely. A mentor helps you grow day to day, learn from your past, and plan for your future. Having a mentor doesn't mean that you will not make mistakes, but it does mean that you are likely to make fewer and less costly mistakes. Mentorship benefits everyone: beginning with the project manager, but including important stakeholders, project members, the client, and the company.

Mentorship is a profoundly beneficial business tool that is enormously underutilized.

Let's Talk: Questions & Answers

Q4.1   *You focus on mentors for project managers. Are mentors a good thing for any project member or employee?*

A4.1   Yes. Any employee can benefit from a mentor. The most progressive organizations have various levels of mentorship programs for their employees.

A mentor accelerates the process of "experience."

Q4.2   *Is it okay for a project manager to have more than one mentor?*

A4.2   Yes. A project manager can be mentored in more than one skill area and can have a mentor for each. For example, a project manager could have a mentor related to (1) the "hard" skill areas of planning, tracking, and risk management, (2) the "soft" skill areas of negotiating, communicating, and leadership, and (3) surviving and thriving in the political quagmires of an organization. Moreover, a project manager could have more than one mentor in the same general area as a check-and-balance. For example, when you are about to make a major decision related to your job or career, consulting with more than one mentor can be beneficial.

Q4.3   *Why do you say that it is best to seek out a mentor who is not your boss or in your management chain?*

A4.3   The mentorship works best when there is total trust in the relationship. There will be times when it is helpful to the mentorship experience to "bare all"—to expose your weaknesses and reveal your inner thoughts. If those private experiences were reflected in your performance evaluation, then it would totally shut down the trust relationship and the mentoring process would greatly suffer.

Most performance evaluations involve elements of subjectivity and the benefit of the doubt typically is in favor of the employee. However, if your boss is also your mentor, he or she may use the knowledge gained in confidential meetings to justify a lower evaluation rating, or worse, to negatively affect your future job assignments, salary, and awards. If your mentor is outside of your management chain, then the knowledge gained by your mentor will have no negative bearing on your assessments.

Q4.4   *How should I go about finding a mentor?*

A4.4   You first must decide in which specialty area(s) you would benefit from a mentor's assistance. Look for a person in your company to whom you have fairly easy access.

People outside your company may also be candidates. They could be an academic from a local learning institution, a qualified friend, or even a family member. A local project management group such as a PMI® chapter can be an excellent place to network and potentially find a willing mentor. Some PMI® chapters are actively developing mentorship programs. (See *www.pmi.org* to locate a chapter near you.) If you choose a mentor outside of your company, you may need to have him or her sign a nondisclosure agreement to protect information that your company considers proprietary.

Perhaps the best place to begin the search is through your resource manager. Your resource manager likely has people connections beyond yours and will generally be willing to work with you in finding a qualified mentor.

Q4.5   *Is it okay for me to approach a person and ask them if they are willing to be my mentor?*

A4.5   This approach may be fine; however, be prepared to articulate to the potential mentor what it means to be your mentor in terms of duties and time. Moreover, because people who are sought after as mentors are typically among the busiest people in an organization, be prepared if the person declines the request.

Be sensitive about keeping your manager in the loop. For example, your resource manager may want to know of the mentorship if he or she sees you spending otherwise unexplained time with the mentor.

Q4.6   *What if I choose a mentor who is not in my company and is not easily accessible? Can this work?*

A4.6   Yes, but with stipulations. For example, at any given time, I mentor about a dozen people across almost as many companies. Although I have many of the skills to make a good mentor, my inability to be immediately available can be a handicap. For example, if a mentee has a crisis and needs to contact me immediately, I may be traveling, in the middle of conducting a workshop, or consulting. This means that the mentee may have to wait until the evening for me to return the call. However, most times when a mentor seeks advice, it is not during a crisis that must be handled within minutes or hours.

Q4.7   *How much time is required of a mentor?*

A4.7   The answer depends on many factors, such as the experience level of the mentee and the specialty area of mentorship. For example, if a project manager is relatively new to project management and requests direction in creating a project plan, this could take days of mentoring. However, if a mentee is looking for advice on dealing with a difficult project member or client, perhaps an hour or less of counseling would do. I often work with mentees that I haven't heard from in several months, yet their next call may require several hours of assistance spread over a week or two.

Q4.8   *As a mentor, what is something that surprises you about working with mentees?*

A4.8   A big surprise to me is that in perhaps as many as 80 percent of the calls I receive for mentoring, the mentees have the "right" answer for the situation. The major value I add is often nothing more than validating that the mentee is on an effective path. Often, just the reassurance of an idea or action can make all the difference in boosting the confidence of a mentee and encouraging him or her to follow through.

Q4.9 *Should I look for a mentor who has made many mistakes and learned from them, or is it better to have a mentor who has made very few, if any, noteworthy mistakes?*

A4.9 This is a subject for debate. I fall in the camp that recognizes value from practitioners who have suffered through failures, but demonstrated their resilience to learn and grow from them. There's perhaps no better teacher than firsthand experience with hardships. I should add, however, that the best mentors need to have some successes behind them to help validate their approaches.

Q4.10 *Is a formal mentorship development plan (MDP) required for a mentee?*

A4.10 Not necessarily. People being mentored are at different stages of need and the formality of a plan can vary. However, in most cases, both the mentee and the mentor can benefit from understanding and discussing the information that typically would appear in an MDP. When goals are formalized, the mentee is more likely to attain those goals and measurements can be identified to help quantify the progress being made.

Q4.11 *Who owns the MDP, the mentee or the mentor?*

A4.11 The mentee owns the plan and is responsible for its creation, contents, and timely implementation. The mentor assists in validating the contents and reasonableness of the plan.

Q4.12 *Is there a tool that you have found to be especially helpful while mentoring?*

A4.12 *Day shadowing* has proven to be a highly effective tool when mentoring leader types such as project managers. The mentor shadows (accompanies) the mentee throughout a day. The mentor observes, firsthand, the effectiveness of the mentee in participating in meetings, conducting meetings, resolving conflicts between parties, facilitating or performing escalations, and in a myriad of other settings. At the end of the day, but preferably at the end of each event, the mentor discusses the mentee's style and effectiveness. This approach offers the mentee immediate feedback in the actual work environment rather than getting bogged down by theory and what-ifs.

Q4.13 *I would like a mentor, but feel uncomfortable exposing my mistakes—my vulnerability. Any advice?*

A4.13 Get over it, if you want to be all you can be. Look at the people who have achieved the most around you, even those in front of the public in sports, business, science, politics, TV, and movies. They are people who are vulnerable to criticism from all those around them. However, mature professionals look beyond their egos and don't focus on what others think about them. Instead they focus on growth, improvement, and mastery of their specialty. They seek to open "exterior" doors so that they might better understand what's behind their "interior" doors—to better understand themselves and how to break out of self-imposed perceptions.

Here again, you can see why the mentor you choose must protect your confidentiality and have your best interest in mind. Go open that door! You will grow from the experience.

Q4.14 *Should I always take my mentor's advice?*

A4.14 An effective mentor can easily expand your thinking and options, and can significantly help you be more successful. So you want to listen thoughtfully to his or her words of experience and wisdom, and engage in an appropriate dialogue. After all, that's why you are working with a mentor. However, there is no substitute for you thinking for yourself. You are responsible for your domain of responsibility along with the decisions that affect its success. You are the final arbiter.

CHAPTER 5

Is Your
Professional Behavior
Respected?

 *Nothing so conclusively proves a man's ability to lead others as what he does from day to day to lead himself."*

—Thomas J. Watson, American industrialist,
entrepreneur, former chairman of IBM

As a project manager—a leader—do you both preach and practice professionally mature behavior? Are you role-model caliber? You should be! In my experience, most leaders have a credibility gap with coworkers in this area. By coworkers, I mean the full range of the organizational hierarchy, from people who work under you, to your peers, to higher-ups.

Here's a starter list of professional behaviors to embrace that can help you be a more effective—and respected—leader:

- *Develop great working relationships.* Make relationships with your stakeholders not just work, but work well. Remember, leadership is the art of getting things done through people. The best leaders have nurtured great relationships with others.
- *Make your boss and your project sponsor look good.* Your actions are a reflection on your boss (resource manager) and your project sponsor. Your job includes helping make them look good and helping make their jobs as easy as possible. If you want to improve your working relationship with your boss and project sponsor, this technique is sure to get their favorable attention.
- *Be a role model to your peers.* Strive to act and behave in a manner that motivates people to emulate your style. You want your peer stakeholders to look forward to being in work meetings with you or including you as a welcomed contributor who can help bring harmony and effective resolutions to the challenges at hand.
- *Be a role model to your project members.* Show your project members—those you lead as a project manager—how you expect them to behave. Showing them through your actions is far more effective than merely telling them. You want them to ask themselves often, "How would [your name] handle this?"

- *Count to that proverbial 10 before saying or doing something that will cause problems.* Once the words leave your lips or your actions have been shown, you cannot pull them back. Moreover, it can take weeks, sometimes months, to recover from a moment of indiscretion. For example, consider not sending potentially inflammatory emails at the end of the day. Your patience is lower and you may not be at your best in demonstrating good judgment. Write the emails, but wait until morning to reread them. More often than not, you will change the wording or not send the emails, and will decide to handle the problems in a different way.

In the midst of great joy do not promise anyone anything. In the midst of great anger do not answer anyone's letter."

—Chinese proverb

- *Meet your commitments.* Don't make a commitment unless you can achieve it. Whether to your boss or another stakeholder, meeting a commitment is one of the best things you can do to establish a great reputation. If you cannot meet a commitment, then realign expectations before the original due date, so that collateral damage can be minimized. Projects and business are all about commitments. You should not take lightly the importance of making and managing commitments effectively, nor do you want others to form that perception from your behavior.
- *Ask others for their advice.* Bouncing ideas off others serves two great purposes. First, it improves relationships. People are flattered and feel important to be asked. Second, you will learn in the process. Sometimes the lesson learned is a validation of your original approach, but other times you will walk away with a better idea.
- *Look for solutions.* Don't become an obstacle. Search for all the reasons that something can be made to work, rather than focusing on why it cannot. You are always better off knowing the problems that you face, and knowing them as early as possible. Be especially vigilant against focusing primarily on who's at fault. We want to learn from our past, but not at the expense of instilling fear and distrust in those with whom we work.

    The higher your position in an organization's hierarchy, the more you are expected to solve problems without requiring help from higher-ups. If something you did gets back to your superiors or senior stakeholders, you want it to be because of the good it provided, not because of a problem you caused, contributed to, or could have defused.

- ***Maintain a great attitude.*** It's wonderful that we have control over our attitude; no one can choose it for us. If our attitude stinks, we have only to gaze in a mirror for the culprit. If you doubt the benefit of demonstrating a great attitude, try it for a day. Your day likely will go more smoothly, more effortlessly, and you will feel a greater sense of comfort and satisfaction with your actions and effectiveness. Take charge of your attitude; don't let someone else choose it for you.

 The greatest discovery of my generation is that a human being can alter his life by altering his attitudes of mind."
—William James, American psychologist and philosopher

- ***Expect from yourself what you expect from others.*** Hold yourself to the same high standards that you expect from others. Practice what you preach. Some examples: Arrive to meetings on time and prepared. Be timely in returning phone calls. Increase person-to-person communications while decreasing overreliance on emails.

This is not an exhaustive list, but it is a start in identifying professional behaviors to embrace. Think about the project managers and other leaders you know whom you admire the most. Many of them may already routinely practice these behaviors. It's not just about being nice; it's also about being effective.

You know when you are making headway in practicing these behaviors when someone compliments your behavior or action, especially if you have disarmed them because they did not think that you would have reacted so effectively. It's a great feeling to see that your professionally mature behavior is having a notably positive impact on others.

You get from others what you invest in others.

We all demonstrate these behaviors from time to time. The key is to embrace them on a routine basis. Adopt them as a part of the professional you choose to be. The investments you make in others will be returned multifold.

You get to choose the professional you most want to become.

Let's Talk: Questions & Answers

Q5.1 *The item, "Make your boss and project sponsor look good," makes me a bit uncomfortable. Isn't this going to be viewed as kissing up?*

A5.1 There's a difference between flattery and genuinely making your boss look good. It's not about "kissing up"; it's about doing your job. You come to work every day to move your company forward by focusing on your domain of responsibility. (See Chapter 1, Mind Your Own Business.) The more effective you are in performing your job, the better you and those who depend on you look. If you were the boss or project sponsor, wouldn't you like to have employees who consistently made your job easy—made you look good?

> *When your boss or project sponsor looks good, you look good.*

Q5.2   *It seems that you are expecting project managers to be superhuman. For example, look at the item, "Meet your commitments." In any given day, I must be in so many meetings, return so many calls, deliver so many emails or documents, and so on, that it is all but impossible for me to do all that I said I would do when I said I would do it.*

A5.2   We all are works in progress. Nobody does all this stuff flawlessly when they enter the workforce. Even after years of experience and striving to exemplify the best side of what it means to be a professional, we all have our moments. Don't be too hard on yourself.

Having said that, you have control over your commitments and actions to achieve those commitments. If you have a poor track record for meeting commitments, then you need to look at your busy day and decide how to change your behavior so that you will be more effective. For example, make fewer commitments and give yourself more time. Keep in mind that because of the influential position you hold, those around you will tend to mimic your behavior—good or bad.

> *Don't beat yourself up for past behavior; instead, use those lessons for improvement and move on.*

Q5.3   *You say to be accountable for your commitments and performance, but what if a commitment was not of your own doing?*

A5.3   Commitments are almost always of our own choosing. Picture this:

> *Your boss gives you an additional assignment that requires a level of effort of one month, but the assignment is not due for three months. You tell your boss that your plate is "pretty full," but you will do what you can.*
>
> *Your boss will interpret this as a commitment, even though you may think you are sending a different signal. You may feel frustrated that your boss dumped this assignment on you. You may begin to feel less conviction to prior commitments, while slowly building resentment toward your boss.*

Where's the problem in this scenario? You! When your boss first approached you with the additional work, you should have shown a great attitude by saying that you will do whatever the boss requests, but you need his help. You identify the top three to five assignments on your plate. You then ask where the new assignment should fall in terms of its priority. Something will have to give. If a commitment you made earlier to your boss will have to slip, then you negotiate for it to slip. If a commitment to another party will have to slip, then you let your boss know that you are looking for his support when you inform the other party of the situation.

You control and manage your commitments. No one, not even your boss, can know for sure when your capacity to take on more work has been exhausted. Your job is to manage your commitments candidly and maturely.

> *You manage your commitments; nobody manages them for you.*

Q5.4 *As a project manager, I like to inject some light-heartedness, some humor, into my day. Is this okay in a professional work environment?*

A5.4 Yes, assuming it is in good taste and at an appropriate moment. Picture this:

> *A meeting has just been called to settle a dispute between two parties. As people assemble in the meeting room, an uncomfortable silence is felt. Everyone has arrived and the meeting is about to start. There's instability in the air, a feeling of tension that one wrong word or action could ignite into an emotional explosion. The first words are spoken and a round of laughter fills the room.*

A well-timed bit of humor is often sorely needed. All too often we fail to loosen up and find the humor in ourselves and our situation. How terribly depressing for a team to resist expressing the lighter side of the daily problems we face. As a leader, support a healthy dose of humor. Displaying a sense of humor also helps you remain cool under pressure and keep problems in perspective. Humor has been shown to preserve the health of individuals; it also can promote the health of a project or organization.

 It is my belief, you cannot deal with the most serious things in the world unless you understand the most amusing."
—Sir Winston Churchill, British statesman

Caution: Don't use sarcasm in your humor. While some may view your comment to be amusing, it may leave others feeling uncomfortable and unsettled. Sarcasm also can hurt the trust you have developed with others.

Q5.5 *Can a project manager with an oversized ego be consistently successful?*

A5.5 Although it is possible, an oversized ego can easily backfire. We all have an ego. For some, that ego can inhibit the quest for growth and opportunity.

Here is the paradox: Often the person who insists on attention is the one least likely to receive the type or amount of attention sought. An overactive ego does not help win the recognition, admiration, and approval that the egotist seeks. Instead, it has a repelling effect that causes others to limit their association with the egotist. Furthermore, it leads others to question the real value and substance behind all the verbal arm-waving.

An oversized ego can also interfere with recognizing others for their contributions. And it can bias decisions being made, favoring *who* is right rather than *what* is right.

> *The less approval you demand from others, the more you are likely to receive.*

Having an exaggerated ego doesn't mean you will never get to be a leader. But it does mean that fewer people will trust you or want to work for and with you. It will also make your job harder and less effective than it needs to be.

Q5.6 *This chapter is helpful for recognizing what constitutes professionally* mature *behavior, but it's easy to behave in professionally* immature *ways and not be aware of it. Any ideas for recognizing professionally immature behavior?*

A5.6 Glad you asked! I have included a chapter to address professionally immature behavior: Chapter 6, Recognizing and Dealing with Professional Immaturity.

Q5.7 *Although this chapter appears to be targeted to project managers, the principles discussed are relevant to all project members. Any ideas on how best to share these ideas with the team?*

A5.7 Yes. Chapter 19, Create the Desired Culture for Your Project, reveals an effective method for doing so near the beginning of a project.

CHAPTER 6

Recognizing and Dealing with Professional Immaturity

*P*rofessional immaturity is behavior that is disruptive, destructive, or otherwise void of benefit in a business environment. It often manifests itself through behavior such as weak personal initiative, weak accountability, self-absorption, and low awareness of the impact of one's own behavior.

Achieving professional maturity is not a condition that automatically happens to us as we enter the workforce. It's something that we must be taught. Unfortunately, most of us were not adequately taught. Moreover, many of us do not realize it for years—and some never get it!

The increasingly *handholding, coddling, I'm-not-responsible-for-my-own-actions* world in which we live is having a devastating impact on preparing people for the workforce—the *real* world. While students learn technology skills, they often lack the business skills based on "soft" areas like accountability, resourcefulness, and leadership. We see far too much emphasis on whining, finger-pointing, and effort—and far too little emphasis on solving problems, being accountable, and achieving results.

Most people in the workforce have not been properly prepared and don't recognize their handicap: They are professionally immature.

Professional immaturity undermines projects and organizations. Moreover, many employees do not realize the negative impact that their behavior is having on their own performance and careers. Professionally immature individuals:

- Believe that effort is more important than results
- Wait to be asked to work overtime
- Expect management or others to initiate needed change in areas that affect their own work output
- Complain rather than constructively work issues to closure
- Avoid escalating issues that are at an apparent impasse
- Escalate too hastily or too often
- Bring problems to senior management without any recommendations for solutions
- Believe that commitments are transient
- Wait to be blessed with empowerment and authority by a higher-up rather than take the initiative
- Delay in asking for help when needed
- Take no accountability for their own actions

- Believe that the grass is greener in the next organization or company
- Look out for the company at the expense of their own domain of responsibility
- Believe that their boss is responsible for their career.

Professional immaturity is strikingly common and widespread.

Do you see beliefs that you support or exhibit? Are you surprised to see behaviors that you thought were acceptable? Perhaps you never gave some of the items a second thought. Professionally immature behavior is often not obvious to a person who has never been taught otherwise. Moreover, you can be professionally immature *at any age!*

When employees have not learned what it means to be professionally mature, the responsibility lies with the managers—the resource managers—of these employees to teach them. However, all too often, these resource managers either demonstrate similar professional immaturity or place a higher priority on work other than their key assignment: nurturing their employees. (See Chapter 15, Duties of the Effective Resource Manager.)

A resource manager's primary objective is to nurture his or her staff, which includes teaching them professionally mature behaviors.

The result is a tremendous burden on project managers. In addition to planning and executing a successful project, they must spend the time and energy teaching their project members what constitutes proper behavior—professionally mature behavior.

As a project leader, you may be thinking, "It's not fair for me to perform the job that the resource managers aren't stepping up to." Don't go there! In the real world, it's not about what's fair; it's about results. If you want a winning project, then you need to deal with the people side of issues. By all means, work with resource managers where appropriate—but ineffective resource managers are not an excuse for project failure.

Project managers must deal constructively with professionally immature project members to ensure consistent project success.

Many companies state, as part of their company core beliefs, that their most important asset is their employees. I contend that a company's most important asset is its leaders. If a company has mediocre leaders and the best staff, it will be doomed to be a mediocre force in its industry. However, if a company has the best leaders and mediocre staff, that company will be a formidable force in its industry. Why? Because employees rise to the expectations of their leaders: Companies with the best leaders will ultimately have the best employees.

Project managers are leaders and, therefore, teachers. If you are unsure how to proceed with a soft issue, then seek counsel, but avoid doing nothing. Do not allow professionally immature behavior by your project members to negatively impact the success of your project. The professional maturity of project members will improve based on your awareness of this pervasive problem and your willingness to become part of the solution.

> *A company's most prized asset is its leaders.*

> *Leaders are teachers.*

Let's Talk: Questions & Answers

Q6.1 *Why do you say that "some never get it," referring to what it means to be professionally mature?*

A6.1 Most of us, as youngsters growing up, are not taught what it means to be professionally mature. Moreover, it is not something that students are likely to pick up in college. We are most likely to learn it in the workplace—if we learn it at all.

As stated, resource managers are the primary persons in a work environment charged with teaching professional maturity. Younger minds appear to be more agile and open to learning these lessons. For many employees who are not sufficiently taught professional maturity traits early in their work experiences, it can be more difficult for them to be open to and accept these ideas later.

For example, if an employee grows more cynical over the years about his or her job, management, compensation, and so on, that employee may dismiss lessons of professional maturity that are targeted at employees as playing into management's hands and the "political system." That employee may not be motivated or open to understanding that we have control over how we think and behave—that we are not victims unless we choose to be.

> *Pity parties, while convenient and self-serving, keep a person detached from learning, growing, and achieving.*

Q6.2 *If a person ever behaves according to any of the examples of professional immaturity, does that make the person professionally immature?*

A6.2 If a person behaves according to *one* of those examples, then that person is demonstrating professional immaturity *in that instance*. It doesn't necessarily mean the person is across-the-board professionally immature. However, a frequent pattern of such behaviors does constitute general behavior that is judged to be professionally immature.

Q6.3   *Most of us commonly display some types of professionally immature behavior. Are you, therefore, saying that most of us are professionally immature most of the time?*

A6.3   My experience is that most employees demonstrate professional immaturity most of the time. I am not saying that these employees are not mature human beings away from work or that they are not good community members. I am saying that they are professionally immature in many of their actions while performing their work.

Q6.4   *You appear to be setting the bar too high. It's not easy to avoid some of the behaviors you consider to be professionally immature.*

A6.4   I never said it was easy to be professionally mature. But for a project or organization to work at its optimal effectiveness, its members must strive to achieve behavior that is consistently professionally mature.

Q6.5   *Is there ever a time when a person can demonstrate professionally immature behavior and actually be doing the right thing?*

A6.5   Yes, if you have been directed to behave in a certain way in your work environment.

For example, professionally mature employees typically initiate working overtime if their commitments demand it. However, your boss may have requested that you never work overtime unless it is first approved. Of course, demonstrating professional maturity in this case is to approach your boss when you first realize that overtime will be necessary.

> *It is not always easy to consistently demonstrate professionally mature behavior.*

Another specific example is that professionally mature employees should not just be raising problems, but they should also be recommending solutions. However, you may have a hands-on boss who wants to know about problems immediately—even before a solution is found. Professional maturity in this case is being involved constructively in arriving at the appropriate solution.

Be careful here. I can continue to cite exceptions, but don't fall into the trap of thinking that your world is full of exceptions and that, therefore, it is acceptable to continue professionally immature behavior. In almost all cases, exceptions don't hold up.

Q6.6 *What can employees do when they are not sure of the behavior expected of them as professionally mature employees and project members?*

A6.6 Ask. There are a multitude of people to approach, depending on your position and the situation. You can ask your resource manager, team leader, project manager, or even consult with a mentor. (See Chapter 4, What Good Is a PM Mentor?)

Q6.7 *What happens when people are professionally immature?*

A6.7 Plenty. For example, it can stunt their personal growth, cost them respect, harm their projects and organizations, cut short their careers, and damage the organization and company.

Q6.8 *Is there more material that reinforces professionally mature behavior according to your belief system?*

A6.8 Yes, this book is loaded with direction on behaving in ways that support professionally mature behavior and thus support achieving consistently successful projects. In fact, many of the chapters in this book focus on how to overcome professionally immature behavior. Here are some examples:

- Chapter 1, Mind Your Own Business, addresses the item "Looks out for the company at the expense of their own domain of responsibility."
- Chapter 3, Ask for Help—or Become Part of the Problem, addresses the item "Delays asking for help when needed."
- Chapter 19, Create the Desired Culture for Your Project, addresses the item "Expects management or others to initiate needed change in areas that affect their own work output."
- Chapter 31, Escalate Is Not a Dirty Word, addresses the item "Avoids escalating issues that are at an apparent impasse."

Q6.9 *As a project manager, I didn't take this job to wipe noses. I resent having to do the job of resource managers by developing their employees. I have enough on my plate. What do you say to that?*

A6.9 Stop acting professionally immature yourself! If you have project members who are not pulling their weight or are disruptive, you have every right to request that their resource managers get involved. If they don't, you can escalate over the resource managers until you get the needed help. However, in some cases, you

> **Ineffective resource managers are not an excuse for project failure.**

may have to wait until hell freezes over if you expect the problems to be fully resolved.

Your job as a project manager is to make things happen so that you deliver the promised project successfully. This will, more times than not, require you to deal with bouts of professional immaturity as they arise. As a leader, you also have the responsibility to set an example—to be a role model.

CHAPTER 7

Behaviors to Master When Dealing with Your Leaders

Your leaders want you to know—*need you to know*—the behaviors they consistently expect from you. Just because you have a leadership role doesn't mean you are living up to the expectations of your leaders. Routinely adopting behaviors that your leaders expect from you, but often do not see fulfilled, can enhance your image, effectiveness, and career—and make your leaders' jobs easier. Here's a starter list:

- ***Don't dump and run.*** When you have an idea for an improvement, don't transfer that idea to your leader and then wash your hands of it. Be willing to be its champion and become part of the solution. Your leader has neither the duty nor the bandwidth to personally take on and work every good idea to closure.
- ***Make it brief.*** When you are dealing with your peers you can speak in sentences, sometimes in paragraphs. But higher up the food chain, speak in sound bites. Your leaders don't have time for the unabridged version. They know you are capable and worthy or you would not be in your position.
- ***Don't complain.*** People who habitually complain are a bore and a waste of time and energy to those around them. If you are complaining, you are not solving; you are part of the problem. For example, if you complain to Person A about something that Person B can fix, then you just wasted your time and that of Person A. But if you "complain" directly to Person B, who can fix the problem, it is not complaining; it is the first step in moving toward a solution. By the way, if you get a reputation as a complainer, people will eventually stop listening.
- ***Bring solutions with problems.*** When you are faced with a problem and need help, articulate both the solution and the specific help required. Tell your leaders exactly what you need from them (e.g., funding, letter of support, escalation support, lifting the freeze on hiring, approval for new tool). You are far more likely to secure their support when you have a solution in hand and they know precisely what you expect from them to help you carry out the solution.
- ***Wear one face.*** Don't be one person when your leaders are around and someone different the rest of the time. Choose the same face regardless of the audience.

- *Close issues.* Don't allow issues to linger, to drift. Close them with the business urgency that they deserve.
- *Meet commitments.* Do what you have committed to do. Show others that you can be counted on, that you are reliable.
- *Promote dialogue.* Don't be a "yes" employee—or more specifically, a silent employee. Don't just take notes, nod, and leave your boss' office. Listen thoughtfully, ask good questions, raise concerns (if any). Your leaders need your response, your ideas, and your participation. It's far more important to be able to ask the right questions than it is to know all the right answers.
- *Make your leaders look good.* Satisfying the needs of your leaders—fulfilling their expectations—is your job. That makes them look good, which makes you look good.
- *Keep your leaders informed.* Don't work in a vacuum. Keep your leaders informed of important news. Avoid surprises. Don't let them hear about your newsworthy actions from someone else.
- *Offer professional criticism.* If your views run counter to your leaders', then constructively and discreetly share those views. Your value increases when your interest, honesty, and passion are apparent.
- *Offer praise.* When you observe noteworthy ideas, actions, or deeds by your leaders, show that you appreciate their behavior. Do not focus only on criticism—as constructive as it may be.
- *Demonstrate integrity.* Know the difference between right and wrong—and do the right thing. Do not support or condone illegal, unethical, or immoral behavior.
- *Don't take it personally.* Your leaders may not handle stress any better than anyone else. Occasionally, they may be abrupt, impatient, argumentative, unappreciative, or simply not thinking clearly or effectively. Cut them some slack as you hope others would for you.
- *Solicit feedback on your performance.* Ask for constructive criticism as well as praise based on your actions and behavior. Make it easy—be a willing student—for your leaders to work with you and professionally "shape" you into a more effective leader.
  - *Support your peers.* Be quick to support noteworthy ideas and actions by your coworkers. Choose the collaborative path rather than the competitive or contentious path. Build bridges instead of burning them.
  - *Show you can be trusted.* Don't have loose lips. Earn the reputation of being a trusted confidant. Support the company mantra and work to continually improve its effectiveness.

Just because you have a leadership role doesn't mean you are living up to the expectations of those who lead you.

• *Be a role model.* Without fanfare or recognition, behave in a manner that others can emulate. Promote an organizational culture that supports continual success.

If you are relatively new as a leader, this starter list may appear daunting. But to your leaders, it represents what they strive for when recruiting, coaching, and mentoring. It is my experience that far more leaders are made than born. You have the ability to shape your behavior and, therefore, your effectiveness.

"Made leaders" are more abundant than "born leaders."

Let's Talk: Questions & Answers

Q7.1   *The list of behaviors appears daunting. But isn't this really just common sense?*

A7.1   No. Common sense can vary widely among cultures. Often the cultures across town can be as diverse as the cultures across the world. Don't assume you know what the accepted culture is for your leaders. If in doubt, approach them to discuss a starter list of these behaviors. Also discuss what may be missing from the list that is especially important to them.

Q7.2   *You say to "Make it brief," but I am concerned that my leaders will not understand the full magnitude of what I say. Most of them are not as technical as I am, nor do I expect them to be. What do you say about that?*

A7.2   You need to learn to "read your audience." People send signals when they've "got it." Learn to recognize those signals, then move on. Use your best judgment. You may be doing just fine. If in doubt, ask your leaders for feedback.

Q7.3   *When you say "Bring solutions with problems," do you mean we should come with multiple solutions for a single problem?*

A7.3   It is usually a good idea to have more than one solution to offer; however, my style, in most cases, is to offer one solution but have one or more tucked away in case I need to fall back on them. I generally believe it is not a good idea to offer up many solutions and have your leaders choose. This smacks of transferring responsibility to them. Take a position. Tell your leaders what you want them to know. If they are not satisfied, they will let you know.

Q7.4   *By "Wear one face," do you mean do not talk destructively behind your leaders' backs?*

A7.4   For starters, yes. But I mean much more. I want you to maintain a positive attitude about all you do and your relationships with others. Wearing two or more faces not only undermines the best interests of your leaders and the organization, but it also damages your credibility.

Q7.5   *Under "Meet commitments," what if you cannot always meet your commitments?*

A7.5   Then fess up as early as possible and put a recovery plan in place. But do not surprise key stakeholders such as the project sponsor, client, or your senior manager or executive. Once you have made an external commitment, you no longer have the freedom to change it arbitrarily. You must openly work with the stakeholder with whom you initially negotiated the commitment.

Q7.6   *Under "Promote dialogue," when my leaders have given me direction I don't feel I have the latitude to question their marching orders. Do you?*

A7.6   If the direction is unclear, contradictory, incomplete, or misleading, you must professionally speak up to ensure that the proper action results. If you owned the company, would you want your employees to blindly follow your directions—especially if they are confused or need information that could change your direction? Speaking up (with a tone of respect, of course) does not have to be interpreted as insubordination. It should come across as the opposite: showing that you care about your job and doing the right thing.

Q7.7   *Under "Make your leaders look good," what if I make my leader look good and he takes all the credit and leaves none for me?*

A7.7   This could happen, but it will not in most cases. Most leaders know that their success depends on those around them—that they look good in large part because of the many shoulders they are standing on. It is my experience that most leaders will share the limelight of their successes with those who are deserving. Occasionally, there is the bad apple who is interested only in his or her career or, frankly, may be in the wrong job. Fortunately, this is far less common than the opposite case. Over the long haul, my experience shows that the major contributors to the success of others will be recognized.

Q7.8   *Under "Don't take it personally," where do I draw the line between reasonable behavior and abusive behavior?*

A7.8   There are so many scenarios that it's difficult to give a general answer. My experience is that you will know the difference when it occurs.

If the uncomfortable behavior exhibited by a leader is an exception from that leader's typical behavior, then in most cases it may be best to let it go. If the behavior is followed by an apology, then, again, chalk it up to the leader having bad day.

If the unsettling behavior is frequent or personally crosses a line, then you may need to deal with the issue. We all have different thresholds when it comes to taking things personally. What may not be a big deal to me could be unacceptable to you. Play this one carefully. Better to err on the side of cutting too much slack than not enough.

If the situation is a legal or ethical issue, then immediately distance yourself. You should also consider alerting your legal team, human resources department, or other proper authority, depending on the specifics of the issue.

Q7.9   *Apparently you believe that leaders can be made?*

A7.9   Absolutely, yes! But even those who are "born leaders" need help along the way to fine-tune their craft. We all get better at what we do if we stick to it, care about the outcome, and understand what is expected of us.

 *Contrary to the opinion of many people, leaders are not born. Leaders are made, and they are made by effort and hard work."*

—Vince Lombardi, American football coach

CHAPTER 8

Are You Too Soft?

> " *A true leader has the confidence to stand alone, the courage to make tough decisions, and the compassion to listen to the needs of others. He does not set out to be a leader, but becomes one by the quality of his actions and the integrity of his intent."*
>
> —Unknown

It is my experience that most project managers are not willing to make the tough and unpopular project-related decisions, even though their instincts warn them that they are not taking the most effective action. These project managers are not leading their project teams to resolve their project's most important problems quickly. They frequently allow the project team to operate on consensus and what seems to please the most people—or to please the most vocal, influential people. To avoid or reduce conflict, they tend to make decisions that often are not in the best overall interest of the project.

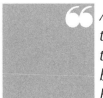

Most project leaders are too soft most of the time.

Being *too soft* is demonstrating behavior that results in being consistently less effective than what is otherwise possible—and needed—in performing responsibilities.

Examples of project manager actions (or inactions) that are indicative of too-soft behavior include:

- Holding back from providing constructive criticism to project members
- Avoiding escalating project-related problems that are at an apparent impasse for resolution
- Being unwilling to passionately defend the *right* project plan to the project sponsor, executives, or client
- Behaving as if there is little or no authority to support responsibility
- Putting off insisting on and driving good project management practices throughout the project
- Loosely inspecting what is expected from others
- Delaying asking for help when needed

- Being lax in holding project members accountable for their commitments and actions
- Complaining rather than constructively working issues to closure
- Taking on too much work instead of assigning tasks to the appropriate project members
- Being remiss in seeking out and obtaining needed project management training of both hard and soft skills
- Avoiding taking a position on an issue out of fear of alienating project members
- Avoiding or excessively delaying making key decisions
- Focusing predominantly on other than the top three problems.

If you routinely exhibit these types of behaviors, then you are too soft—you tend to take the easy way out rather than do the right thing by demonstrating effective behavior. If you only occasionally slip into this behavior, then that may not be serious cause for alarm.

Project success is about *results*—delivering a product that satisfies the customer and offers the organization an appropriate return on investment. The project manager's job is to lead the project's members in the pursuit of a successful project and product. In most cases, a project's success is directly related to the impact the project manager had on the project team throughout the project.

> **Project success is about results, not just effort.**

The most effective project managers behave as if they are running their own business. They believe—and their actions demonstrate—that *the buck stops here* and that they are fully accountable for the project. They must make and be accountable for many decisions, and they frequently and respectfully draw upon the knowledge, experiences, and insights of those around them so that they make the most informed decisions. But they are careful not to rely too heavily on consensus management; they recognize their duty to be fully accountable for the outcome of the project. This can mean that the most effective project managers will at times stand alone with what they believe to be the right decision.

> **The best project leaders are "the-buck-stops-here" accountable.**

Avoiding being too soft doesn't mean you have to be rude, insensitive, abrasive, arrogant, or a bully. None of these attributes is acceptable—ever! On the contrary, an effective project manager must strive to demonstrate behavior for others to model. For example, make yourself available and approachable to coach and support others through their problems and setbacks, be a constructive catalyst when change or a given action is required, and demonstrate respect and dignity for all project members. It is not about finding fault or making someone feel uncomfortable; it's about helping the project's members and encouraging them to help each other so that the prevailing attitude is that *we all are successful together.*

> **Project leaders that demonstrate too-soft behavior are performing a disservice to all stakeholders.**

If you believe that too-soft behavior will win friends and influence others, don't go there! It will have the opposite effect long-term. Those around you will lose respect for you as a leader, your project's outcome will be negatively impacted, and your career can become stagnant—or even shortened.

If you have difficulty making unpopular decisions, if you allow what others think about you to be more important than what you think about yourself, if you follow the "squeaky wheels" around you rather than your own inner compass . . . then you might not be ready to be an effective and successful project manager.

> **Anyone can learn to be an effective leader—if they choose to.**

But don't despair. Almost all project managers who perform their roles effectively today had these challenges to overcome yesterday. You too can persevere if it is important to you and you take the initiative to make things happen.

Let's Talk: Questions & Answers

Q8.1 *You assert that most of us as leaders are too soft most of the time. Why is this?*

A8.1 There are many reasons. For example: Many of us have never seriously focused on the too-soft issue so it has escaped our attention; many of us are afraid of alienating others and concerned that people will not like us; we don't understand our job well enough to realize that it's about results, not a popularity contest; and we are concerned that tougher behavior will burn bridges and be career-limiting.

Although it helps to understand why we may be too soft so that we can be more deliberate in correcting our behavior, *why* we may be too soft is never an excuse for performing ineffectively. What matters is that we, as leaders, take accountability for our performance and drive ourselves and our stakeholders to achieve the needed results.

Q8.2 *Can you elaborate on your example of too-soft behavior that especially resonates with me: "Evades taking a position on an issue out of fear of alienating project members"?*

A8.2 Here's an example.

> *I am mentoring a project manager I will call "Mike." Occasionally I shadow him for the day while he performs his duties. We*

are early heading to a meeting one afternoon when we encounter two of Mike's team leaders in the hallway discussing an issue. The issue has to do with a disagreement they had among themselves and they were not making any headway in resolving it—an issue that would harm the project if not resolved fairly quickly. We joined them to understand the issue.

A short while later, Mike motions to me that we have to leave to get to the meeting on time. I observed that Mike had remained quiet throughout the encounter as the frustrations between the two team leaders were reaching a boiling point. I ask Mike why he didn't join the discussion to help it to an appropriate resolution. Mike said that if he voiced his desire, then he would have alienated one of them. He explained that he tries his best not to get anyone upset with him. I shared with Mike that he obtained a worse outcome: Both are upset because Mike demonstrated behavior that is too soft—he didn't demonstrate the leadership, the backbone, required to help bring the issue to an acceptable resolution.

Mike's job as a project manager is to facilitate, when necessary, such problems so that they can get resolved reasonably quickly and with an acceptable outcome. More times than not, project members can accept a decision; what they cannot accept is inaction and indecision. On the off-chance that Mike's decision would have alienated one of the team leaders, that was not a valid reason for Mike to refrain from appropriately addressing the issue. Again, the reason why we may be too soft is never an excuse for performing ineffectively.

Q8.3 *Would you say that being too soft is a major contributor to project failure?*

A8.3 Let me make this absolutely clear. It is my experience that the No. 1 reason project managers—and all leaders—fail is that they are too soft. The No. 1 reason *projects* fail is that we don't effectively manage to the top three problems. (See Chapter 28, Manage to Your Top Three Problems.)

> **The No. 1 reason *project managers fail* is that they are too soft.**

Q8.4 *Your list of too-soft behaviors is daunting. There don't seem to be many people who can live up to the expectations you are placing on project managers.*

A8.4 Most of us have been guilty of being too soft at some point in our careers. I know I have. That's okay. All of us are works in progress. What's not okay is when we do not learn from ineffective past behavior and apply those lessons going forward.

It's not that I have raised the bar too high for what's expected of a project manager; it's that the bar needs to be that high for consistently effective behavior.

If you look around you and identify the people you respect the most as effective leaders, you will see the role-model behavior that I am talking about. These leaders have learned how to be effective—how to make things happen. From my experience over the years, I know that some of you reading this are already performing at the raised-bar level.

Q8.5   *What is your take on empowering yourself?*
A8.5   "Empowerment" is an overused word these days, but an underused concept.

Empowerment is understanding your job, taking ownership of your job, and doing whatever is necessary—within legal and ethical parameters—to accomplish that job.

All too often I hear, "I have all the responsibility, but I don't have the authority!" The problem is that most of us do not *take* the authority. We do little more than grab the tip of the iceberg of authority, of behaving boldly. When was the last time your boss (resource manager) called you on the carpet for exceeding your authority? Most people cannot remember a time. If you can, and you did nothing illegal or unethical, then you are to be applauded.

Q8.6   *What is your take on empowering others?*
A8.6   New leaders commonly resist giving up some of their "power" by empowering others—giving them full responsibility and accountability for key tasks. They often believe that they can do the job better or faster themselves, or fear giving others too much work. They also allow society's work ethic—being independent and self-reliant—to interfere with their duties as a leader of others. Resist these attitudes and transfer some of your work, some key tasks.

 No man will make a great leader who wants to do it all himself, or to get all the credit for doing it."

—Andrew Carnegie,
American industrialist and philanthropist

A successful leader knows that he or she achieves goals through the dedication, skill, and efforts of others. You must learn to work with others in ways that allow them to grow and achieve their dreams. After all, you appreciated the opportunities that others gave you to learn. Give others their chance as well. Doing so is good for you and good for your team members.

> **Empowering others frees you to lead and frees them to learn.**

Q8.7   *As a project manager, I feel I have difficulty being decisive. Any thoughts on this?*

A8.7   Your project members react to your actions. When you delay making crucial decisions, you also delay the time that will be needed to implement those decisions. Many projects and organizations have the capacity to increase their productivity and effectiveness. By putting off decision-making, you are not driving your team efficiently. If you delay your own decision-making, you are also preventing the next tier of decisions from being made. This decision queue can build to a point where progress within the project is seriously affected. The result is a sluggishness that spreads throughout the project—and that only you, the project manager, can correct.

Once the WHAT is decided, the HOW always follows. We must not make the HOW an excuse for not facing and accepting the WHAT."

—Pearl S. Buck, American novelist

It's better to make decisions early—when their pain and cost to the project are relatively minor, yet when they can have a major, long-term, positive effect. Some decisions will, in hindsight, prove to be less than the best. However, if you wait until absolutely no risk remains before taking a position on a problem, then you will lose all competitiveness.

Q8.8   *As a project manager, I am the busiest person on the project. When members whine about taking on duties or action items that are within their domain of responsibility, I often step in and perform them. The result is that I am working a lot of overtime, facing burnout, and am even considering giving up being a project manager. Any advice?*

> **Project managers should avoid becoming a project's critical path.**

A8.8   You have set yourself up to be the critical path on the project. Instead of being the critical path, you should be free to help navigate others who are on the critical path. You need to hold others accountable for performing their work. If they need help, then work to obtain that help, but do not take on their duties.

Q8.9   *Can you expand on the positive behaviors we should embrace to overcome the negative behaviors listed?*

A8.9   Many of the behaviors you seek are the focus of chapters in this book. These include:
- Chapter 2: Are You a Benevolent Dictator? You Should Be!
- Chapter 3: Ask for Help—or Become Part of the Problem
- Chapter 5: Is Your Professional Behavior Respected?
- Chapter 10: Turn Criticism into an Asset
- Chapter 14: Duties of the Effective Project Manager
- Chapter 18: Are You Learning from Project to Project?

More information about too-soft behavior is available in another one of my books. If you're interested, see Chapter 15, Are You Too Soft? in *The EnterPrize Organization: Organizing Software Projects for Accountability and Success* (Newtown Square, PA: Project Management Institute, Inc., 2000). © 2000, Project Management Institute, Inc.

CHAPTER 9

Foster Interpersonal Communications

 *Too often we underestimate the power of a touch, a smile, a kind word, a listening ear, an honest compliment, or the smallest act of caring, all of which have the potential to turn a life around."*

—Leo Buscaglia,
American motivational author and speaker

There has been a disturbing trend in recent years to slot people as objects, as commodities, rather than treat them with the respect, dignity, and nurturing that are both sought and required. We are not objects or machines. Nor are we low-maintenance. We have great aspirations and, therefore, high needs. In fact, we are high-maintenance whether we like to admit it or not.

When you get past the surface—the veneer that so many of us spend a lifetime developing, molding, shaping, and refining—we all are remarkably similar. We all want the same things from life: We want to be loved and appreciated; we want security and health; we want to contribute, to achieve; we want to dream and pursue those dreams to their imagined end.

When the veneer is removed, we all are remarkably alike.

 If you treat employees as if they make a difference to the company, they will."

—Dr. Jim Goodnight, CEO and founder, SAS

The dignity and value bestowed upon and felt by each individual are central to the overall continued success of an enterprise. The best-run projects and organizations—and often those with the highest morale—typically are those where individuals demonstrate a basic respect for one another.

The core principle underlying effective interpersonal communications is the Golden Rule: "Treat others as you would like to be treated." There is no better rule to follow when working with or serving others such as project stakeholders.

A rule for all seasons: "Treat others as you would like to be treated."

Some key actions to adopt that will foster and improve effective communications among project members include:

- **When you are wrong, admit it.** We all make mistakes, and to varying degrees will continue to do so, especially as our work environments and the challenges we face increasingly change. But how we handle the mistakes will be closely observed by those around us and can affect our relationships. Admitting when you are wrong often can change the interaction from one of confrontation to one of cooperation. Moreover, the general level of respect that people have for you typically increases after you have admitted that you made a mistake. We continually look to see ourselves in others and when others show humility, grace, and maturity, we embrace them more closely.

> *When you are wrong and admit it, you are demonstrating social maturity.*

- **Exercise tolerance; be quick to assist.** More than ever, your job requires you to know more, resulting in a greater dependency on the knowledge and experience of others. Conversely, others have a greater dependency on us. We need to exercise tolerance of others when they come to us for help. After all, we will need their help from time to time. As members of a project willingly share their knowledge and experiences, the collective strength of a project increases. Moreover, "helpers" are frequently the most respected and admired members of a team. *Caution: Do not voluntarily assist others at the sacrifice of your own responsibilities and commitments.*

> *Four words to speak if you want to be remembered: "I will help you."*

- **Make direct contact.** Interactive communication is still the best there is. Go out of your way to meet the people on whom you depend or who depend on you. Talk to them via telephone or face to face. Invite them to your meetings; ask to attend theirs when appropriate. E-mail has great value, but do not overlook the need to build relationships and bonds that only your voice or presence can cement. An especially effective action is "management by walking around"; that is, build into your routine informally "checking in" with your project members. You not only will learn a lot about what's really happening, but you will build closer relationships.

> *The more human the contact, the greater the investment in the relationship.*

- **Use tact.** The message you send may not be heard as loudly as the manner in which you send it. Keep emotion out of your discussions, focusing on the facts at hand. Show people that you are willing to work with them where appropriate, and that you are working to add value to the product or process.

> *Saving face for another can save face for you as well.*

- **Let go of bad news.** Whenever possible, dispose of bad news discreetly. The preferred approach is in private, where its impact can be better assessed by clearer thinking minds with fewer emotional complexities taxing their attention. Moreover, release the bad news as soon as reasonably possible. The longer you delay in revealing the bad news, the greater the potential for harm to the project's stakeholders.

> *Bad news happens; learn to deal with it effectively.*

- **Write an note of appreciation once each week.** Recall how much a letter of appreciation that you received meant to you. What a great feeling. Many of us save those letters and notes, which can help us regain our confidence, our self-esteem, our sense of worth. However, make sure not to write wholesale appreciative notes from a template that you distribute to most people you encounter. Be selective and sincere in identifying the truly noteworthy events. As appropriate, remember to copy the resource manager of the person receiving your praise. Or, send the appreciative note directly to the resource manager and allow the resource manager to share the note with his or her employee.

> *One of the greatest rewards is to help people realize that they are worthwhile.*

- **Go out of your way to do something kind for one person each day.** It may be offering a compliment or performing a service or an act of aid. The more you practice this behavior, the more people will enjoy your presence. Moreover, this behavior can become contagious to those around you. Performing "random acts of kindness" can be among the most rewarding moments a person experiences.

> *The more you give, the more you receive.*

- **Close problems.** Lingering problems between people or groups have a negative effect on communications. Important problems should be logged in an accessible data base, assigned an owner, given a target close date, and tracked to closure. Closing problems in a timely and effective manner shows that you care about your word, your commitments, your relationships, your success—and the success of those on whom you depend and who depend on you.

> *Routinely closing out the old problems will help you focus your energies on new problems.*

- **Be a good listener.** Communication is a two-way process. To be an effective communicator, you must be able to send *and* receive information. Helpful tips include: Maintain frequent eye contact, voice brief responses to show you are listening, don't prematurely change the subject, ask questions, and restate what you heard. We learn through listening.

> *Everyone gains when you listen.*

- **Be willing to break with tradition.** We live in a rapidly changing world. All of us must be more open than ever to new ideas and new ways of thinking. Tradition can cause us to narrow our thinking and to jump to erroneous conclusions. It can cause us not to grow, to be less effective, to be unable to see what is possible and even necessary. Be open, even eager, to new ideas and methods. However we performed yesterday, we must perform better today and still better tomorrow.

 Insanity is doing the same thing in the same way and expecting a different outcome."

—Chinese proverb

- *Ask questions; never assume.* Have you ever assumed something and later learned you were wrong? We all have. Incorrect

Asking questions is not dumb; not asking is.

assumptions that you make on the job can cost your project considerable rework, lost time, and ultimately, lost revenue. Asking a question at the appropriate time can help you avoid missing a commitment, save money, save time, and even save face—yours or someone else's.

Although one person can influence change in an organization, the more members that rally behind a cause, the stronger impact it will have. To this end, consider developing a set of people principles to be adopted across your project or organization. Because a project consists of people of diverse backgrounds and experiences, these principles may not be intuitively obvious to everyone. If they were, projects and organizations would not have so many people-related problems. We need each other. Let's start by appreciating and celebrating one another.

Let's Talk: Questions & Answers

Q9.1   *You say that the core principle underlying effective interpersonal communications is the Golden Rule. Are you making a religious statement?*

A9.1   No. I respect and honor each person's right to believe as long as it does not interfere with the well-being of others. I am no religious scholar, but I suspect that the Golden Rule is fundamental to many of the world's religions. I happen to find the Golden Rule to be, by far, the best philosophy to embrace in working and living with others. Projects and organizations benefit greatly by its application.

Q9.2   *When you say to dispose of bad news discreetly, sometimes it seems that there is little choice. Can you cite an example?*

A9.2   Here's an example where there's a choice:

> *You and your resource manager have a meeting scheduled at 8:00 a.m. in your resource manager's office. A few minutes before the meeting, you discover some really disturbing news about your project. The news appears to be serious enough that you are surprised it escaped your radar for so long.*
>
> *When you walk into your resource manager's office at 8:00, you find that your resource manager's boss is also there. In most cases, you should politely ask your resource manager if you could chat with him for a moment outside his office. You then may choose to share the disturbing news. Your resource manager now can make the decision to share the disturbing news with his boss or wait until more information is available.*

If you surprised your resource manager with the bad news in front of his boss, then you might be undermining your resource manager by making him appear ineffective. Being discreet with your resource manager doesn't mean that he will like the news, but he will appreciate your sensitivity regarding the manner in which you shared that news.

Q9.3   *Why do you say "in most cases" you should discreetly take your resource manager aside? What could cause you to behave differently?*

A9.3   If you, your resource manager, and your resource manager's boss have a great working relationship, it may not matter that the information is shared the first time with all parties present. I would like everyone to have the good fortune of working in such an environment; however, for many people, that level of supportive environment is elusive.

Q9.4   *I have a hard time imagining that a person can ever justify holding back important information from senior management. What's your take on this?*

A9.4   If you ran to your resource manager or senior management every time you discovered a potentially serious problem, you would be wasting their time as well as yours. Many problems are not as serious as they first appear. Many times it is more professional to invest time and energy in understanding the importance and impact of the problem and its resolution before passing the information up the management chain. Some call this *due diligence* or *completed staff work.*

Q9.5 *Sometimes I write a letter of appreciation and receive no thanks afterwards. Why should I bother?*

A9.5 Do not do a good deed for a "thank you." You take action because it is the right thing to do and that is who you choose to be. Moreover, it is behavior that you are role-modeling so that others can learn from your actions. It's also called *integrity*.

Q9.6 *I believe the project manager, as a role model, should always be kind, humble, and helpful to others. When you recommend the actions, "Go out of your way to do something kind for one person each day," and "Perform random acts of kindness," it sounds like you are encouraging the project manager to show these attributes only occasionally rather demonstrate them consistently. Am I interpreting you correctly?*

A9.6 No, I need to clarify. You should always treat others with respect and dignity—as you would like to be treated. I am referring to making a habit of reaching further than you need to or further than what is expected. Let's look at an example.

> *You are waiting for a fax to arrive. You walk from your office to the fax room and find your fax. However, you also see a fax that is for a coworker. Even though the coworker's office is in the opposite direction from where you need to go next, you carry the coworker's fax to her office. The coworker is not there. You leave the fax on the coworker's chair without leaving your name as the person to thank for the delivery.*

This is what I mean by going out of your way to do something kind each day that is beyond your expected duties. Such behavior takes almost no time and can have a far-reaching impact on the overall health of a project, organization, or company.

Q9.7 *Related to the action, "Be a good listener," what do you recommend if you are listening to someone—say, in a hallway or a small meeting—and they drone on and on?*

A9.7 If you and others already have obtained the information you need, then politely move on, either with the next topic or by ending the conversation or meeting. Don't view yourself as a victim, with no choice but to continue listening. You have choices; just make sure you behave in a professionally mature manner and demonstrate respect for others.

Q9.8 *Why be so willing to break with tradition when tradition often has persevered for so long?*

A9.8 Just because a belief has endured for hours, weeks, or centuries does not make it right or the best approach. It is healthy to question our past actions so that we can learn and grow. Having said that, I am not espousing that you thoughtlessly discard conventions that work—or that you reinvent new traditions with each new project. Here is an example that may explain this further.

You must always be willing to constructively examine the past so that the future can benefit.

When you were 18 years old, you were doing your best to identify what career option to choose. Most of us have changed our career choice more than once since we were 18. At your age today, would you take vocational guidance from an 18 year old? Neither would I.

Q9.9 *You say to break with tradition and explore new ideas and methods. How can one do that if the organization is stuck in the dark ages?*

A9.9 Every organization will change eventually, or it will go the way of the buggy whip and the crank telephone. Among those organizations that survive, some change far more quickly than others. Therefore, we know that change is possible. The question is "Who will champion the change?" It could be you as well as another. This book is loaded with ideas to help you be a catalyst for change, for making things happen. (For example, explore Part Seven, Promoting the Advancement of Project Management beyond Your Projects.)

Q9.10 *I sometimes criticize hastily. Any ideas for me?*

A9.10 Resist the temptation. When you suspect poor work, ask questions and listen carefully to the answers. Once a wrong or regrettable word is spoken, it cannot be taken back. After you understand the reason behind a problem, attack the problem, not the person.

Give others the same courtesy that you would like shown to you. Take this opportunity not only to help someone resolve a problem but also to help him or her benefit from the experience. Also, work at increasing the bond and trust between you and the project member. If you demonstrate constructive behavior and resist attacking the person, you may find yourself with a more loyal and dedicated project member.

Q9.11   *You say to ask questions rather than assume. But doesn't doing so makes me look stupid?*

A9.11   Better to have the misperception of looking stupid than proving stupid because you failed to ask sufficient questions.

Earlier in my career, there was a person new to our project. He was a senior level technical employee, but seemed to ask more questions about the product and project than all the other project members combined. Some of his questions seemed elementary and made him look "stupid." Some members privately questioned his value and wondered why he was recruited to be on the project. In a few short months he became one of the most valuable members of the project. He turned out to be a sponge for information and all those questions resulted in a reservoir of knowledge that proved invaluable both to him and others.

Turn Criticism into an Asset

Criticism is something we can avoid easily—by saying nothing, doing nothing, and being nothing."

—Aristotle, Greek philosopher and scientist

Who isn't familiar with criticism? It comes from everywhere—friends, family, coworkers, supervisors, and even strangers. While there is little we can do to prevent criticism from coming our way, there are ways of dealing with criticism that can make it a positive experience. As project managers and leaders, it is essential that we deal effectively with criticism.

For many of us, criticism has the effect of penetrating our fragile self-esteem, often leaving us to analyze and question the truth behind the image we have of ourselves. For some, criticism can cut even deeper, and depression can seep into our being and leave us with a sharp sense of desperation—we just want to hide, to be left alone.

Why does criticism affect so many of us in this negative way? Some reasons for the control it appears to have over us are:

- We fear rejection by the people who are part of our world.
- We are afraid that the criticism has merit and that we are wrong and look stupid.
- We don't like the image we have of ourselves and the criticism reinforces our negative self-image.
- We fear that our self-perceived feeling of self-control will crumble as people whittle away at its foundation
- We are frustrated because people won't give us a chance to see how effective we really can be, but often seem to focus on the "bad" parts of us.

Three Practices to Adopt

We can overcome the reasons for allowing others to affect us negatively, but we will never escape criticism. More often than not, we have no control over the criticism that comes our way. So, what can we do? We can adopt three practices:

1. Learn to expect criticism.
2. Learn to recognize, accept, and welcome constructive criticism.
3. Never allow criticism—constructive or destructive—to negatively impact our thoughts or performance.

Learn to Expect Criticism

Criticism is going to happen. It is part of the reality in which we live. You are not likely to experience a full day around people without being on the receiving end of criticism for something. If you learn to expect criticism, you are far less likely to be caught off guard and far more likely to remain in control when the criticism arrives.

If you acknowledge that receiving criticism is a fundamental byproduct of living around people, then you can prepare yourself to deal effectively with it.

Learn to Recognize, Accept, and Welcome Constructive Criticism

Criticism can be either *constructive* or *destructive*. You should welcome constructive criticism; that is, criticism that is well-meaning and intended to be useful. Constructive criticism should leave you with the feeling that you have been helped, that you have learned something about yourself and the impact that your actions are having on others.

But what about destructive criticism? Destructive criticism is criticism you receive that might have malicious overtones. This type of criticism offers no value that enables the recipient to learn and grow from the experience.

Know the difference between constructive and destructive criticism.

A cautionary note: By far, most of the criticism we receive is constructive. However, many of us may not perceive this as true. There are two primary reasons why we may believe that criticism is *destructive*, when, in fact, it is *constructive*. The first reason is that the criticism has been delivered in a destructive tone even though the criticism itself is constructive. Some people have difficulty expressing thoughts in a nonaggressive, tactful, and articulate manner.

The second reason why we may believe the criticism to be destructive is because it hurt us in some way. For example, it may have embarrassed us, hurt our pride or feelings, or shown us in an unfavorable light to others and to ourselves. The truth often hurts, but it is still *truth* and we can learn and benefit from it. Practice listening carefully to apparently destructive criticism for useful information that it might be disguising.

Never Allow Criticism—Constructive or Destructive—to Impact Your Thoughts or Performance Negatively

At some time or another, you will find people who disapprove of your behavior or your decisions. (You might even project those feelings toward others from time to time.) Even the people you love, and who love you, will at times disapprove of your actions. Keep in mind that other people's opinions are just that—opinions. If you allow what other people say about you to immobilize you—to impact your thoughts or performance negatively—then you are saying, in effect, that what other people think about you is more important than what you think about yourself.

 *The trouble with most of us is that we would rather be ruined by praise than saved by criticism."*

—Norman Vincent Peale,
American religious leader and motivational author

If you need the approval of others before you can feel good about yourself, you are giving permission to others to control you. If you don't think well of yourself, it will show through in the relationships you have. People would rather be around those who feel good about who and what they are. It is okay and healthy to think well about yourself. This is not a selfish, uncaring action. Quite the opposite: You have more to give to others if you think and feel good about yourself.

> *What you think about yourself must always be more important to you than what others think about you.*

Changing How We Deal With Criticism

For many of us, our families, our friends, school, and work environments have taught us that if we want another person's approval—if we want to be liked and accepted by others—then we need to alter our behavior to accommodate our critics. This view is so widespread that it has become ingrained into our makeup, as part of the core of what we perceive ourselves to be. Intentionally or not, people use criticism as a form of controlling our actions, controlling us. And we use criticism as a tool for controlling or hurting others.

> *Being negatively affected by criticism is a learned behavior.*

How can we change the way we deal with criticism? Every time you receive criticism—constructive or destructive—ask yourself the following question and respond accordingly:

"Can I benefit in any way from the criticism?"

- If the answer is *yes*, then welcome the opportunity to learn and grow, to be stronger tomorrow than you are today. If appropriate, show appreciation for the criticism.

- If the answer is *no*, then discard the criticism and proceed with your plans.

When you receive criticism, make sure you give it careful thought before rejecting it. Criticism is often related to aspects of our behavior that we at first do not understand—we don't understand what we don't know. Work at keeping an open mind. For example, if a boss or someone you respect gives you criticism and you do not immediately understand why, dig deeper to understand it. There likely are valuable messages that you need to understand and internally process.

> **We don't understand what we don't know.**

You might think that this sounds too easy. It's not easy. It requires practice, and lots of it. But then, you have all kinds of opportunity to practice—each time you receive criticism. Criticism should be viewed as an opportunity to learn, to improve yourself, and to enhance what you can offer to others. Criticism is truly a potent learning aid, if we view it in the positive light that it deserves.

> **Criticism is a potent learning aid; you can either grow from it or be controlled by it.**

Criticism is here to stay. You can deal with it or be intimated, wounded, or destroyed by it. You can learn and grow from it or slowly withdraw and fall apart from it.

Here's an exercise that can help you distinguish between constructive criticism and destructive criticism—and help you learn to deal effectively with any criticism when it occurs. You may find that your capabilities for dealing with criticism are greatly diminished when you are in a high-stress situation.

List every piece of criticism you received over the past day or two. List everything, no matter how insignificant the remark or action seems to be. Follow your journey throughout the day and recall the people you had contact with, whether in person, on the telephone, through email or snail-mail. Develop a list of at least 10 incidents of criticism.

Now examine each item and mark whether it is an example of constructive (C) or destructive (D) criticism. If you can learn anything at all of value from it, mark it as constructive. As you mark each entry, recall how you felt when you received the criticism. Did it bother you? If so, recall what was said earlier in this chapter about never allowing criticism to impact your thoughts or performance negatively. Visualize, as if the incident was being replayed, how you could have maintained your inner control. Repeat these actions for each item on the list.

The more you visualize yourself maintaining your inner control and acknowledging the lessons you receive from constructive criticism, the more you are programming your mind to behave effectively in dealing with criticism. Practice this enough and it will become part of the way you think and operate.

As project managers and leaders, it is essential that we deal effectively with criticism, both when receiving and when transmitting criticism. Our performance, as well as the performance of those within our domain of responsibility, will benefit greatly. By the way, the more responsibility you take on as a leader, the more you will receive criticism from those around you. Be prepared to deal with it effectively.

Let's Talk: Questions & Answers

Q10.1 *Are you, in effect, saying that with each new promotion of added responsibility a person should expect to encounter more criticism?*

A10.1 Yes. If the promotion requires you to work with more people, make more decisions, or perform more actions, then there will be more opportunity for those around you to judge your behavior and actions. The higher a person is promoted up the corporate ladder, the more criticism that person can expect from those around him. As you would expect, if a person has difficulty dealing with criticism, that person's career can be seriously stunted.

Q10.2 *As a project manager, don't you think that project members should just accept what I direct them to do, instead of questioning or criticizing it? After all, I am accountable for the outcome of the project.*

A10.2 The project manager definitely should be held accountable for the launch, execution, and successful completion of the project. However, the project manager needs to solicit opinions as well as listen to what others have to say. Collectively, the project members are likely smarter than the project manager about many issues. The project manager must learn to skillfully request opinions, assess those opinions, and then make the appropriate decisions. It is healthy for project members to offer alternative approaches, but once a decision has been made/blessed by the project manager, it's time for everyone to work off the same page. (See Chapter 2, Are You a Benevolent Dictator? You Should Be! for more on decision-making in a project environment.)

Q10.3 *Do you believe that criticism has played a big role in who we are today?*

A10.3   Absolutely, a profound role. We are in large part the sum total of all the criticism that we have received throughout our lives—criticism that we have chosen to reflect upon and change our behavior correspondingly. The power that all that criticism has had in shaping our behavior is truly profound for each of us. It can be even more profound as we learn to deal with it effectively. Constructive criticism should always be welcomed. From it, we learn, we grow, we change, and we prosper.

We are today defined by the impact of the criticism we have received throughout our past.

CHAPTER 11

Dealing with Difficult People

We all encounter difficult people in the workplace. We may be that way ourselves from time to time. By *difficult* I mean a person who routinely exhibits one or more of the following behaviors: hard to work with or manage; doesn't want to play by conventional social or organizational rules; or is a disruptive and disturbing element to others.

By difficult, I do not necessarily mean someone who doesn't agree with us. Disagreement is often healthy and good for business. It serves as a check-and-balance to help ensure that the best ideas and decisions are considered; it stretches the players to perform at their best. It is not always important that we agree. It is, however, important that we can work reasonably well together despite our different points of view.

> *Don't assume that a person who disagrees with you is necessarily a difficult person.*

A person who *routinely* exhibits one or more of these behaviors can be a disruptive and disturbing element to the well-being of the team:

- Misses meeting commitments
- Does not return phone calls or emails
- Communicates rudely
- Refuses to follow directives
- Treats others abusively
- Undermines team cohesion
- Is overly aggressive and self-serving
- Is overly passive and indifferent.

Why Are Some People Difficult?

Everyone has reasons for being the way they are. As noted, we all can have our moments of difficult behavior. But why do some people *routinely* exhibit difficult behavior? Perhaps they are:

- Reacting to your behavior, however unintentional you may have been
- Lazy
- Uncaring
- Without sufficient skills

- Overworked
- Unaware of their improper behavior
- Reacting to some misfortune in their professional or personal life
- Insecure
- Unhappy in life
- Rebelling against some event from their recent or distant past.

What Can We Do When Faced with Difficult People?

We have many options for dealing with difficult people, depending largely on the underlying reason for the difficult behavior.

If the reason for a person's difficult behavior is that he or she is reacting to your behavior, then your next actions may help remedy your earlier behavior. Look closely at your own behavior to determine if you are the problem. If you are, then admit your mistake and repair the situation as best you can. Occasionally a third party may be necessary to help break an impasse between you and the other party. The Golden Rule—*Treat others as you would like to be treated*—can go a long way to-

Don't expect everyone to practice the Golden Rule— including you on occasion; first look within to see if the problem lies there.

ward helping you avoid becoming or remaining the problem.

If the reason for the difficult behavior is that the person is lazy or uncaring, then you may choose to follow a two-step approach. The first step is to work with the difficult person in an attempt to allow him or her to correct the behavior. Sometimes showing that you care about the person and his or her performance can positively affect behavior. If the behavior does not change sufficiently, then you invoke the second step: Inform the person's resource manager (boss). If the person's resource manager is not effective in turning the person's behavior around, then you must escalate the issue higher to seek an acceptable solution.

In almost all cases, you should attempt to work with the difficult person before proceeding with an escalation.

If the underlying reason for the person's difficult behavior is that the person lacks sufficient skills, then you again may choose to follow a two-step approach. The first step is to work with the person to help him or her learn what he or she needs to know. You personally can work with the person or seek out assistance from one or more project members. If the person requires more help than is reasonable or available, then step two is implemented: Get the person's resource manager in-

volved to help bring the person along through training, mentoring, or a buddy system. If these options are not reasonable or do not work, then the resource manager must find another person to take on the committed duties.

If "overworked" is the problem, then the person's workload must be addressed. In most cases, this will require involving the person's resource manager. For example, perhaps the resource manager must assign some of the person's duties to others—whether temporarily or permanently—so that the person's duties are sufficiently handled.

If the person is unaware of his or her improper behavior, then constructively confronting the person may be all the action needed to correct future behavior. If that doesn't work, then the person's resource manager may need to be involved to deal with the behavioral problem. A project manager is expected to go only so far in teaching the project members proper behavior. The brunt of that task falls to the person's resource manager.

> *The person charged with the primary role of developing the professional behavior of employees is the resource manager.*

If any of the last four items appears to be the reason for the difficult behavior, then the underlying problem is more deeply rooted and you may be ineffective in turning the situation around. You must inform the person's resource manager so that the person can obtain proper help.

Are We Accountable for the Disruptive Behavior of Others?

You are not accountable for the disruptive behavior of those assigned to your project. However, you are accountable for dealing effectively with disruptive behavior that harms your project or impacts your performance or duties. If a person refuses or is unable to take an action, perform a service or duty, or make or fulfill a commitment, then you must take the action necessary to correct the situation.

If you require some action from another and that person's attitude and behavior are getting in the way of your needs, then you must not allow the person's negative behavior to cause you to miss your commitments or obligations. You have the responsibility—the duty—to continue to move forward even if that means pursuing an escalation to get the person to focus on your needs. If you avoid taking appropriate action, then you become the problem and will be held fully accountable. Don't allow yourself to become the fall guy. Everyone is counting on your leadership to prevail so that the project is successful.

> *You are responsible for your actions and commitments, regardless of the actions of those around you.*

Let's Talk: Questions & Answers

Q11.1 *What do you say about dealing with someone who generally is not difficult, but is having a bad day?*

A11.1   Generally, I would cut them some slack. After all, we all may have an off day occasionally. You may decide to lend an ear or be a friend to help. But whatever you choose to do, it is important that you not allow the event to have a lasting harmful effect on your commitments and the project.

Q11.2   *What if I am unsure about the reason behind a person's difficult behavior? How do I know the proper course of action to pursue?*

A11.2   Of course, you want to avoid making incorrect assumptions that could be unfair to or offend the person. In general, if you are unsure of the reason behind the difficult behavior, approach the person professionally and discreetly to discuss the situation. Be open to the possibility that the misunderstanding could be of your doing. Professionally approaching the difficult person can defuse an apparent growing problem before it has a chance to fester and become bigger than it currently is.

  If you believe that it is inappropriate to confront the person demonstrating the difficult behavior, then you can seek counsel from your resource manager or the difficult person's resource manager. In all cases, try your best to use good judgment and approach the situation as you would want someone to behave if you were the offending party. However, also remember that you are responsible for your actions and commitments, regardless of the actions of those around you. If the person's behavior is an impediment to you fulfilling your commitments, you must take action.

Q11.3   *Is it acceptable to use email to attempt to work out the conflict with another person?*

A11.3   Careful! Depending on the level of rapport between the two parties and the nature and urgency of the issue, use email thoughtfully and sparingly. In many cases, email may make the situation worse. The tone of an email can easily be misinterpreted and can escalate the tension between the parties. In most cases, face-to-face contact is the best approach for defusing possible hostilities and encouraging both parties to reach out to one another. If face contact is not practical, then try a phone call.

Q11.4 *When you believe it is necessary to go to the resource manager of the difficult person, do you inform the person before contacting his or her boss?*

A11.4 Whenever possible, you should first try to work out the problem with the person. If that action is not yielding the necessary results, then you must escalate to the person's resource manager for help. I recommend informing the person that you are about to involve his or her resource manager. You might even suggest that the two of you see the boss together. Of course, there may be situations where the disruptive behavior should immediately be reported to the person's boss without further contact with the person.

Q11.5 *When you go over a person's head, aren't you making the situation personal?*

A11.5 As a professional, be candid and respectful. Tell the person of your project goals and your need to address the issue at hand—even if it requires involvement from upper management. Escalation is not your first choice, but it is a viable option.

Never intentionally make an issue personal. It's business. If a person's difficult behavior is harming the project or your ability to manage the project effectively, then you must confront the problem. If you allow the problem to drift unresolved, then you become part of the problem. (See Chapter 31, Escalate Is Not a Dirty Word.)

Q11.6 *Is the difficult person's resource manager always the right point-of-contact for escalating the disturbing situation?*

A11.6 The proper position to escalate the issue to is usually the person's resource manager. However, depending on the project or the organizational structure in your environment, a project sponsor or other designated person may be more appropriate.

Q11.7 *What do you do if you have escalated the problem to the difficult person's resource manager, but the boss is ineffective in resolving the problem?*

A11.7 Then you escalate higher up the escalation chain according to the escalation process described in Chapter 31, Escalate Is Not a Dirty Word.

Q11.8 *What do you do if the difficult person happens to be your resource manager?*

A11.8 This is the worst-case scenario because your resource manager typically controls your salary, promotions, awards, and job opportunities. Obviously, it is in your and your resource manager's best interests for the two of you to have a good working relationship. When you don't, the fallout can be a high price on your satisfaction with both your job and your company.

In most cases, I recommend that you professionally maintain open and honest communications with your boss so that he or she understands what bugs you. But it is a two-way relationship. You also have a duty to work hard at meeting your resource manager's needs and expectations.

If the difficulty with your resource manager is related to a legal or ethical issue, then run—don't walk—to take the issue up the management chain. However, compared to other issues that require escalation, legal and ethical issues are rare. Going over your resource manager's head for other than legal or ethical issues can be career-limiting, so consider the fallout carefully before taking that step.

Q11.9 *I read all you said about what we can do when faced with difficult people, but sometimes the negative vibes can resonate all day and even come home with us. Any further advice on this?*

A11.9 When we encounter difficult people, sometimes they can have an emotional lingering effect on a good part of our day. Even worse, we might bring the emotional discomfort into our personal lives. The vast majority of people that we work with are reasonable and well-intentioned. But even though the difficult people are, overall, relatively few in numbers, they make up for it by the upsetting impact they can have on our day and our productivity.

> *You have the power to not allow difficult people to negatively affect your day and your performance.*

Do not allow difficult people to have any significant negative effect on you. Instead, recognize their behavior for what it is and do not lose control of yourself, your duties, and your day. Professionally confront the problem and then move on with your responsibilities.

> *You will encounter difficult people throughout your professional and personal lives, regardless of the respectful behavior you demonstrate.*

You will never be able to rid your world of difficult people, but you can learn to deal effectively with their behavior so that they do not negatively impact your performance or attitude. Always maintain control over your thoughts and performance despite the undesirable actions of those around you.

CHAPTER 12

Don't
Fear
Failure

 *If you have made mistakes, even serious ones, there is always another chance for you. What we call failure is not the falling down but the staying down."*

—Mary Pickford, Canadian-born
American movie actress and producer

The fear of failure—or inversely, the fear of success—prevents many of us from realizing our dreams. When we are bitten by the failure bug, we recoil—we want to go into hiding. We withdraw from taking big steps with our dreams and endeavors; we become content with baby steps or no steps. We become overly cautious and seek the safe ground. We become anxious. We churn inside and nervously look over our shoulders in fear that failure is close by. We cower at change; we become immobilized and can essentially lose our effectiveness.

Why do so many of us have such an unhealthy inhibition toward failure? Common reasons include:

- Looking stupid
- Losing respect from our coworkers
- Remembering bad experiences
- Losing out on future opportunities and job growth
- Disappointing our leaders
- Fearing reprisal
- Losing our job
- Being marked a failure by others
- Being marked a failure by ourselves.

Ironically, without failure, we cannot grow, learn, and master those things that are important to us. Many of the things that you do easily today (e.g., swimming, riding a bike) are things that you failed at repeatedly as you were learning to master them. Many more accomplishments are intangible, such as improving soft- and leadership-related skills like communicating, negotiating, organizing, planning, working well with others, and making things happen.

Once you allow the fear of failure to dominate your thinking and actions, you have placed yourself into a box that is rocked from side to side from the wake caused by life passing you by.

Continuous progress is not possible without failures along the journey.

What many of us view as failures are not failures at all but instead are steppingstones to progress—to success. Without these steppingstones we could never arrive at the many destinations and goals we have attained. In the end we call it *experience*.

We have all marveled at the athlete who wins an Olympic Gold Medal, the master painter who creates a priceless work of art, the genetic biologist who discovers the defect-causing gene, the Oscar winner, the Nobel Prize winner, the Pulitzer Prize winner. We wouldn't dare think of any of these great achievers as failures. Yet, what often escapes us is that each of these champions of champions failed many, many times before achieving their victory.

Failures are steppingstones to success.

But none of these people saw their failures as indications that they themselves were failures. Instead, they grew stronger from each attempt. They realized that they were producing results that offered them opportunities for learning, for assessing, for growing, for achieving. The failures represented lessons, not defeat. They were not even viewed as setbacks as much as they were viewed as necessary steppingstones in reaching their personal summit.

Failure is necessary in achieving those things that are important to you.

All achievers—but especially great achievers—meet with failure along the way. In fact, great achievers not only learn from their own mistakes, but they also learn from the experience and advice of others. They know that no one lives long enough to make all the mistakes themselves. They know that the only real failures are the experiences we don't learn from, particularly when they are our own.

The only real failures are the experiences we don't learn from.

One of my favorite famous-failure stories is of an American who:

- Failed in business
- Was defeated for the legislature
- Failed again in business
- Suffered a nervous breakdown
- Was defeated for state elector
- Was defeated for Congress
- Was defeated for Congress again
- Was defeated for a Senate bid
- Was defeated for a Vice President bid
- Was defeated again for Senate.

He then became 16th president of the United States. His name was Abraham Lincoln.

All of us have our own failure-to-success stories, though perhaps not as lofty as Lincoln's. The next time you are confronted with an opportunity, or have a dream, or feel an inner signal to set a higher goal, to go beyond what you have already achieved, remember that failure is a necessary ingredient for achieving.

Failure is, in a sense, the highway to success, inasmuch as every discovery of what is false leads us to seek earnestly after what is true."

—John Keats, English poet

When all is said and done, people never remember the failures when they are looking at a person who is accomplished at something. And, most importantly, it doesn't matter what anybody thinks about your stumbles; it only matters what you think and how you choose to process the so-called "failure."

Let's Talk: Questions & Answers

Q12.1 *I have a hard time disassociating my failures from thinking about myself as a failure. Any advice?*

A12.1 There is no connection between failing and being a failure. Your failures are lessons to aid your growth and success. We all not only make mistakes, but also will continue to make mistakes. Once you learn to view failure in the positive light it deserves, you will be better prepared not to fear failure or associate failure with you being a failure. Successful people look at mistakes as feedback, outcomes, results; unsuccessful people look at mistakes as defining who they are, their self-worth—they make it personal.

Q12.2 *I can deal with small failures; it's the large ones that haunt me. Comments?*

A12.2 Failures can be small—an email sent with a word typed incorrectly—or large—your project came in 40 percent late and 50 percent over budget. Yes, we naturally feel heightened emotion from bigger failures, especially when they affect many other people. Even so, it is important that we learn what we can from these valuable lessons, apply those lessons going forward, and move on.

> **Without failures our growth would be tragically stunted.**

Some of your biggest successes will come out of your biggest failures.

Q12.3   *Even if I do not fear failure, shouldn't I still work hard to avoid it?*

A12.3   Yes. You should want to make as few mistakes as possible. However, depending on the circumstances, it is possible and likely that some of us will find ourselves in a position in the business world where failures are inevitable. In fact, it is often preferable to accelerate the discovery of failures so we can get to the successes more quickly.

Some of our biggest successes come out of our biggest failures.

> " *Whatever humans have learned had to be learned as a consequence only of trial and error experience. Humans have learned only through mistakes.* "
>
> —Buckminster Fuller, American architect, designer, and inventor

Q12.4   *Do you believe that being able to deal effectively with failure—to not fear failure—is an attribute of an effective leader?*

A12.4   Absolutely. If you watch closely the leaders you admire the most, their careers are littered with failures, invariably some large ones. Yet their ability to rise from the ashes and move on makes them all the stronger and more valuable. People tend to be judged by what they make of their life today, not their failures along the way.

Your success tomorrow, in large part, reflects on your failures of yesterday.

Q12.5   *I have made a lot of mistakes throughout my career. Shouldn't I feel bad about them?*

A12.5   Don't carry the burden of mistakes forever. Learn from them, do your best to avoid repeating them, but move on. A person who is not failing is a person who is not growing.

Q12.6   *What about the person who believes he can do it, but fails. Tries again and again, but fails again and again. Is this person justified in blaming the "system"?*

A12.6   Probably not. The problem likely rests with the person. When a person gets to the point of blaming everything and everyone in his path, he may be in denial; he just doesn't get it. This person may be delusional about his skills and talents.

Q12.7 *Should I be tolerant of project members who fail?*

A12.7 You should hold them accountable for their commitments and actions. You should inspect what you expect. You should be there for them and help them to the degree reasonable and possible. But you should also recognize that we all have made and will continue to make mistakes along our journeys. This is business. Don't make it personal. Once people have failed, allow them to learn and move on.

> *When people fail and stand accountable, allow them to learn and move on.*

CHAPTER 13

A Silver Bullet?

We are always on the lookout for that *silver bullet* in project management. We upgrade to "better" planning and tracking software, continually improve documented processes, review lessons learned at the end of projects or phases of projects, routinely seek to improve our knowledge and skills through training and mentoring, and obtain project management certification or the equivalent. All these things can help, but none can match the power of applying passion, boldness, and focus to our duties. This is as close to a silver bullet as I know!

> *Without passion, boldness, and focus, consistent success is elusive.*

What is so remarkable about passion, boldness, and focus is that they are within reach of each of us. They come from within. It's not about your educational level, gender, race, wealth, age, religion, ethnic origin, or who you know. It's about who and what you choose to be.

By *passion*, I mean an intense inner drive or feeling that compels you to achieve a specific objective. It is a steadfast enthusiasm and eagerness you demonstrate in the pursuit of a cause. It is a spirited embrace of a mission. It is behaving as if you own the company and the company is defined by your domain of responsibility.

By *boldness*, I mean the act of responding to a situation in a manner that may be viewed as daring to some, but is essential to address the issue at hand. I do not mean being rude, reckless, insensitive, or arrogant. I mean doing whatever is necessary to achieve the objective (provided, of course, that it is legal and ethical). It's about demonstrating integrity and doing the *right* thing.

By *focus*, I mean concentrating on a handful or fewer of the most important problems (including risks), even to the exclusion of most other problems. The most effective leaders always know their top three problems and focus most of their time each day on solving these problems.

> *It's not about the ability of those around you to lead. It is about your ability to lead despite what is happening around you.*

All too often project managers maneuver in the shadows of their leaders waiting for—even expecting—these attributes to be exhibited. But most of us are disappointed most of the time. It's not about the ability of those around you to lead. It is about *your* ability to lead despite what is happening around you.

Think about people in the public eye who are viewed as the best. They may have been awarded a Congressional Medal of Honor, an Olympic gold medal, an Oscar, a Super Bowl ring, a Nobel Prize, or *Time* Person of the Year. They don't whine that they can't get the job done. They don't complain that life is unfair. They don't blame every Tom, Dick, and Harriet in their path. They just do it! They get the job done.

It's a lonely job being a project manager—a leader, a teacher, rallying others when you may not be receiving from your superiors the care and feeding you consistently and continually provide others. You are a professional. It is your job. Get a backbone. Believe in something. Make things happen. It's not about your intentions; it's about your actions. Your project members expect it of you. Your higher-ups, clients, and sponsors also expect it of you. Moreover, they are all within their rights to expect it of you.

> *It's not about your intentions; it's about your actions.*

The most effective leaders are driven from within themselves: their inner signals, their conscience, their integrity. It takes courage and boldness to sometimes stand alone with our beliefs. But true leaders are no strangers to adversity or finding themselves alone with their convictions. We all have a great source of strength within ourselves.

> *Who and what you choose to be comes from within.*

On your project, all eyes are on your behavior and your ability to lead. You should run your project with the same passion, boldness, and focus you would if it were your own personal business. You just might be surprised at the great potential that lies within you waiting to be unleashed.

Let's Talk: Questions & Answers

> *Most problems that fester on a project can be linked directly to a project manager who does not consistently exhibit passion, boldness, and focus.*

Q13.1 *What if you start the day with passion, but you constantly have the wind knocked out of your sails by your coworkers, boss, or client? After a while, it's hard to muster the wherewithal for passion.*

A13.1 My response is simple: It's not about the ability of those around you to lead. It is about your ability to lead despite what is happening around you.

 Only passions, great passions, can elevate the soul to great things."

—Denis Diderot, French critic, philosopher, and encyclopedist

You are handily hiding behind an excuse. You must take responsibility for your thoughts and actions, and not place blame on others. Nearly every workday you will encounter obstacles. You must rise above them. The more you practice this in your mind and actions, the easier it will become. After a while, it can become second nature to you.

Occasionally you will encounter a day when your passion may fade. It's not a big deal if it is only occasional. It is a big deal if it is the norm. Other chapters in this book can help you get and stay in control. Some examples are:

- Chapter 2, Are You a Benevolent Dictator? You Should Be!
- Chapter 6, Recognizing and Dealing with Professional Immaturity
- Chapter 7, Behaviors to Master When Dealing with Your Leaders
- Chapter 11, Dealing with Difficult People.

Q13.2   *How strong a role do you believe persistence and perseverance play in the consistent success of a project manager?*

A.13.2   Perseverance is a universal characteristic of successful leaders. This attribute can propel a so-called "common" person to achieve uncommon feats. Perseverance pushes a chemist to try that 10,000th mixture that finally succeeds, an athlete to achieve an Olympic-class victory, an artist to create a masterpiece, and a medical biologist to locate a disease-causing gene. Perhaps the most inspiring effect of perseverance can be seen in a person who overcomes a major physical handicap and goes on to accomplish a feat that would be difficult for even a fully functioning person to achieve.

 Great works are performed not by strength, but by perseverance."

—Dr. Samuel Johnson, English poet,
critic, essayist, and lexicographer

Intellectual and physical capabilities vary widely among people. However, it is encouraging to know that we all have the innate ability to exercise perseverance and determination in achieving those goals that are important to us. Being persistent can make all the difference between dreaming and seeing the dream blossom into reality. Act like it is impossible to fail. You can achieve nearly anything you set out to make happen if you are persistent in following your dreams.

You can't build a reputation on what you are going to do."

—Henry Ford, American automobile manufacturer

For a project manager, persistence is crucial for consistent success. It's not how smart you are; it's what you do with what you have. Persistence levels the playing field for everyone. Walter Elliot, American Catholic priest and writer, summed it up nicely when he said, "Perseverance is not a long race; it is many short races one after another."

> **It's not how smart you are; it's what you do with what you have.**

Q13.3 *Is boldness really all that necessary and important? And won't others see it as being too offensive?*

A13.3 Picture this: You are observing two equally talented and skilled individuals. One person has a consistent performance record of demonstrating boldness, while the other exhibits little or none. What is the difference between them regarding their achievements?

The person who consistently displays bold behavior will far outperform the other. Boldness helps propel a person beyond what he or she might otherwise achieve. In fact, boldness has such a profound impact on performance that I find it curious that this trait is not talked about more in the leadership and project management arenas.

As for your boldness being offensive to others, remember: Boldness is not about being rude, disrespectful, condescending, or abusive. None of these behaviors is ever acceptable. It's about making things happen, but with integrity.

Observe the people around you who are making positive change in their organizations or projects. Their actions require boldness. After a while, you may not think of the coworkers as bold, but simply as effective leaders. Boldness is an essential element of all consistently effective leaders.

 Whatever you can do, or dream you can, begin it. Boldness has genius, power and magic in it."

—Johann Wolfgang von Goethe,
German poet and playwright

Q13.4 *You say that passion, boldness, and focus are as close to a silver bullet as you know. What about many of the other noteworthy ideas you promote throughout this book?*

A13.4 I view all the items identified in this book as noteworthy; otherwise, they would not be included. In looking over all the ideas, however, I find that it is the combination of passion, boldness, and focus that represents the champion of champions, the best of the best. It is through passion, boldness, and focus that the other noteworthy items are made possible.

PART TWO

Roles and Responsibilities

CHAPTER 14

Duties of
the Effective
Project Manager

The *project manager* directs the planning and execution of a project and is held personally accountable for the success of the project. The project manager is a nurturer of projects.

Truly effective project managers are not easy to find. Although many people have the potential to become successful project managers, a person must first understand the duties of a project manager before being sufficiently effective in that role.

The duties of a project manager must be understood before a project manager can be effective.

The project manager holds the single most important and visible position on the project team. Along with the position comes a significant level of responsibility, accountability, and authority, the last of which is often undersought and underutilized. The project manager is accountable for the successful launch, execution, and outcome of the project. Every problem that surfaces for attention—that threatens the well-being of the project—will, either directly or indirectly, fall to the project manager. Because this role is so critical, project managers must be carefully selected, trained, and nurtured to give them and the project every opportunity to be successful. (See Chapter 4, What Good Is a PM Mentor?)

A major reason why many project managers are not more effective is that they do not fully understand their duties—their roles and responsibilities. Almost all of us will rise to the occasion if only we understand what is expected of us. The more significant duties of a project manager include:

If a wheel represents the collection of project members, then the project manager is the hub of that wheel—the hub that holds the spokes together and operates to ensure a smooth roll to the wheel's destination.

- **Is fully accountable for the project.** The buck stops with the project manager. Any and all problems with the project lead back to the project manager. The project manager is directly responsible and accountable for problems that emanate from within the project team as well as for problems that must be worked through with stakeholders from outside the core team, such as the client, sponsor, or company executives. The project manager, fully responsible and accountable for the outcome of the project, is the glue that holds the project together. The project manager leads the project with passion as if it were his or her *own business*. (See Chapter 1, Mind Your Own Business.)

- *Applies lessons learned from past projects.* The project manager studies the lessons learned from earlier recent projects and applies the most important lessons to the new project. This is done regardless of whether or not the organization has an established practice for doing so. (See Chapter 18, Are You Learning from Project to Project?)
- *Ensures that project roles and responsibilities are well-defined.* The project manager is responsible for ensuring that project members understand what is expected of them and what they should expect from one another. Only after project members truly understand their duties can they be expected to excel at them. To this end, the project manager drives ownership of decisions to the level where the accountability of the decision must lie. With proper training and coaching, project members will almost always rise to the expectations placed on them.
- *Leads the project planning activities.* The project manager directs the creation, approval, and ongoing maintenance of the project plan—which should be aggressive but *achievable*. (See Chapter 22, Do Not Make Long-Term Project Commitments.)
- *Leads the project tracking and problem management activities.* The No. 1 reason for tracking a project is to discover potential problems *before* they occur. The project manager applies this proactive approach in routinely tracking project members' progress against their project commitments. (See Part Five, Project Execution and Control.)
- *Promotes project management best practices.* The project manager—not senior management—is responsible for defining/obtaining, teaching, and enforcing the use of good project management practices. (See Chapter 19, Create the Desired Culture for Your Project.)
- *Manages to the project's top three priorities.* The project manager understands that the top reason that projects run into trouble is that a project's most important problems are not managed effectively, nor with the sense of urgency they require. The project manager, in dedicating most of his or her time each day to addressing the project's top three to five priorities, continuously performs project risk assessment and reduction/mitigation. (See Chapter 28, Manage to Your Top Three Problems.)
- *Ensures the proper level of client involvement.* The project manager recognizes that project success is directly related to satisfying the client; therefore, client involvement throughout the project

cycle, but especially at strategic points, is essential to ensure that the *right* product is built.

- *Encourages and supports escalations.* The project manager establishes a project culture where escalations to resolve "stagnant" problems are viewed as good business, not as personal. Of course, a reasonable attempt at negotiating a resolution should be made before initiating an escalation. (See Chapter 31, Escalate is Not a Dirty Word.)

- *Communicates project status to project stakeholders.* No significant project status leaves the boundaries of the project without the project manager's approval. Typically, project status is captured each week and distributed to the appropriate stakeholders. (See Chapter 26, The Project Tracking Meeting.)

- *Enforces effective change control.* The project manager ensures that scope creep is carefully managed. No features/functions are added/modified/deleted without being assessed through an appropriate change control process. (See Chapter 25, Scope Creep: Runaway Train or Good Business?)

- *Promotes good working relationships.* The project manager serves as a role model in promoting good working relationships across a project. The objective is to work and pull together as a team. The prevailing theme is that *we are all in this together*. (See Chapter 9, Foster Interpersonal Communications.)

- *Makes things happen.* You don't have to be the smartest, most knowledgeable person on the project to be the project manager. You do, however, have to have the knowledge, skills, and experience to be able to recognize when problems surface or potential problems are looming. You must be able to articulate those problems, bring the right people together to solve those problems, and know when the problem has been properly addressed and closed—all this with the proper sense of urgency that the problem requires. The project manager also performs as a teacher and helper. (See Part One, Leadership, Soft Skills, and You.)

> *"Project manager" is a job for those who want to make a difference.*

Let's Talk: Questions and Answers

Q14.1   *You list a lot of duties for a project manager. Are there more?*

A14.1   This is not an exhaustive list of the duties of a project manager. However, I view the more significant duties listed here as essential for a consistently successful project manager. Depending on how you or your organization defines the roles and responsibilities of a project manager, this list can be expanded further. For a more exhaustive list of project manager duties, see Chapter 3, The Project Manager, in *The EnterPrize Organization: Organizing Software Projects for Accountability and Success* (© 2000, Project Management Institute, Inc.).

Q14.2 *I don't see mention of "budgets" anywhere in the list. Is that intentional?*

A14.2 My view is that the project manager should create, defend, and manage to a budget throughout the duration of the project. This is implied by the listed items of "Leads the project planning activities," "Leads the project tracking and problem management activities," "Promotes project management best practices," and "Enforces effective change control." Many project managers, rightly or wrongly, manage to a budget weakly because their senior management does not require a more detailed level of budget accountability.

Q14.3 *You say that the project manager is fully accountable for the project. Is this realistic?*

A14.3 It can be, depending on the leadership and initiative of the project manager and the support provided by senior management. Far too many project managers are wimpy from the start and expect someone else to tell them what to do. Then when the project manager is constantly feeling micromanaged, he or she becomes resentful. Most senior management and clients do not want to micromanage, nor do they have the time or skills. They are expecting, hoping, *begging* for the project manager to take the lead in driving the project through to successful completion.

Q14.4 *Why do you place the burden of promoting project management best practices on the project manager? Isn't this more the duty of senior management?*

A14.4 Promoting project management best practices is the duty of the project manager. Moreover, in most cases, I would expect the project manager to know far more about these best practices than senior management.

Q14.5 *You say that the project manager must encourage and support escalations. Escalations are taken personally in my organization. Any suggestions on dealing with this?*

A14.5   Escalations are good business. If you owned the company, wouldn't you rather that an escalation occurred to resolve a conflict between two parties than allow the conflict to continue to drift unresolved? The members of a project must be trained to know not only that escalating is sometimes necessary but also when and how to escalate an issue to closure. (See Chapter 31, Escalate Is Not a Dirty Word, for more on this essential business tool.)

Q14.6   *You seem to leave the impression that the sun rises and sets on the project manager. Don't you think that the success of the project, as well as the success of the project manager, depends more on the contributions of the other project members than on just the project manager?*

A14.6   The success of a project is clearly a team effort. Everyone's contributions are key. But without leadership at the helm, the ship may not successfully navigate the rough seas and make it to port intact. Everyone on the team is looking to the project manager to lead the way. The team members are ready, willing, and able, but they need someone to lead the crew so that they are all pulling together.

For example, have you noticed how common it is for a project to be made up of very competent and seasoned members, yet continually stumble and display elements of failure—occasionally total failure? It happens all the time. The primary reason is weak leadership. The other project members will never get their due credit with a weak project manager at the helm. An effective project manager, however, allows everyone to shine as the project reaches a successful completion. Project success often comes down to a leader—the project manager—who is held accountable in driving a team effort and yielding team results.

Q14.7   *What do you mean when you say that authority is often undersought and underutilized?*

A14.7   All too often I observe project managers waiting for their boss or senior management to tell them what to do, how to do it, when to do it, and where to do it. I believe that project managers already have the authority; they just don't seize it often enough. If project managers are uncertain of their authority and fear overstepping their positions, then they should consult with their resource manager (boss) or project sponsor. But too many project managers create an imaginary box around themselves and then impose this as their field of authority and control.

Q14.8 *Do you really believe that a person can learn to become a successful project manager?*

A14.8 Absolutely yes! Although some people may have more potential than others in terms of managing very large, complex projects versus smaller ones, if a person truly has an interest in being a consistently successful project manager, there is no doubt that he or she can become one. Of special importance can be Chapter 4, What Good Is a PM Mentor?

 It's never too late to be who you might have been."

—George Eliot, English novelist

CHAPTER 15

Duties of the Effective Resource Manager

The *resource manager* hires, fires, makes job assignments, coaches, counsels, evaluates, awards, promotes, and secures future work opportunities for direct reports.

The No. 1 reason why employees leave a company is that they *don't feel appreciated.* They don't feel like anyone is championing their cause, looking out for them. Resource managers are the primary nurturers within an organization and company. They support their direct reports in helping them be successful in two key areas:

- Meeting their project commitments
- Helping them discover and achieve their potential in the organization.

The project manager's primary job is to nurture the project and ensure that it is launched, executed, and completed successfully. The resource manager's primary job is to nurture people. Together, these two positions are critical to an organization's continued success.

> **The resource manager is a nurturer of people.**

With the prominent role that is becoming increasingly popular for project managers, resource managers are becoming less sure of their role. The resource manager's key roles include:

- **Hires and fires.** The resource manager must invest the time to hire qualified people who can help projects achieve their goals. Also important is the need to address poor performers appropriately.
- **Performs resource planning and allocation; makes job assignments.** Only resource managers can make job assignments. (Project managers can, however, assign tasks and action items as they relate to a project member's assigned job.) Resource managers must anticipate and plan for future demands for their resources (their direct reports).
- **Defines roles and responsibilities.** Resource managers ensure that their direct reports not only understand their jobs, but also understand how they will be measured in performing their jobs satisfactorily.

- *Supports direct reports in meeting their commitments.* Resource managers work with their direct reports to help them be successful. This includes reviewing their plans and routinely tracking their progress.
- *Teaches professional maturity.* Most direct reports are not professionally mature; that is, they have learned technology skills but lack the business skills based on "soft" areas like accountability, resourcefulness, and leadership. The resource manager is responsible for ensuring the ongoing development of the professional maturity of his or her direct reports. (See Chapter 6, Recognizing and Dealing with Professional Immaturity.)
- *Evaluates performance.* Although verbal input from others can and should be solicited, the resource manager is fully accountable for working closely enough with his or her direct reports to evaluate their performance fairly.
- *Compensates and awards.* The resource manager has the duty to compensate and award appropriately. (Better to err on the side of too many and too large awards, than too few and too small.)
- *Provides career counseling and development.* Each direct report needs to be nurtured to reach his or her potential. The resource manager must be available and accessible to work with and help develop direct reports, which includes the areas of training and job opportunities.
- *Promotes a productive work environment.* The resource manager is responsible for ensuring continual improvement in his or her direct reports' productivity, both on long-term projects as well as from project to project.
- *Serves as channel for company communications.* The resource manager serves as a conduit for the dissemination of company-related information to direct reports. The resource manager puts a "face" on the corporation with which the direct reports can communicate.
- *Executes company policies and practices.* The resource manager is the enforcement arm for company policies and practices as they relate to the resource manager's domain of responsibility. This includes ensuring compliance with legal issues in areas such as products and services, workplace safety, and contractor relationships.
- *Secures future work opportunities.* The resource manager strives to practice a full employment policy for direct reports whose performance is satisfactory. The best resource managers do not resort to downsizing as a standard or convenient method of managing the business. Instead, they accept responsibility for seeking and devel-

oping new business opportunities, while the direct reports focus on driving the day-to-day operations.

The job of resource manager is one of the most difficult jobs in a company. It is a nearly impossible job—with demands coming from every imaginable direction—yet it is a job that can have a profound impact on an organization's success.

Let's Talk: Questions & Answers

Q15.1   *You list a lot of duties for a resource manager. Are there more?*

A15.1   This is not an exhaustive list of the duties of a resource manager. However, many of the more significant duties are listed here, all of which are essential for a consistently successful resource manager. Depending on how you or your organization defines the roles and responsibilities of a resource manager, this list can be expanded further. For a more thorough list of the duties of the resource manager, see Chapter 7, The Resource Manager, in *The EnterPrize Organization: Organizing Software Projects for Accountability and Success* (© 2000, Project Management Institute, Inc.).

Q15.2   *If this book is focused primarily on the project manager, why do you include this chapter about the duties of the resource manager?*

A15.2   Understanding the duties of resource managers can make project managers more effective. Resource managers have roles to perform regarding projects to which they have assigned resources. Their roles are related to the assignment and performance of their direct reports. Project managers and resource managers need to work well together to ensure the success of both of their jobs.

Q15.3   *Can resource managers also be project managers?*

A15.3   It is not advisable to mix the two unique jobs of resource manager and project manager. They have very different focus as well as require different skills. It is typical for a person holding both positions to focus predominantly on the position of project manager (in response to organizational and company pressures) and to sacrifice the much needed nurturing of employees.

Q15.4 *Are you saying that assigning one person to be both a project manager and a resource manager will not work?*

A15.4 It can work. However, it places a hardship on that person as well as on the direct reports and the projects that person manages. Depending on the resource manager's number of direct reports and the number, size, and complexities of projects, the job demands on that person can become overwhelming.

For example, if a resource manager has only five direct reports and also is managing only one project, which includes only the direct reports, combining these two positions—while still not recommended—can be made to work reasonably well. However, if the resource manager has 15 direct reports and is simultaneously managing several projects that include not only the direct reports but others as well, then something's going to suffer—the personal development of the direct reports, the success of the projects, or both.

Q15.5 *You say that both the project managers and the resource managers have responsibility for "roles and responsibilities." Can you clarify this?*

A15.5 Resource managers make *job assignments*. For example, they decide if an employee will perform design work, perform test work, or write technical documentation—all *job*-focused. Resource managers also ensure that their employees understand their jobs and how they will be measured in performing their jobs satisfactorily.

Once employees have been assigned to projects—become project members—project managers have the authority to *assign activities, tasks, and action items* related to their *job assignments*. Project managers are charged with ensuring that project members fully understand their duties as they relate to their project.

If it were left to project managers to determine the *job assignments* of project members assigned to their projects, they would almost always place project members in jobs that reduce the risk to the projects, even though these jobs may not be in the project members' best career interest. Therefore, resource managers decide *career-related jobs*. However, as stated earlier, project managers can *assign activities and action items* related to the *jobs* that the project members have been assigned by their resource managers.

Q15.6 *Does a project member get tracked by both the project manager and the resource manager?*

A15.6 Yes, but for different reasons. Project managers track their project members (1) to determine progress against the original plans, and (2) for proactive purposes of anticipating problems on the projects before they happen. Resource managers track the progress of their direct reports to ensure that (1) they are proceeding satisfactorily with their commitments on their assigned projects, and (2) their career potential is being properly developed.

Any tracking that the resource manager does with a direct report that is related to a given project will also benefit the project manager. In fact, resource managers can be thought of as behind-the-scenes partners with project managers. As a project manager, wouldn't you welcome the resource managers of your project members caring enough about their commitments on your projects that they stay in close touch with their direct reports on how well they are performing on your project? I would!

Q15.7 *You say that the resource managers evaluate the performance of their direct reports. The project managers do that in my organization. Is this okay?*

A15.7 In most cases, it is not okay. Project members will be at various job levels within the organization and their performance can be assessed differently within each level. Project managers typically do not have the knowledge, skills, or training to evaluate the performance of their project members fairly. It is an unwise distraction to saddle project managers with this chore; it takes them off their main objective of nurturing their projects.

Q15.8 *But how can resource managers know enough about how their direct reports are performing to evaluate them fairly?*

A15.8 That's a big reason why resource managers stay closely connected with their direct reports. Moreover, it is expected that resource managers will draw from performance information that they receive verbally from the project managers and others.

Q15.9 *Which is more important: attitude or skill?*

A15.9 Both are important, but let's put them in perspective. Let's say that I am looking to hire a new employee with exceptionally high skills in a certain field. I narrow the selection to two candidates. One candidate is clearly outstanding in the field, but has a poor attitude. The other candidate has an acceptable level of skills in the field and a great attitude.

I would hire the candidate with the great attitude. Why? Because someone in a leadership position with a poor attitude can easily undermine a project or organization. If I have a project or organization made up of people with great attitudes, I can accomplish nearly anything with that team. I am so certain that I would hire the person with the great attitude because earlier in my career I hired the other . . . and had to perform damage control for the life of the project.

Q15.10 *Your response to the previous question appears to support the notion of emotional intelligence. Do you agree?*

A15.10 Yes. Daniel Goleman, in his book, *Emotional Intelligence: Why It Can Matter More Than IQ* (New York: Bantam, 1995), makes the case for "emotional intelligence" being the strongest indicator of human success. Goleman defines emotional intelligence in terms of personal traits such as self-motivation, self-awareness, persistence, social skills, and empathy. He makes the case that people with high emotional intelligence succeed in their careers as well as in their personal relationships. This book contains a plethora of practices that support making the most of emotional intelligence for project managers.

Q15.11 *If an organization or company has a high rate of employees leaving the company, is this indicative of weak or ineffective resource managers?*

A15.11 Yes, more often than not. Organizations that experience high turnover of staff are typically ineffective at creating consistently productive, interesting, and nurturing places to work. It can be that resource managers are also working as project managers and have inadequate time for nurturing their employees. Or it can be that resource managers assign their direct reports to projects and then "walk away"; that is, they all but cease a nurturing connection with their employees. It can be for a number of similar reasons that have a single-thread connection: The employees don't feel appreciated. No one champions them. No one is looking out for them as they are tossed from one project to the next.

Of course, there can be reasons for high staff turnover other than weak or ineffective resource managers. These reasons can include: (1) many of a company's employees reaching retirement age and leaving, (2) the company being in a cyclical, seasonal industry where staff turnover is predictably high, and (3) the company doing work that is contract-based, which inevitably leads to sporadic employee turnover. Nevertheless, more often than not, the problem is ineffective resource managers.

CHAPTER 16

Duties of
the Effective
Project Sponsor

The *project sponsor* champions the project from a business perspective and helps remove obstacles that might impede its overall success.

Every project should have a sponsor. Project sponsors typically are members of senior management who exert a respectable level of influence and authority and serve as proponents of projects. Project sponsors are sometimes called product sponsor, project director, account manager, or business unit manager.

Some projects do not have clearly defined project sponsors. Even more common are projects that have sponsors, but the sponsors' duties are not defined and documented. If a project has no apparent sponsor, or a weak sponsor, the project will suffer a severe handicap whenever senior management support is needed.

> *The project sponsor is the designated senior-level champion of the project.*

As a project manager, if your project does not have a project sponsor, you can work to cultivate that role with a likely senior manager. If your project has a designated project sponsor, but the duties are vague, it is in both your and the project's best interest to define and document a proposed set of duties and negotiate them with the sponsor.

The project sponsor's key duties include:

> *The duties of a project sponsor must be understood before a project sponsor can be effective for the project manager.*

- *Ensures the strategic significance of the project.* The project sponsor endorses and defends the project as a valued investment of organizational resources—an investment that serves the organization's strategic objectives.
- *Provides approval and funding for the project.* Organizations have more opportunities than funds and people to work them. The project sponsor lobbies for the approval and subsequent funding of the project.
- *Promotes support from key stakeholders.* The project sponsor maintains a good working relationship with major stakeholders such as the project manager, client, and senior project players from other internal and external organizations and companies.
- *Supports broad authority for the project manager and team.* The best project sponsors do not micromanage a project. Instead, the project manager enjoys great flexibility to promote best practices in planning and managing the project and making day-to-day deci-

sions. However, decisions related to scope, schedule, and costs that affect changes to external commitments must include the project sponsor.

- **Resolves appropriate conflicts.** The project sponsor resolves conflicts that require senior management involvement, such as funding, priorities, external commitments, cross-organizational boundaries, and clients. The project sponsor strives to buffer the project team from political issues. Timeliness to close issues is critical.
- **Is accessible and approachable.** The project sponsor must be available to the project manager and other stakeholders on relatively short notice. The project sponsor should be viewed as a stakeholder who is always willing to listen and get involved as needed—to serve as a sounding board and to provide advice and guidance.
- **Supports periodic reviews.** The project sponsor weighs in and approves the need and frequency of project reviews. (Project reviews are independent reviews performed at specified intervals in a project to assess the health of the project. Actions are then recommended to immediately address any significant problems that are identified.)
- **Supports post-project review.** The project sponsor promotes the implementation of a post-project review upon project completion or following a major phase of a long-running project. (A post-project review identifies what went right, what went wrong, and where improvement can be made on future projects. The objective is to learn from past project experiences so that future projects can benefit. For more on this subject, see Chapter 35, Conducting a Post-Project Review.)
- **Encourages recognition.** The project sponsor, working with senior management and the project manager, supports the timely recognition of noteworthy individual and team achievements.

The project sponsor provides ongoing, on-call support for the project manager, who is, in effect, the project stakeholder charged with planning and executing the project plan—which leads to successful delivery of the product/service. A close-working, supportive relationship between the project sponsor and project manager can greatly benefit the performance of the project manager and project team and thereby the overall success of the project.

Accessibility, timeliness, and closure of issues in support of project managers are key attributes of successful project sponsors.

As we have seen, the project manager's primary job is to nurture the project and ensure that it is launched, executed, and completed successfully, and the resource manager's primary job is to nurture people. The project sponsor's primary job is to nurture products and services, in large part through the support of projects. All three of these positions are critical to an organization's continued success.

> *The project sponsor is a nurturer of products and services.*

Let's Talk: Questions & Answers

Q16.1 *Are there more duties for a project sponsor than those you list?*

A16.1 While this is not an exhaustive list of the duties of a project sponsor, I consider it to be a solid starter list of essential duties.

Q16.2 *I have a project sponsor in "name," but the person doesn't come close to performing the duties you list. What can I do?*

A16.2 Depending on the industry and company in which you work, the expectations of a project sponsor may be somewhat different. I suggest customizing the duties listed in this chapter to meet your "needs" and "wants." Then meet with your project sponsor and discuss the benefits to the sponsor. You may not achieve everything you hope for, so focus on your "needs" and be prepared to back off on your "wants." Make compliance for your sponsor as easy as possible. Your job is to help the sponsor look good.

> *The project manager should make compliance with the project sponsor's duties as easy as possible.*

Q16.3 *My project sponsor is well-intentioned, but is spread thinly across many other projects and endeavors. Any recommendation for how to stay connected beyond the initial meeting where duties are discussed?*

A16.3 Based on your initial meeting with your project sponsor, you will have a good sense of the types of information your project sponsor would like to receive. Make sure that the information is being communicated adequately to your sponsor throughout the duration of the project. If you plan an action that you feel could have an effect—positive or negative—that your project sponsor should know about beforehand, then make sure your project sponsor has been overtly informed. Burying the information in a project status report or email that may or may not be timely read by the project sponsor is not an effective form of communicating important issues; face-to-face meetings or telephone contact will be required.

Q16.4 *When you say "The duties of a project sponsor must be understood before a project sponsor can be effective for the project manager," what exactly do you mean?*

A16.4 Project sponsors can be viewed by their senior-level peers as effective and successful even though the project managers may have less complimentary views. This book focuses on project managers, and it is important that project managers work with their project sponsors to derive benefits from the relationship. Of course, any benefit to the project managers also benefits the projects, project sponsors, and all other stakeholders.

Q16.5 *Does a project have to have a project sponsor?*

A16.5 Most projects will have a sponsor; otherwise, they would not be funded and assigned resources. But many sponsors are so weak that they appear to be nearly invisible. Special situations sometimes allow projects to exist without sponsors. So while a project does not necessarily have to have a sponsor, not having one can severely handicap the project manager if support for the project is ever needed.

CHAPTER 17

How Technical Must a Project Manager Be?

In Chapter 14, Duties of the Effective Project Manager, we discussed that the single most important position on a project is that of the project manager. The person holding this position is ultimately accountable for the successful planning and execution of the project. The leadership exhibited by the project manager will directly influence and impact more people than any other position, and can profoundly impact the outcome of the project.

As more individuals, organizations, companies, and institutions come to recognize the great benefits of adopting project management practices, more people are being placed in project leadership positions without sufficient technical training, mentoring, or experience. A question increasingly being asked today is, "How technical must a project manager be to be effective?"

Technical is defined as the capability of a project manager to understand the terminology, technology, and processes relevant to the product being built or the service being performed sufficiently to yield an effective and successful outcome. Having sufficient understanding of these areas can help a project manager earn the respect of his or her team and can significantly help in the planning, execution, and problem management activities required on a project. Being sufficiently technical helps a project manager understand the project dynamics and be better qualified and prepared to: know when to ask questions, know what questions to ask, understand the responses, and know when to seek help.

Of course, some projects require a greater level of technical capability than others. On projects like software development, commercial building construction, or missile defense systems development, not being sufficiently technical can be a handicap, perhaps a serious one.

On the flip side, projects that are not technically intense or as technically challenging (e.g., launching a new ad campaign, developing and rolling out a new training workshop, communicating policies to company employees) typically require less technical prowess to plan and run effectively. Even on projects that are not technically intense, however, the project manager benefits from having knowledge and experience with the terminology and processes involved.

Even on projects that are not considered technically intense, the project manager benefits from having knowledge and experience with the terminology and processes involved.

Strong Project Management Skills; Not Sufficiently Technical

Consider a scenario where a project manager is well-versed and experienced in the application of project management principles, yet relatively new to the industry (e.g., software development, missile development, nuclear reactor development) where the principles will be applied. An experienced project manager will be considered handicapped due to his weakness in the technical aspects of the project. Depending on how intensely technical the project is, the handicap can be very serious. Of course, the project manager can eventually learn to become sufficiently technical, but that may not happen on the first project.

The project manager who is not sufficiently technical in his or her chosen industry will be working with a handicap.

Let's look at an example.

I sometimes ask the participants of project management classes that I conduct if they think that I would be an effective project manager of a project to build the next generation of commercial aircraft. The class participants know that I have around 30 years of experience in software development and IT projects, project management, and leadership assignments. They assume that I am proficient in project management, having written five books related to the subject. Most participants usually respond "yes"—that I would be a good project manager candidate.

I would *not* be a good candidate!

You don't have to be the smartest, most technically knowledgeable person on the project to be the project manager.

You don't have to be the smartest, most technically knowledgeable person on the project to be the project manager. You do, however, have to have the knowledge, skills, and experience to be able to recognize when problems surface or potential problems are looming. You must be able to articulate those problems, bring the right people together to solve those problems, and know when the problem has been properly addressed and closed—all this with the proper sense of urgency that the problem requires.

With essentially no experience in building aircraft, I would make costly mistakes that an experienced aircraft-related project manager would have easily avoided. I might still complete the project and it might be viewed as reasonably successful, but a seasoned project manager experienced in building aircraft very likely would complete the project in less time and with lower costs.

Weak Project Management Skills; Not Sufficiently Technical

To make matters worse, let's look at another, but more pervasive, situation. Picture a person who is relatively new to both the project management profession and to a discipline, say, software development. Would that person be an effective project manager of her first software development project, particularly one of a respectable size?

Not likely! Why? Because, in addition to having weak project management skills, that person would not understand the terminology and technology being employed on the project and would have difficulty dealing effectively with questions such as:

- What is a reasonable software development process to follow?
- What are reasonable productivity rates for performing design, code, test, and documentation work?
- How important are design and code reviews?
- What testing is essential to perform?

A project manager, in addition to having a workable grasp of project management concepts, must also be sufficiently astute in the technical aspects of the discipline within which these concepts must be employed. If the project manager is not sufficiently technical, then you can expect cost, schedule, quality, and functional problems to occur that would otherwise have been avoided or reduced in magnitude by a more technically astute project manager. Training, mentoring, and evolving experience can help a project manager gain the necessary technical skills to be effective. Are you sufficiently technical? If not, what are you doing to compensate?

Let's Talk: Questions & Answers

Q17.1 *Are you saying that a project manager with a good working command of project management principles cannot effectively run a project that is highly technical?*

A17.1 The project manager will likely experience a handicap; that is, it will be unlikely that the project will be as well run as it would have been had a project manager experienced with the domain knowledge of that industry managed the project.

Q17.2 *If a highly skilled project manager is put in a position to plan and manage a project that is outside of his domain knowledge (e.g., is in a technically intense industry unfamiliar to the project manager), why can't this project manager be effective? After* *all, the project manager has developed the soft skills to tap into the knowledge, skills, and experience of the stakeholders around him.*

A17.2 Being a successful, seasoned project manager is certainly a great asset. However, the project manager will not always know the right questions to ask, when they should be asked, if the responses are appropriate, or when to seek help. Relying on the project members to come forth with the right information at the right time or expecting the project members to consistently volunteer information is not a reasonable expectation. In the best of all worlds, the project manager could be effective, but it is not a typical outcome.

Q17.3 *On several occasions you use the word* sufficient, *such as in describing being* sufficiently *technical, being* sufficiently *effective, being* sufficiently *astute, or* sufficiently *understanding something. Can you expound on its meaning a bit?*

A17.3 *Sufficient* is not a precise, quantifiable term, but it does represent "that which is needed." In reference to this chapter, *sufficient* is intended to represent that which is needed to yield an effective and successful outcome. If a project manager is not *sufficiently* technical, then his or her level of technical astuteness is less than preferred and may result in the project manager being less effective than expected or required.

Q17.4 *If I am placed in a position where I am not sufficiently technical, what can or should I do?*

A17.4 Get help. The help can come in the form of additional training and/or mentoring. The training can be classroom, online, from books/articles, or from participating at conferences. Mentoring is typically the most effective tool. (See Chapter 4, What Good Is a PM Mentor?) You can have more than one mentor depending on the subjects with which you seek mentoring.

You can always learn to be sufficiently technical. The question typically comes down to "Is there time and are there accessible, qualified persons who can help bridge the technical gap until that gap is sufficiently filled?" Another action you can take is to ensure that your team is made up of strong technical members.

Q17.5 *You don't expect the project manager to be the most technical person on a project, do you?*

A17.5 Absolutely not! In fact, the project manager might even be the *least* technical person, yet still be *sufficiently* technical. Again, it is a matter of having a sufficient level of project-related domain knowledge regarding terminology, technology, and processes.

Q17.6 *From your experience, which do you think is best: a project manager who is strong in project management skills but weak technically, or a project manager who is weak in project management skills but notably strong in technical skills?*

A17.6 As a general rule, it is far better for the project manager to be strong in project management skills and weak technically than to be strong technically and weak in project management skills. It has been my experience that some project managers who are very strong technically can actually be handicapped because of their interest and natural lure to getting more involved in the technical aspects of the project at the expense of properly applying good, sound project management principles.

> *The project manager can be the least technical member of the project, but still be sufficiently technical.*

> *First and foremost, a project manager should strive to be strong in project management skills.*

Q17.7 *Are you saying that a highly technical person cannot be an effective project manager?*

A17.7 A highly technical person, who also has a strong command of project management skills, can be a very effective project manager. However, it has been my experience that of the four possible permutations shown in Figure 17-1, quadrant "1" is

Project management skills

	Strong	Weak
Strong (Technical skills)	1	3
Weak (Technical skills)	2	4

Figure 17-1 Four Permutations of the Mix of Project Management Skills and Technical Skills

the least common, but likely the most favored scenario. The quadrant numbers represent the order of preference for the mix of project management and technical skills.

Q17.8   *As a project manager, I am more technical than most and can do the work better and faster than most of those on my team. Is it wrong for the project manager to do the work of the project members sometimes?*

A17.8   Be careful here. If you occasionally help out in a pinch so that major commitments can be fulfilled, then that may be fine. But if you often find yourself performing work that was defined to be another's, then you are out of line. Project members cannot grow or feel a sense of self-worth if you perform their work. Moreover, they will not want to work with you.

> *Give others the opportunity to learn and grow—to feel a sense of being needed and contributing.*

The parable about fishing applies nicely here. Rather than provide your hungry project members with the proverbial fish occasionally, you will have a far greater positive impact on everyone if you teach them how to fish. If they have weak skills, then give them the opportunity to develop those skills.

By the way, when you are out doing the work of others, who's running the project? Remember where your primary responsibility—and value—lie.

Q17.9   *How can a project manager know if he or she is sufficiently technical?*

A17.9   Many project managers probably already have a good sense of whether they are sufficiently technical. However, your boss or a peer project manager, as well as some project members, should be able to offer insight. Mentors, both from the project management perspective and the technical perspective, also can help gauge your level of proficiency.

Whether or not a project manager is sufficiently technical can become apparent when reviewing how well the project plan has been developed and observing the effectiveness of the weekly project tracking meetings. It also can become apparent by how timely and effective project issues are being identified and resolved. The stronger his or her project management skills—including the leadership and soft skills components—the more quickly and effectively the project manager can overcome, or at least productively work with, any lack of technical expertise.

Project Initiation

CHAPTER 18

Are You Learning from Project to Project?

If you are among the 95+ percent of us who fail this simple test—but shouldn't—you could be in a position of weakness, to the detriment of your current and upcoming projects.

This test consists of only two questions. Answer *yes* or *no* for each question and see how you do:

> **Question 1:** *As a project manager, do you always insist on (or is it required of you) performing a post-project review when your project or a major phase of a lengthy project of yours has completed?*

> **Question 2:** *As a project manager of a new project, do you insist on (or is it required of you) going before a small review board to demonstrate that the lessons learned from post-project reviews will be applied to your new project?*

If you answered *yes* to *both* questions, you are in a very, very small minority. Yet, the benefits for a project manager who can answer *yes* to both questions can be striking. If you can answer *yes* to only the first question, what's the point? Where's the improvement occurring? Where are you applying the lessons learned?

There's little point in performing post-project reviews if the lessons learned are not applied to follow-on projects.

Too many project managers complain that there is little they can do to improve the application of project management practices on their projects. This antiquated and unimaginative thinking perpetuates the myth that only management can truly lead the charge for change in an organization or even on one's own project.

It's your project! You can insist on post-project reviews for your projects. You also can initiate using a review board as a means to validate that you are applying lessons learned from past projects to your next project.

"Learning is not compulsory . . . neither is survival."

—W. Edwards Deming,
American business advisor and author

Mandatory Directives

Here are two project-related activities that should be mandatory in organizations:

1. Post-project reviews must be conducted within a week of projects ending.
2. At the start of new projects, project managers must convince a review board that they have reviewed the findings from the most recent post-project reviews from across the organization and have satisfactorily applied those findings to the benefit of their new projects.

Of course, the organization gets to decide the criteria a project must meet before these activities become mandatory. For example, the criteria may apply to all projects consisting of at least three members and being at least two to three months long, or projects of at least 1,000 hours of effort, or $50,000 budget, or whatever best applies for your line of business.

> *Sometimes leadership means requiring mandatory actions before change can become institutionalized across an organization.*

Benefits to an Organization

The benefit to an organization that appropriately applies these two directives can be enormous. Picture the following:

> *You work for a company that is five years old. Each year 10 projects are undertaken, each of one-year duration. Today, at the end of five years, your company has the experience of having completed 50 projects. The founders of the company had the foresight to insist on learning from both their mistakes and their successes; therefore, it was mandatory to perform a post-project review at the end of each project. Furthermore, it was mandatory, at the start of a new project, for the project manager to convince a small review board that the most important lessons learned from recent projects would be aptly applied to the new project.*

At the end of the first year of this scenario, 10 post-project reviews were held, highlighting a plethora of lessons to learn. The 10 new projects for the second year benefited from the lessons learned from the first year. At the end of the second year, the post-project reviews revealed the next layer of lessons to learn. Again, the 10 projects started in the third year benefited from the most recent lessons learned. And so on, until the organization has experienced five years of consistent improvement.

It is my assertion that the company depicted in this scenario will become a major force in whatever industry it serves. The products and

> *There is no better way to perpetuate self-improvement for an organization than to perform post-project reviews and apply those lessons to future projects.*

services produced will be among the most advanced and successful, the employees will be among the most skilled and productive, the quality of the work will be among the best, employee morale will be among the highest, and the customers will be among the most satisfied. Why? Because we consistently get better in designated key areas by deliberately analyzing, measuring, and improving our performance.

The initiation phase of a project is especially important. If a project starts weakly, it may never fully recover; if it does "recover" there will be a "burden cost" to pay in increased costs, slipped schedules, lower client satisfaction, and likely lower quality. Moreover, how well a project is planned can have a direct impact on the quality that must be repaired during the maintenance periods of the product's life cycle. It should be imperative not only to perform post-project reviews on completed or failed projects, but to apply lessons learned to new projects to avoid or significantly reduce the burden costs.

> *When a project starts weakly, there is a "burden cost" that forever remains associated with the product that resulted.*

Your Personal Leadership

> *You don't have to wait for management to initiate actions that fall within your domain of responsibility.*

You do not have to be a member of an organization that enforces mandatory post-project reviews and ensures that the lessons are applied to new projects to benefit from these concepts. You, independently, can apply these concepts within your domain of responsibility. You have the authority—perhaps duty—to manage to these practices on your own projects. Remember, true leaders are those who do the right thing despite what's happening around them.

> *The great thing about being the problem is that you have control over the solution.*

As a project manager, if you are not learning from project to project by examining the past and applying lessons to new projects, then you—not your organization or your management—are the problem. The good news is that recognizing that you are the problem has its advantages: Now you know what to work on and you have control over the solution.

Let's Talk: Questions & Answers

Q18.1   *What is your recommended approach for project managers going before a review board?*

A18.1   Although there can be many variations, the approach I favor is the following. The project manager of a new project must review the most recent post-project reviews conducted within his or her organization. Then the project manager, working as needed with other project members, determines how best to apply the lessons learned to all relevant aspects of the new project. Afterwards, the project manager meets with a review board consisting of three peers (i.e., other project managers).

The project manager must then defend how the project has applied—or plans to apply—the relevant lessons learned so that similar problems will not occur on the project, or if they do they will be lesser in magnitude. If the review board is satisfied that sufficient important lessons have been learned and applied satisfactorily, then the board approves the project manager moving forward with the planning and implementation of the new project.

If the review board is not satisfied, then the project manager does not receive the board's approval to move forward with the project. The project manager must now reassess the lessons learned and how best to apply them. Then the project manager revisits the board with actions that are more convincing. This process continues until the project manager has obtained the review board's approval.

Q18.2 *How many post-project reviews must a project manager study?*

A18.2 The project manager should study at least several of the most recent post-project reviews. Most of those studied should not be the project manager's own projects. Preferably the projects studied have similarities to the new project.

Q18.3 *Any ideas for helping project managers study the most recent post-project reviews?*

A18.3 Preferably the overall organization will assign a group to archive and manage the collection of post-project reviews. A project management office, quality group, or software engineering process group are good candidates. The group can periodically update a master post-project review summary document that highlights the most important lessons identified across an organization's projects.

Q18.4 *Must the review board be made up only of other project managers? How about members from management, for example?*

A18.4 In the beginning, the review board can include managers so that this critical process is properly sponsored and on its way to becoming institutionalized. However, at some point, I would like the managers to remove themselves and encourage the nonmanagers to learn to behave as mature professionals who can "police" themselves and put self-corrective processes in place as needed.

Q18.5 *How does a review board help an organization improve its project management practices?*

A18.5 Perhaps the most obvious way is for the review board to serve as a check-and-balance to the organization. This role helps ensure that project after project is being managed with continually improving project management practices.

But there is another major benefit. The three project managers on the review board are not necessarily permanent members. The board members can rotate in and out as frequently as the organization chooses. That way, all project managers are continually learning from one another no matter on which side of the review they happen to be participating.

A simple "gate" to trigger the use of the board and obtain its approval is the requirement that all new project plans have an activity called "approval from project review board." This helps ensure that the proper approval has been obtained before a project can advance to its next phase.

Q18.6 *Is there a preferred approach to conducting post-project reviews?*

A18.6 See Chapter 35, Conducting a Post-Project Review, for more on this topic.

Q18.7 *In addition to implementing the review board at the start of new projects to ensure that lessons learned are applied as appropriate, do you have any other ideas for starting new projects off on a strong footing toward being successful?*

A18.7 Yes, see the next chapter, Chapter 19, Create the Desired Culture for Your Project, for a highly effective method to create the most effective culture for your project.

Create the Desired Culture for Your Project

Most projects are in need of a major "culture" makeover. Members are uncertain about the behavior expected of them. Their uncertainty covers all aspects of a project, such as roles and responsibilities, planning, tracking, problem management, processes, interpersonal communications, and accountability. Members commonly complain about the unproductive culture within which they must work. Furthermore, a pervasive myth is that the only way to change the culture within a project is for the direction to come from higher management.

As discussed in Chapter 1, Mind Your Own Business, you should focus your energies and passion within your domain of responsibility. As project manager, you have a captive audience with which to create the most effective culture. Your audience is eagerly awaiting your vision, your direction, your immersion into shaping the project environment toward achieving the desired culture.

> *As a leader, you are expected to drive needed change, not wait for others to do it for you.*

The Culture-Training Class

The culture-training class is a highly effective method you can use to create the most effective culture for your project—and it is a method that doesn't require permission or intervention from higher management.

Culture training is the formal training of all project members in key hard skills, soft skills, and processes that are essential in helping ensure a successful project. Culture training provides all project members with a common understanding of how the project will be run and the role that each team member is expected to play.

A culture-training class should be mandatory at the start of all projects that are made up of at least three members and have a duration of at least two months. All project members should be required to attend. A project management office (PMO) or training organization is a likely organization to conduct culture-training classes or to find suitable instructors to do so. The project manager can teach none, a portion, or all of the class.

Culture-training classes typically are one to two days in length, depending on the size and duration of the project and the "culture maturity" of the project members. Very small

> *Paraphrasing a noted saying: Don't fall into the trap that you and your team can't find time to do it right but can always find time to do it over.*

> *A culture-training class likely can save weeks of effort on short projects and months of effort on longer projects.*

projects of five or fewer members and duration of only a few months may require classes only a half-day long. You say you and your team cannot spare a few hours to two days for a training class? You can't afford not to! My experience shows that a project training class can save weeks on projects of several months in duration and save months on projects longer than six months in duration.

Key Topics to Address

Let's look at some topics to address in a culture-training class:

- *Roles and responsibilities of project members.* These project positions include the project manager, resource managers, product architect (chief technologist), business architect (client's advocate), product manager and/or project sponsor, team leaders, and team members.
- *Process methodology.* This includes the methodology to be followed in building the product or performing the service, including the major activities to be performed and the documents to be created.
- *Project planning process.* This includes the process steps to be followed in creating and approving the project plan and how the plan will be maintained through change control.
- *Project tracking process.* This includes discussing project tracking meetings, identifying metrics to be tracked, identifying high-risk/high-priority problems, and creating problem recovery plans.
- *Escalation process.* This includes discussion of the process to be followed when an escalation is required to resolve an issue.
- *Project reviews.* These include how to conduct project reviews and their frequency and timing. Performed at selected points along the project cycle, a project review is an independent review that examines the health of a project. A project review is recommended every three to four months for projects that are six months or longer in duration.
- *Post-project review.* Project members should be alerted that a post-project review will be conducted at the completion of the project. Topics should include a brief description of the process to be followed in conducting the post-project review.
- *People communications.* Common interpersonal communications problems that can arise on a project and how to avoid or deal with them should be discussed. Examples include attacking problems

and not people, asking for help, being willing to help others, giving praise and showing appreciation, and asking questions rather than assuming.

- **Soft skills.** The attributes and behaviors that one can adopt to become a more effective project member should be discussed. Topics include dealing with criticism, conflict, the value of persistence, managing time, making and meeting commitments, behaving as if it is *your* business, and being accountable for one's own actions.
- **Lessons learned.** This includes a discussion of the key, relevant lessons learned from the most recent post-project reviews and how to benefit from those lessons.

Other topics also can be discussed, such as client, vendor, and contractor relationships.

Culture-training classes provide uncommonly great benefits to starting a project and its members on a productive footing toward launching and implementing a successful project. Culture-training classes not only can give new projects a jump-start, but can also help power projects through to a successful completion.

Let's Talk: Questions & Answers

Q19.1 *Do you mean to say that culture-training classes are recommended at the start of all projects, not mandatory?*

A19.1 Culture-training classes should be mandatory for all "designated" projects, but your organization gets to decide which projects must comply. For example, they could be mandatory for projects that have a level of effort of 1,000 hours or more, or a cost of $100,000 or more. Another approach is for your organization to identify its top 10 "most important" projects and require those to adopt culture-training classes.

> *As the project manager, you do not need to wait for your project to be declared a candidate for culture training; you can make the decision to conduct a culture-training class regardless of what's happening around you.*

Q19.2 *When is the best time to conduct a culture-training class for a project?*

A19.2 As soon as possible, but typically after both the requirements and the scope of the project have been defined. Moreover, it is preferable that the critical mass of the project members has been assigned. For some projects, the culture-training class might include what commonly is called the "project kickoff meeting."

Q19.3 *What about training for those project members who were added to the project* after *the culture-training class occurred?*

A19.3 For the greatest effect, all project members need to participate in a culture-training class. This means that, for some projects, you may need to hold more than one culture-training class.

Q19.4 *When you say that all project members should attend the culture-training class, do you mean resource managers, the client, vendors, contractors, and the project sponsor as well? All stakeholders?*

A19.4 For best results, the resource managers, project sponsor, client, contractors, and lead folks from the vendors should attend. You might consider having smaller, more specialized culture-training classes for selected groups such as vendors and the client.

Q19.5 *Why don't you expect project managers to always teach the culture-training class for their projects?*

A19.5 Ideally, I would like the project managers to teach the culture-training class for their projects; however, in many cases, this is not practical. For example, most project managers do not have the time to develop the material required for conducting the class. Moreover, many project managers may not know the culture that they should be encouraging.

The most realistic approach may be to have someone from the project management office or company training organization develop and teach the classes. The same person teaching allows the material and messages to evolve so that both the delivery and the principles taught are consistent and always improving.

If a project manager is comfortable conducting all or a portion of the class, he or she should do so. In all cases, the project manager will play a dominant role in participating in these classes; after all, the classes are intended to help the project manager and other stakeholders increase the likelihood of a successful project.

Q19.6 *Why discuss the details of a post-project review at a culture-training class?*

A19.6 First, it is important that all project stakeholders know that their performance will be studied at the end of the project as a means of learning from the past to improve future projects. If project members know that their actions will be reviewed down the road, they are more likely to perform better. Second, the low-level detail of conducting a post-project review will not be discussed; rather, an overview of what project members can expect from a post-project review will be presented.

Q19.7 *If a culture-training class was conducted early in a project, the project was completed successfully, and a second project was about to begin with most of the same project members, should another culture-training class be conducted at the start of the second project?*

A19.7 Absolutely yes! The most important reason to conduct another culture-training class is to help make the messages "stick." Have you ever seen a movie for the second time and discovered and understood so much more about it than you did the first time? These classes should be conducted at the start of all designated projects so that the desired culture becomes truly ingrained into the culture fabric of all stakeholders. Over time, the classes likely will become shorter in duration.

Q19.8 *Is it a project manager's job to change the culture in the organization, not just for the project?*

A19.8 The project manager—first and foremost—should focus on his or her domain of responsibility, which, in most cases, does not include what happens outside the project. (See Chapter 1, Mind Your Own Business.) But keep in mind that if you want to change the culture in an organization, it can be done project by project.

Q19.9 *Can the culture across an organization truly be changed based on culture-training classes conducted project by project?*

A19.9 Yes, remarkably so! As project stakeholders participate in culture-training classes from project to project, their behavior—as well as the behavior they expect from others—is being shaped. Moreover, they carry this behavior with them from project to project and assignment to assignment. Once they experience the positive results, many stakeholders will demand culture-training classes on their future projects.

Q19.10 *What do you say to those who believe that project culture is very much the responsibility of management?*

A19.10 This is outdated, old-school thinking. It is a trap in which many· project managers find themselves. If project managers believe that the overall culture on their projects is the responsibility of management and not themselves, the project managers are doomed from the start. Once you believe that you are not accountable for your project's culture—that you have no or minimal control over your project's culture—then you significantly handicap yourself. It's your project! Its success is largely a reflection of your leadership and influence; so too is its failure.

Projects will be planned, tracked, communicated, and nurtured according to the best practices that the project manager promotes. No one is in a better position to shape the project culture than the project manager. In fact, everyone is waiting, sometimes *begging*, for the project manager to take the lead and make things happen. What use is the project manager if not to make things happen? Senior management cannot be expected to understand project management as well as project managers, so why leave it up to management to shape the culture on *your* project?

> *The client, senior management, and project members are waiting—even begging—for you to take the lead.*

CHAPTER 20

Should You Be Given a Project End Date?

Ever have your boss, client, project sponsor, or someone else in a position of authority give you the delivery date for a yet-to-be-planned product or service? This is common practice, but is it good practice? Should you be given a target date or should you be left to determine the most appropriate date for you and the project team?

In almost all cases, it is good business to provide the project team a target end date. An end date yields two primary benefits:

Providing a target project end date almost always demonstrates good business and good leadership.

- **The target date will likely have special meaning to the business.** For example, it may coincide with an important trade show, allow revenues to be earned before the fiscal year ends, meet or beat a competitor's date for the launch of a similar product, or meet a legal deadline such as a regulatory date.
- **The target date will stretch the project team to be more creative.** Left to our own preferences, many of us will take the path of least resistance; that is, a comfortable plan rather than a more aggressive (but achievable!) plan. We often perform our best work when we are being challenged.

Let's consider a scenario:

The boss directs you to put a plan together to build product JKL and to present the plan for approval. The boss does not provide a target end date. You and your team spend considerable time over the coming weeks creating a plan. The plan's duration comes in at 12 months. You present the 12-month plan to your boss. She says, "I can't live with a 12-month project duration. I need it in eight months."

What are you feeling? Disappointment? Annoyance? Frustration? You may be thinking, "I don't know if we can build the product in only eight months, but I wish my boss would have declared the eight-month target in the beginning. It sure would have saved my team and me a lot of time and energy. Now we must perform considerable rework on the plan."

In this scenario, it was unproductive for the boss to imply that the end date was open-ended when it wasn't. There was no apparent value to be gained by the boss holding back the eight-month requirement. Quite the opposite: Schedules, productivity, costs, and morale can all be negatively affected by the poor leadership style exhibited by the boss.

A target project end date should reflect business needs and help stretch the project team to perform at its best.

Let's examine a scenario where an improbable target end date is given:

> The boss provides a target end date of six months. This gives your team a solid goal upon which to focus. Planning decisions are balanced against the requirement to complete the product in six months.
>
> But what if the best plan that you and your team can create requires eight months, not the six months requested? What do you do? You present the eight-month plan to your boss and articulate why the plan's duration cannot be reduced. You identify the negative consequences that are likely to result if it is reduced. However, be prepared for an onslaught of questions about whether you and your team have fully exhausted options such as outsourcing, acquiring off-the-shelf components, reducing the features offered, and hiring proven experts to help in the implementation.
>
> *It is bad business for a decision-maker to insist on an unachievable plan— all stakeholders lose!*
>
> If you can defend your eight-month plan professionally, then most bosses will yield to your due diligence and accept moving the end date out an additional two months. However, some bosses will say, "I want it in six months! Find a way to make it happen or . . . ." ("I will find someone who can" is the inference). This is bad business! All stakeholders lose! Demanding that the proverbial 10 pounds be placed into a five-pound sack does not make it possible. Laws of physics will not change just because someone wants them to and has demanded or legislated it to be so.

As a project manager, it is important that you create the best possible plan. All stakeholders will recognize the business importance of building an aggressive plan, but the plan must be achievable or it likely will be considered bad business.

The project manager must champion a plan that is aggressive but achievable.

It's All About the Target

It is good business to be provided a *target* end date. It is bad business to be driven to meet an end date that is not achievable.

I recall working with an executive who told a project team to build a specified product in 12 months. He knew that it would take 18 months but believed that by demanding 12 months it would be ready in 18. The executive further believed that had he allowed an 18-month plan to be created, the delivery date would creep an extra 6 months and become 24 months.

This executive believed he had human nature figured out. *He missed on this one!* When a project team is mandated to build a product in 12 months, yet an 18-month plan is required, the product will be built in 18 months. However, the quality almost certainly will be poor. Why? Because so many corners will be cut in trying to achieve the impossible duration of 12 months that those cut corners will impact the quality of the deliverable for the remainder of the project—and long after the project has completed. The best approach is to allow an 18-month plan, but manage to that plan.

> *The best leaders do not play games with stakeholders; instead, they ensure that the right plan is in place and hold the project manager accountable for achieving that plan.*

Target dates are good business—as a starting point. Moreover, the project manager, while working with the project team, can apply the same concept to creating a project plan. For example, say the boss requests a target date of six months for the delivery of an improved product. Working backwards from the six-month delivery date, the project manager determines target dates for the project's major milestones. These target milestone dates help the project members focus on building a plan that can meet the six-month end date. Most project members likely can meet the target milestone dates. The project manager works with those who cannot meet a date creatively to either meet or modify the date somewhat to achieve the best possible delivery date for the project. (See Chapter 22, Do Not Make Long-Term Project Commitments, for more about the use of major milestones.)

> *To help ensure that the best project plan is created, the project manager should provide the project members with target dates for the project's major milestones.*

Setting target end dates for final delivery or for intermediate major milestones is good business, enabling the best plans to be created. But be prepared to defend your plan, especially if you believe that you cannot achieve the target dates. Offer alternatives; *do something!* As a project manager, all eyes are on you to ensure that the right plan is in place and the team is committed to achieving it.

Let's Talk: Questions & Answers

Q20.1 *Is a target end date really that big of a deal?*

A20.1 Most project managers will encounter a higher-up or client who tells them the project end date at the start of a project. However, many of these project managers will resent or may show an "attitude" at being given the "answer" before they have a chance to see if the date is even possible. It's important for project managers to understand that being provided a target end date is *good* business. In most cases, this is precisely what should happen, so *get over it* and channel the potentially negative energy into the positive direction of building the best plan.

Q20.2   *What can a project manager do if directed to create an un-achievable plan?*

A20.2   The project manager has the duty to articulate why the too-aggressive plan is not achievable. It's not enough to say, "Gee, this plan will be awfully hard to achieve." The project manager must identify the problems, or cons, of the plan in specific terms. These may address quality, project member burnout from too much overtime, low client satisfaction with the final delivery, and high maintenance costs eating away profit. The project manager also must identify one or more alternative plans and list the pros of choosing one of these plans.

Q20.3   *What if senior management insists on a delivery date that the project manager "knows" is not achievable, despite the project manager's attempt to drive toward a more reasonable plan?*

A20.3   We can all read an organization chart. The project manager likely will create the "unachievable" plan. However, here are five items for the project manager to consider:

1. *Request that someone from outside the project, but well respected by senior management, be called in to review the "unachievable" plan.* The goal is for the project manager to gain an ally who will support the creation of a more achievable plan. (Of course, this approach could backfire if the outsider agrees with senior management and not the project manager.)
2. *Include an activity called "Perform project review" in the new project plan* to occur every three or four months. The findings of this independent "audit" to assess the health of the project may support the project manager's views that the project is not achievable.
3. *Immediately identify a set of metrics to be tracked weekly* that can be used as an early warning to all project stakeholders in the likely event that the overly aggressive project plan begins to come apart.
4. *Agree on a fixed date for a near-term major milestone* and negotiate to leave the end date as a target date. Then adopt item #5 below.

5. *Include an activity called "Re-evaluate project plan" in the new project plan at the end of each major milestone.* This creates the opportunity to factor new information into the project plan and adjust it as needed. (See Chapter 22, Do Not Make Long-Term Project Commitments, for more on re-evaluating project plans.)

Although it is possible that none of these five actions will change senior management's position on insisting on an overly aggressive project plan, the information gathered will certainly provide more data that can show that the proverbial light at the end of the tunnel is really a train heading your way.

Q20.4   *Is it always bad business to build an unachievable plan?*

A20.4   In almost all cases, yes. However, exception scenarios can be imagined. An example: A company "goes for broke" with a new product or service in terms of winning a foothold in an industry. It creates an unusually aggressive project plan. Everyone involved in the plan understands that it is full of risks, but its achievement may mean the difference between retaining your job or facing massive layoffs.

The objective is to avoid overly aggressive, unrealistic project plans, and to create the best aggressive, *but achievable*, plans—and then manage appropriately to ensure that those plans yield success.

Q20.5   *Instead of creating a project plan by starting with the end date, how about temporarily ignoring the target end date, planning from beginning to end, and seeing what dates naturally arise? Then, if your schedule runs past the imposed target, you have more accurate durations to analyze.*

A20.5   In almost all cases, I favor the technique discussed in this chapter. However, the approach followed can depend on the reasonableness of the originally targeted end date. If the end date is achievable, or achievable with some stretch, then working back from that date can be more efficient in driving toward the right plan the first time. However, if the end date appears to be far from reasonable, then temporarily ignoring the target end date could be more beneficial. Either way, it is important that the project manager, leading the charge in creating the right project plan, ensures that the team commits only to an achievable plan.

> *The project manager is accountable for leading the charge in creating and defending the "right" project plan.*

CHAPTER 21

Meet Minimum Requirements—Anything More Is Too Much

Does this conversation between a project manager and a project outsider sound familiar? It was a Y2K project, but it could have been any project.

Outsider:	*"Will your project complete on time?"*
PM:	*"We have no choice."*
Outsider:	*"I didn't ask if you had a choice. I asked, 'Will you complete on time?'"*
PM:	*"This is an important project. There's a lot riding on the success of this project. We must complete on time."*

Translation: *"No, we won't complete on time. Anybody with any project experience knows this."*

One of the most common problems with projects is taking on too much work; that is, attempting to exceed requirements rather than *meet minimum requirements*. We allow ourselves to get trapped by overcommitting. What makes this so bad is that most of what we overcommit to often are requirements that are nonessential; thus, we allow nonessential requirements to interfere with a successful delivery. This contributes to a number of classic problems such as late deliveries, budget overruns, low morale, poor quality and, sometimes, canceled projects.

> *Nonessential requirements often impede completing a project on schedule.*

One solution is to build products that meet minimum requirements. You may be thinking that such products will not interest your clients— that "meets min" equates to building a C- or D-level product. I disagree: Building a "meets-min" product is building an A-level product.

Meeting minimum requirements means providing the client with a product or service that satisfies the client's essential requirements—the mission-critical requirements.

"Meets minimum requirements" means giving the client what he or she needs to be successful, but not providing nonessential requirements. If you want to provide requirements beyond meets-min, that's what future releases and future business opportunities are all about. Practicing meets-min helps

> *Products or services that meet minimum requirements provide the essentials—the mission-critical requirements—for your client's success.*

you continually meet your commitments to your clients—and build a reputation of reliability.

You say you *always* provide only essential function? For most of us, most times, that's not true. When a project is in trouble and at risk of missing its delivery date, one of the first things a project manager tries to do is reduce the requirements that make up the product. If the product already has been defined as meets-min, then there likely will be little or nothing that can be downsized. It seems that most times we nevertheless manage to find requirements to remove or tailor.

> *Do not commit to exceed minimum requirements at the expense of meeting those requirements.*

Let's look at an example.

> *A software product is to be developed for a client. The client has identified 100 requirements to be satisfied. Working with the client, the project manager prioritizes the 100 requirements into two categories of essential (meets minimum) and less-essential-but-desirable requirements.*
>
> *Although the client has recognized the priority of the requirements in the essentials list, he nevertheless requests that some of the requirements from the less-essentials list also be included in the new product. Consequently, the client budgets monies for more than just the essential requirements.*
>
> *The project manager then creates two project plans (see Figure 21-1). This means that there will be two projects—a primary project that addresses the essential requirements, and a secondary project that addresses the less-essential requirements. These two projects could have different project managers or be managed by the same project manager. Some of the less-essential requirements that are not being addressed are potential candidates for future product enhancements.*

Let's examine what just happened. Why have two plans? Simply, because the essential requirements are the most important requirements for the client's business. We do not want anything to happen that might jeopardize the new product being available with these requirements; thus we create the primary project plan, where we dedicate a team exclusively to developing a product that includes these requirements.

> *Commit to a project plan that includes only essential function, with an optional secondary plan for less-essential function.*

But because the client has provided monies to address some of the less-essential requirements, another project plan—the secondary project plan—is created to resist contaminating the primary project plan with less-essential work.

Note that two special relationships exist between the two project plans. The first relates to problems that may develop in the primary project plan. If the primary project is in trouble and is at risk of meeting its delivery on schedule, then the secondary project—or a portion thereof—is sacrificed and the appropriate people and monies are diverted from the secondary project to the primary project. Everything reasonable must occur to protect completing the primary project on schedule.

The other special relationship between the two project plans works like this: Any of the requirements of the secondary plan that have been satisfactorily designed, coded, inspected, and tested by a certain predetermined date (say, the date that a major test begins for the primary plan) are moved out of the secondary project plan and into the primary project plan—assuming the project manager of the primary project considers them to be low-risk. You might be thinking that if these requirements were going to end up in the primary project plan, then they should have started there. However, they should *not* have started there because they would have added risk to the primary project plan.

Reducing Rework

A major problem on some types of projects—certainly software projects—arises when less-essential requirements are included in a project plan. Then when serious problems appear on the project, requirements often must be removed—in effect reducing the product's requirements. In theory, this is easy to do, but in reality, it can be catastrophic. The

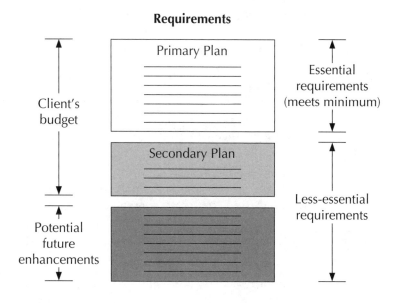

Figure 21-1   Relationship between Primary and Secondary Project Plans

less-essential requirements targeted for removal were designed into the product. It's not as simple as flipping a switch to remove them. They must now be designed out of the product.

Planning to meet minimum requirements can significantly reduce rework, which is common for projects that get in trouble and must reduce embedded requirements.

Talk about wasted time, money, and resources. All these less-essential requirements had been heavily invested in by way of designing, coding, documenting, inspecting, and testing. Now some degree of rework of design, code, documentation, inspection, and test must occur to remove the requirements.

Rework is a major problem on projects that negatively affects schedules, budgets, and quality. We need to build a plan that significantly reduces rework, which means that the original plan—the primary plan—must be only essential requirements.

In the meets-min model, problems of performing major rework are mostly avoided because the less-essential requirements were never in the primary project plan to begin with. Only after less-essential requirements have been separately and successfully developed are they allowed to be moved into the primary project—if the project manager of the primary project approves. So having a secondary project plan is a great way of managing risk away from the primary project plan.

The secondary project plan provides for managing risk away from the primary project plan.

Protecting the Client's Investment

You may wonder about all the investment that the client and the secondary project team made on the less-essential requirements that never made it into the primary project plan. Not a problem. That investment remains intact as the product is prepared for its next release.

Most of us have been conditioned to believe that providing a client "meets minimum requirements" will be bad business because it will be viewed as unexciting and noncompetitive. I believe it to be the opposite. The benefits of adopting the meets-min model include:

- Reducing risk to the primary project
- Reducing rework and saving time, money, and resources
- Setting client expectations that have a greater likelihood of being met
- Beating client expectations by potentially including some less-essential, noncommitted requirements
- Overall, delivering a product sooner and with less expense.

If you care about your client's consistent success, not to mention your own, you must take the initiative to drive your projects to meet minimum requirements. Everyone will win.

Let's Talk: Questions & Answers

Q21.1 *When you list requirements in two categories—essential and less essential—why don't you call the* less-essential list *the non-essential list? Wouldn't this be more to the point?*

A21.1 I agree with your logic and occasionally used the term *non-essential* at the start of the chapter; however, I do not recommend using the term *nonessential* when working directly with clients. As it is, clients are going to have a difficult task placing any requirements in a *less-essential list*. To call it a *nonessential list* would make it all but impossible for clients to place requirements there. The result would be that too many less-essential requirements would be added to the essentials list.

Q21.2 *You began the chapter with a Y2K-related example. For Y2K types of projects, wouldn't all problems appear in the essentials list?*

A21.2 Not at all. All problems that can cause serious harm to the company or its clients would make the essentials list, but many legitimate Y2K problems were minor annoyances at worst. We would not want to fix all problems (essential and less-essential) in the primary project plan if there were any chance that some less-essential problems could divert resources from resolving the essential problems according to the required schedule.

Q21.3 *In the example, you say that there could be two different project managers—one for the primary project and the other for the secondary project. What's the benefit of having two project managers? Why can't one project manager manage both projects?*

A21.3 In most cases, it is fine to have one project manager manage both projects. However, let's look at a prime example of when two project managers would be preferred. If the two projects are of the size or complexity that causes them to be particularly time-consuming, then the project manager's time spent on the secondary project may harm the care and feeding required on the primary project. Having two project managers would obviously resolve this.

Q21.4   *In your example, it appears that your approach may result in surprising the client with less-essential requirements being added to the primary project. Is it a good idea to surprise the client—even with enhancements?*

A21.4   At the start of the project, the client participates in creating both the essential (meets-min) list and the less-essential list of requirements. But the client and all other stakeholders are kept informed of the progress being made on the requirements being worked on the secondary project. Not only will the client know about any requirements being considered for movement from the secondary project to the primary project, but he or she will approve any movement of requirements before it can occur.

Q21.5   *Your example is of a software project. Does it also hold up for projects in other industries?*

A21.5   Building products based on meeting minimum requirements is almost always a good thing. However, there are differences to take into account depending on the industry. For example, if the project is building a commercial building or a nuclear submarine, it is generally not practical to have pieces of that building or sub developed as secondary projects. However, some equipment for the commercial structure or the sub can be built as part of secondary projects and this equipment can be added to the primary projects if it is available in time. Of course, you must use good judgment regarding the degree of applicability a secondary project has to the primary project.

Q21.6   *If a product has been defined strictly by meets-minimum requirements, is it ever possible for some requirements to be removed when the project is in trouble?*

A21.6   Technically a product defined by a meets-minimum requirements list cannot have its list reduced; however, in the business world, exceptions can occur. Creative and resourceful ideas emerge when projects are in trouble. When a project is in deep trouble and big revenues are at stake, a product's meets-minimum requirements list may be revisited as a means to salvage a damaged project. Of course, this may cause a product to have more limited marketability, but some marketability can be far better than none if the project continued on its destructive path.

Q21.7 *Many requirements documents state that the objective is to "meet or exceed minimum requirements." Do you concur with this wording?*

A21.7 No. Which is it? Are we charged with meeting requirements or exceeding requirements? What are the project manager and team going to be measured against? A project plan must be driven by one or the other. I am a big fan of always meeting minimum requirements as the official objective. Anything more is "extra credit." If a project finds the resources to provide extra credit without risking satisfactorily meeting the minimum requirements, that's fine with me, providing that the client and project sponsor are also in agreement.

Q21.8 *How can a project manager (or designated stakeholder) convince a client to focus on identifying meets-minimum requirements when there is such a strong propensity to tag nearly every requirement as a meets-min—an essential requirement?*

A21.8 It's not easy, but you can do it. First you must believe in the benefits of performing this best practice. Then you must convince your client that it is in their overall best interest to adopt this approach for prioritizing and addressing requirements. You must be patient and work closely with the client so that the client knows that you have his or her best interest at heart. My experience is that, more times than not, your client will go along with you on this. However, if you then mismanage the project and allow wholesale budget overruns, missed schedules, and low quality, your credibility will be destroyed and the client will not go along with you again on meets-min. The client will want it all.

Q21.9 *What happens to the secondary project if it loses some of its people and funds to the primary project?*

A21.9 Then the project manager of the secondary project replans the project to account for the loss of people and funds. A project manager should never continue to work to a down-level or broken project plan.

Q21.10 *Early in the chapter you state that one solution to overcommitting on projects is to drive to "meets minimum requirements." What are some other solutions?*

A21.10 There are many additional solutions. For example, project managers can improve their leadership skills, improve their soft skills, perform better start-up activities on projects, improve project planning activities, improve project execution and control, and learn the lessons from project closeouts. This chapter on meeting minimum requirements is but one of many applicable chapters in this book related to project planning.

CHAPTER 22

Do Not Make Long-Term Project Commitments

Most of us have been taught that, at the beginning of a project, we make commitments that carry us all the way to the completion of the project. That's a reasonable directive if the project is up to three months or so in duration. However, projects that are longer should *not* have their end dates committed. You read correctly. Instead, the *rolling-wave commitment model* should be applied.

> *Projects that are longer than several months should not have their delivery dates committed.*

Manage to Major Milestones

Projects should be managed by major milestones, which should be planned every one to two months apart. Why every one to two months? Let's look at Figure 22-1(a), which depicts an eight-month project. The project has been parsed into five major milestones: MM1–MM5, each one to two months apart.

Think of each major milestone as the end of a semester in college (although college semesters are usually longer than two months).The intensity of effort that a student brings to each semester begins at a certain level, as shown in Figure 22-1(b). However, during the last several weeks of a semester, the intensity of effort that a student applies to his or her studies can grow exponentially as finals approach and special projects are due.

> *Manage projects by major milestones planned at one- to two-month intervals.*

This doesn't mean that a student is not working diligently at the start of the semester; rather, it means that a student tends to "pour it on" during the final leg of the semester, studying more, harder, and smarter, and spending less time on non-academic activities.

What happens to a student when a semester has finally completed and there is a weekend or a full week before the next semester begins? The student crashes! Down time is required so that the mind and body can benefit from much-needed rejuvenation. This R&R period is essential for a person's overall well-being. When the next semester begins, the intensity a student applies to his or her studies begins again, but at a lower level—a more comfortable and tolerable level—compared to what will be required as finals again close in. Some mind/body battery recharging also is occurring during this period.

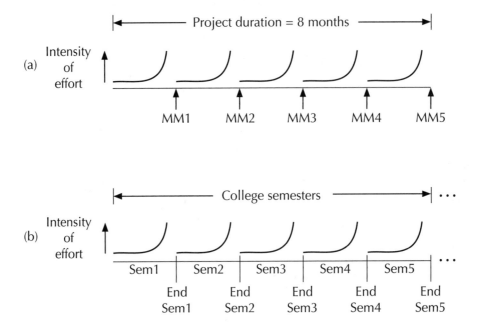

Figure 22-1   Intensity of Effort for a Project's Major Milestones vs. College Semesters

If the semesters were much shorter in duration, then a student could easily experience *burnout* because there would not be sufficient time to recharge the batteries before the next onslaught of finals. If the semesters were much longer in duration, then there could be too little time to "pour it on" in the last few weeks to address all the material covered since the beginning of the semester.

This analogy also applies to projects and their major milestones. As project members begin their trek toward the next major milestone, they are working diligently to achieve their commitments. Because projects should be managed mostly against their major milestones rather than activities, the project manager is not obsessed with project members meeting precisely every activity commitment shown in the project plan. Would the project manager like the project members to meet all their commitments? Of course, but not at the sacrifice of burning themselves out and missing the major milestones. However, when a project is several weeks from a major milestone, the project manager expects the project members to "pour it on," if needed. Meeting a major milestone date is sacred. If we can meet the major milestones, then we most likely can meet the project delivery date.

A project's major milestones are typically one to two months apart because this duration is optimum for project members to rally, if needed, to achieve the next major milestone, yet rejuvenate before the follow-on major milestone comes due. Obviously, if a project is only days or weeks long, then the notion of major milestones being placed every one to two months does not compute. In these cases, good judgment must be exercised in planning major dates with which to pace the project members.

> *Good project planning and tracking can go a long way to help project members avoid burnout.*

Commitment versus Target

When looking at a project plan, the next major milestone is a firm commitment. This means that the members of a project will do everything reasonable to achieve that committed date. All remaining major milestones are targets, including the ultimate major milestone: the delivery date. They are not firm commitments. They are, however, sincere targets and every reasonable attempt should be made to achieve them. It is imperative to estimate these dates for planning and business purposes.

> *The next major milestone is a commitment.*

Looking at Figure 22-2, notice the "X" at the start of the project. If that marks the point where you are now, then MM1 is a committed (C) major milestone and MM2 and beyond are targets (T).

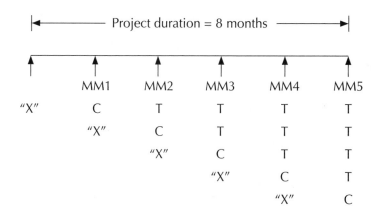

	MM1	MM2	MM3	MM4	MM5
"X"	C	T	T	T	T
	"X"	C	T	T	T
		"X"	C	T	T
			"X"	C	T
				"X"	C

Figure 22-2 Commitments (C) vs. Targets (T)

> *The goal, as well as the intent, is to achieve all major milestones, not just the next one.*

Why differentiate a *committed* major milestone from a *targeted* major milestone if the intent is to achieve both? Simply, to send a pragmatic message to all project stakeholders that all major milestones are not created equal. For example, the closest major milestone has a high probability of being achieved (low risk) compared to the remaining major milestones. Moreover, the further away a major milestone is, the lower the likelihood (higher the risk) that it will be achieved.

Re-evaluate Project Plan

Just after the identification of each major milestone in a project plan, an activity called "Re-evaluate project plan" is added. After a major milestone has been reached, the project manager (working with the project members) determines if the next major milestone and subsequent major milestones are still reasonable to achieve. At that point, major milestones

> *Refine estimates at the end of major milestones.*

can be re-estimated and the relevant portions, if any, of the project plan updated and rebaselined. This approach to planning and estimating follows the *rolling wave* concept, whereby estimates are refined as better data becomes available.

For example, when standing at the first "X" (to the left of MM1) in Figure 22-2, not only is MM1 the only committed major milestone, but the activities leading to the remaining major milestones (MM2–MM5) may be sized with less granularity in the project plan than those activities leading to MM1. After MM1 is achieved, the activity estimates for the remaining major milestones are refined as appropriate, with the activities leading up to MM2—now a commitment—being identified with the greatest level of detail.

> *The rolling wave concept is a realistic, sober approach to estimating project milestones.*

Many types of projects, but especially software projects, get a bum rap for missing schedules. But think about it: Who in their right mind would commit to an end date before knowing what is to be built or how it will be built? *Most of us!* But this is archaic, old-school thinking.

Projects under Contract

Senior management and executives are often heard saying that they can see some benefit to re-evaluating a portion of the project plan at the end of major milestones for noncontract-related projects, but not for contract-related projects. They declare that, "There is no point in re-evaluating the project plan because the delivery date is fixed in a legal document. Why perform a useless, wishful exercise?"

Re-evaluating project plans at major milestones is especially important for contractual projects because of the culture in which they are performed. When asked, "Are you going to complete on time?" a project manager typically answers, "I have to." The next question is, "I know you have to, but are you going to complete on time?" On contract-related projects, no one feels empowered to question or revise dates. Instead, hope and optimism spring eternal.

Contract-related projects especially benefit from re-evaluating the project plan at the end of major milestones.

Unfortunately, hope and optimism are not enough to make a project successful. Good planning and judgment are required. Re-evaluating at the end of major milestones is particularly important for contractual projects to avoid sweeping problems under the rug. Projects need a culture where all problems are visible so that they can be solved effectively. If a person believes that a commitment cannot ever be revised—and the commitment is in jeopardy—then the tendency is to deny or ignore that there's trouble and, therefore, avoid seeking the best corrective action.

Re-evaluating helps minimize the collateral damage that can build up on a project.

Better to admit a problem, create a fix, and potentially be marginally late than to ignore the problem and suffer far greater damage. Importantly, if a project is re-evaluated and its problems are brought into focus for resolution, that still does not guarantee that the project can or will be delivered on time. However, not confronting problems is certain to further delay any chance to achieve the committed delivery date.

Commit to what you reasonably understand, estimate for what you weakly understand, and re-evaluate when new information is available.

Let's Talk: Questions & Answers

Q22.1 *Why not "pour it on" at the beginning of a major milestone period instead of toward the end?*

A22.1 Conventional wisdom is to do just that: If the project manager suspects that overtime may be needed during the last two or three weeks of the major milestone period, then the overtime customarily is started at the beginning of the major milestone period. Resist doing this. Why? Because management and/or the client will see the project team working the overtime and maintaining or possibly exceeding schedule commitments and will be motivated to add more scope to the commitment pile. The earlier and more overtime that is worked, the greater the likelihood that the situation will be met with additional scope.

Overtime serves as a buffer; use it sparingly so that it is available when really required.

Project members need the R&R available to them during the beginning and midway into the current major milestone period. Overtime is a buffer. Use it sparingly so that it is available when really required.

Q22.2 *You say you predominantly manage projects to major milestones rather than activities. Don't you care about tracking activities?*

A22.2 All activities are identified in the project plan and are tracked accordingly. Commonly, however, so much attention is focused on activities that a project manager often loses sight of the bigger picture. It is important for a project manager to keep the project in perspective—to be able to see the forest beyond the individual trees. It is far easier for a project manager to maintain a sense of balance on progress when the major milestones are the key point of focus.

Q22.3 *If you manage a project plan to major milestones, where do you place contingency buffer in the project plan?*

A22.3 An upcoming chapter, Chapter 24, Contingency Buffer: Expect the Unexpected, will discuss the placement of buffer. Generally, I recommend that you place a bit more buffer in the trek toward achieving the first major milestone than all other milestones. Doing this helps ensure that you will meet the first major milestone. If the project team fails to achieve its first milestone, then the team will lose credibility with the client and management—which will be difficult to regain. Moreover, the project begins with boosted morale when the project members reach their first major milestone.

Q22.4 *Isn't it excessive to re-evaluate the project plan at the end of each major milestone?*

A22.4 My experience is that when a major milestone is reached and the re-evaluation activity is underway, only a few project members will need to re-evaluate their work. Most will say that they can still meet their originally targeted dates. In the few cases where replanning is required, the first objective is to be as creative and resourceful as possible to avoid slipping upcoming major milestone target dates. In the case where a major milestone cannot be met, then the movement should be as little as possible. Occasionally, major milestone targets are actually improved!

Q22.5 *If the project plan is re-evaluated at the end of a major mile-stone, you say that it is rebaselined. Do you really mean to change the baseline?*

A22.5 Yes. This is a great benefit of this planning technique. Have you ever been on a project where the project members are behind schedule and there is no chance of recovering, yet everyone is told week after week, month after month, to try their best to improve the schedule? How did you feel? Powerless? Demoralized? Sapped of your drive and passion to keep "pouring it on"?

This planning technique gives hope to project members. They have the opportunity to rebaseline if needed. This improves morale and encourages team members to work harder and smarter to maintain the schedule dates as they drive toward the next major milestone.

Q22.6 *Why would clients and management want to embrace a planning technique that does not commit to an end date?*

A22.6 Because the alternative is worse: committing to an end date at the start of a project and then declaring it will be missed just before the delivery date arrives. Even worse is replaying this scene several times before a delivery is made. Clients do not want last-minute surprises. These last-minute surprises are expensive in terms of budget, people, material, and quality. No client wants a delivery date to slip. But if slippage is unavoidable, clients would, by far, prefer to receive early warning so that they can adjust their business commitments.

Management feels the same way. They would prefer that problems are discovered and mitigated as early in the project as possible, when they are the cheapest to correct. You want to encourage an environment of trust and openness in terms of identifying and correcting problems as early as possible. Re-evaluating the project plan allows project members to factor in news since they last sized their portion of the project plan. It means that delivery dates will have a greater likelihood of being met. Even if late, the delivery dates will be sooner than they would have been if the project had not been re-evaluated at the end of major milestones.

> *The project manager should always welcome the identification of problems; it's the problems that are hidden—intentionally or otherwise—that should be feared.*

Q22.7 *Do you have a hard time "selling" clients on the rolling-wave commitment model?*

A22.7 Most of my clients are outwardly reluctant in the first few moments of discussing this technique. But as we talk about how it is implemented and its many benefits, most adopt it as part of their project management methodology. Their reluctance moves to cautious acceptance to "This makes so much business sense, I cannot believe we didn't embrace this concept earlier."

One client, a president of a sizable worldwide corporation, concluded that if the organization had embraced this planning concept a few years sooner, its last dozen projects that were late would have either come in on time or at least been less late. In either case, the overall costs of the projects would have decreased dramatically as a result of identifying and resolving problems earlier, when their costs were less. Moreover, customer satisfaction would have improved as a result of better communications, earlier warnings, and, of course, the likelihood of earlier delivery dates.

CHAPTER 23

The Effect of Multitasking on Productivity

Consider this scenario:

David is a resource manager with three employees: Anna, Brian, and Carlos. David has three projects going on in his department: Projects 1, 2, and 3. He has assigned each of his employees full time to a different project, as shown in Figure 23-1(a). The number of employees—three—is sufficient to perform the work on the three projects.

David, with the intent of broadening the skills and opportunities of his three employees, decides to reassign them. Now, as shown in Figure 23-1(b), each employee is working a third of their time on each of the three projects.

The result? David no longer has enough people to work on the three projects. He now requires an additional person, indicated by "Other" in Figure 23-1(b), to perform work because employees must multitask across the three projects. How can that be? Because each person pays a price in lost productivity

> **Project members lose productivity when they work across multiple projects simultaneously.**

		Project 1	Project 2	Project 3
	Anna	100%	——	——
(a)	Brian	——	100%	——
	Carlos	——	——	100%

		Project 1	Project 2	Project 3
	Anna	33.3%	33.3%	33.3%
(b)	Brian	33.3%	33.3%	33.3%
	Carlos	33.3%	33.3%	33.3%
	Other	x%	x%	x%

Figure 23-1 Deployment of People across Projects

when working across multiple projects simultaneously. Cumulatively, that price can add up to another employee being required.

Let's look at some reasons why productivity can suffer for the case shown in Figure 23-1(b). Let's say that Anna, while assigned only on project 1, was attending two routinely scheduled meetings each week. Now that she has been assigned to work on three projects simultaneously, she must attend two weekly scheduled meetings for *each project*—six routine meetings per week. But it gets worse, much worse. She also is interfacing with three times more people, reviewing three times more documentation, responding to three times more email messages, and dealing with three times more telephone calls. Notice that these tasks are among those that most *negatively* affect a person's productivity.

Project members need extra time allocated when working across multiple projects—a cost that is easily and often overlooked.

Let's look at another example, that of writing chapters of a book. Typically (and preferably), a writer creates one chapter at a time. Only after one chapter is written, is the next chapter started. But let's look at what happens if the writer works on three chapters simultaneously; that is, each day the writer must perform work on three different chapters.

The writer begins the first morning working on Chapter One. There are start-up delays as her creative juices are being pressed into service. Unfortunately, as her productivity finally begins to move along at a reasonable clip, it's time to put Chapter One aside and turn the focus on Chapter Two. But a chapter cannot just be stopped. There is time required to invest in temporarily placing the work in abeyance until it can be revisited and resumed the next day. Any last-minute thoughts that have not thoroughly been transferred to "paper" must be documented so they are not lost. Files need to be backed up and any relevant notes need to be recorded.

Now turning her attention to Chapter Two, start-up time is required to readjust her thinking and get up to speed on the new chapter. Again, she finally reaches a productive writing pace, but soon it's time to pack it away and begin on Chapter Three. And so on through Chapter Three.

The next day, the writer must begin again with Chapter One. This requires reviewing notes that were recorded during the shut-down sequence performed the day before. Moreover, the chapter, or a sizable portion of it, may need to be reread and "re-absorbed" to help put the writer back into the productive perspective that existed just before yesterday's shut-down of the chapter. Shortly after the pace quickens to match or exceed yesterday's, it is again time to set aside Chapter One and begin work where she left off on Chapter Two. And so on again through Chapter Three. Each day a heavy price is paid for this start-up and shut-down sequence (also known as "switching costs") that must be followed for each chapter.

The writer's productivity would have been measurably higher had she focused on one chapter at a time. This means that she likely would have spent a higher proportion of her time in a high-productivity state instead of cycling up and down so radically each day. Moreover, the sustained high-productivity state might have contributed to an overall higher quality of writing. If you were the writer and were given the choice, would you rather work on a single task until it was completed or multitask across many? My experience is that most of us would prefer the single task approach.

The chapters-of-a-book example shows yet another downside of the impact on productivity with the first example of assigning a person to work across multiple projects. That is, each time a person shifts focus from one project to another, there are start-up and close-down activities that must be performed. Not performing these activities—or not performing them well—likely will harm the productivity of the involved project members even more.

These two examples are indicative of the work environment that many project members experience all too often. They offer a simple look into how multitasking can harm a project member's productivity.

The Goal

The goal should be for resource managers to assign their employees to work mostly on one project at a time. Moreover, the goal for the employees should be to work on one task at a time and go on to the next task only after the first task has been completed. This approach can notably boost an employee's productivity.

> *When possible, project members should work on one project at a time; moreover, they should work on one task at a time until that task has been completed.*

But this approach has another significant benefit: It can reduce the commitment-related risk that a person brings to a project assignment. In other words, when an employee has made commitments across several projects, there is a risk that the commitments made on one or more projects will suffer setbacks that will negatively impact the commitments made on the other projects.

For many people, the choice to work on a single project or to be single-task focused is not an option. Understanding that their productivity will be handicapped can help ensure that people are not spread too thinly, potentially harming project outcomes.

> *Practices that can improve productivity can also reduce commitment-related risk.*

It is typically the resource manager's duty to ensure that employees are not spread perilously thin across projects and that they are making reasonable commitments. This is an example of

A resource manager works as a partner with the project manager.

Project members must be held accountable for making and meeting commitments effectively.

how a resource manager works on the sidelines to support the success of a project manager and his or her project.

But it's not all up to the resource manager. The project members are responsible for making and managing their commitments effectively. Ultimately, the accountability for a commitment rests with the person who is charged with performing the committed task. Project members should not knowingly make commitments that are unachievable or will cause unacceptable hardship and risk to the projects they are assigned.

The Buck Stops with the Project Manager

Clearly, resource managers should make good assignments and project members are accountable for their commitments. It remains the project manager's duty, however, to routinely review (e.g., weekly project tracking meetings) the plans of project members to ensure that commitments are reasonable and are being worked effectively. When a project member is committed to working on multiple projects or must routinely work multiple concurrent tasks, then the resulting negative impact on the project member's productivity must be considered.

Project managers must plan for the reality that many project members will work across more than one project or more than one task simultaneously. Plan for it or be weakened by it.

As a project manager, you are accountable for ensuring the effective planning and execution of your project. Make sure you walk into this common situation with your eyes wide open.

Let's Talk: Questions & Answers

Q23.1   *In the first example where three employees are each assigned to work a third of their time across three projects, you state that an additional employee now is required. Are you aware of a scientific study that supports this assertion?*

A23.1   I have not conducted a scientific experiment that proves this assertion, nor am I aware of any that have been conducted. I base my assertion strictly on experience and on specific observations of the causes behind the negative impact on productivity.

The fact that productivity is harmed is relatively easy to prove; just how much productivity is harmed depends on so many factors that vary from project to project. In the example, the negative impact on productivity could be affected by factors such as the size of the projects, the project management practices adopted, the skill of the project members, and the complexity of the projects. Whether or not a fourth employee is required full time or 80 percent or 60 percent is up for debate; the fact that productivity suffers is not.

Q23.2 *It appears that your first example could depict even more harm to productivity if you had used much larger projects rather than the very small projects you chose to use. Do you agree?*

A23.2 Yes, I do agree. Larger projects have many more variables. When project members work on more than one large project simultaneously, my experience is that many more complications can cause setbacks on one project that can negatively impact the commitments the project members have made to other projects. I used a simple example with the intent of making my main points easier to understand.

Q23.3 *In my organization it is common for project members to be assigned part time on new development work and part time on supporting existing work. I strongly agree that overall productivity suffers when working on more than one project simultaneously. How does a project member performing support work take this situation into account when making plans on new development work?*

A23.3 There are many approaches to this common problem, but I will share with you a common approach that can work in most cases.

Estimate the amount of time each week that your support duties require. For example, you should have a good idea how many problems you typically face each week and each month. You should also be capturing metrics that give you a reasonable estimate of how long it takes, on average, to solve each problem. This should give you a reasonable amount of time that you must set aside each week and each month for working on the support project. Now you also know how much time you can commit to working on the new development project.

The reality usually shows that some weeks are more demanding of your support time. Sometimes you will get a problem to support that causes you to overrun your allotted time on support work for the week, but other weeks will be the opposite. The new-development project manager must keep this all in mind as his or her project is being planned and executed.

Q23.4 *As a project manager, should I have control over how many projects my project members can work on outside of my project?*

A23.4 No. In most cases you must work with the hand you are dealt. However, you must be realistic in committing to a project plan that is made up largely of project members who are working on outside projects. When developing the project plan for your project, you have a fair amount of control over the amount of multitasking that your project members must perform within your project.

Q23.5 *Is a project manager's productivity harmed by leading many projects simultaneously?*

A23.5 A project manager has only so much bandwidth within which to work. She might manage full time a project of 25 members that's a year long, or manage five projects of five members each that are also each a year long. The latter case will be more demanding. Either more time overall may be required of the project manager or less attention to detail may result. Having less time for detail can cause quality on a project to suffer.

> *Multitasking not only harms productivity, but it can cause quality to suffer.*

CHAPTER 24

Contingency Buffer: Expect the Unexpected

*C*ontingency buffer, or *contingency*, is a designated period that is built into a plan to serve as extra time to help absorb unexpected delays.

All projects should have contingency built into their project plans. How much is needed? Where should it be placed? How should it be used?

How Much Contingency Should a Project Have?

A poll asking 10 project managers "How much contingency should a project have?" may reveal 10 different answers. Of course, most answers will likely start with, "It depends." It can depend on any number of factors, including:

- Skill and experience of the project members
- Availability of the project members
- Proven performance record of the project members
- State of the technology involved
- Duration of the project
- Number of members on the project
- Urgency of the project
- Physical remoteness of the project members from one another
- Maturity of the processes being used
- Complexity of the product/service being built/delivered
- Cultural diversity of the project members.

A project manager could argue that a contingency of 100 percent is not enough for building a product that is pushing the state of the art. Or that no contingency is required when planning an activity that has been performed dozens of times before and whose owner is completely familiar with and experienced in its execution.

I have found that for most projects, most of the time, a contingency factor of 25 percent is sufficient. Of course, the 25 percent value can always be altered if the project manager, working with the project members, believes it is too high or too low to apply to the overall project or to each activity on the project. There is no substitute for judgment if information

> *A contingency of 25 percent is sufficient for most projects, but judgment must always be applied.*

is available that suggests a 25 percent contingency is either too much or too little.

Where Should the Contingency Be Placed?

A project's activities should be planned, first, with no contingency. Figure 24-1(a) shows the timeline of a project of four months duration with no contingency. Then a 25 percent contingency is added (or whatever contingency you feel is appropriate). In the example, the four-month project is now stretched to five months with the added one-month contingency (see Figure 24-1(b)).

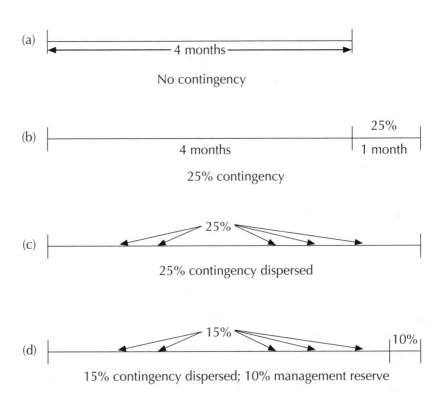

Figure 24-1 Options in Applying Contingency

It is not wise to place the entire contingency at the end of the project. You have added contingency because you believe it will be needed. When the five-month project plan is underway, there will be many instances where project stakeholders will need to dip into the contingency. But because the contingency is not distributed across the project, the project members find themselves behind schedule based on their planned activities that have no contingency built into them.

When this happens, a sense of unease—of frustration, even panic—begins to grip the project members. Moreover, many project members, in an attempt to get back on schedule, take shortcuts, which might include:

- Writing documentation that is a little less complete
- Reviewing documentation produced by others a little less thoroughly
- Compromising processes and standards
- Reducing time to perform design or build
- Not effectively enforcing entry/exit criteria for start/end activities
- Reducing time to perform testing
- Rushing to correct mistakes
- Decreasing or eliminating reviews and inspections.

When project members pay less attention to executing their activities in the quality manner that they instinctively know is required, a bad situation feeds on itself and the project continues to deteriorate.

So what should we do with the contingency placed at the end of a project plan (or at the end of a major phase of a long-duration project plan)? It should be distributed proportionately across all the activities of the project, as shown in Figure 24-1(c). This allows the contingency to be used at the points in the project where it is most needed.

At least some contingency should be distributed across all activities of a project.

Let's look at an example of applying this contingency.

The project manager, Vijay, is working with his project members to develop a project plan. He asks each member to put a plan together that applies to his or her portion of the project. He states that they should not include any contingency in the activities they plan to perform. Instead, they should plan only the time that they can justify; that is, assuming they are productive 100 percent of their day, how much time will they need to complete each activity? They also should include the time required to service any interruptions that they know about, but they should not add contingency—yet.

As Vijay reviews each member's plan, he asks many questions to ensure that each plan is complete. For example, Maria is a programmer who is planning her coding activity. Vijay asks her how much time she needs for coding, assuming that she will not be sidetracked by random interruptions. Maria says that she knows she will need to attend two one-hour meetings a week, but other than that she should be heads-down coding. Maria estimates that she needs four weeks to code. Vijay allows her five weeks, after adding one week (25 percent) contingency.

You may be thinking that Vijay is too easy, giving Maria 25 percent more time. You may be concerned about Parkinson's Law: *Work expands to fill the time available.* This means that if we give Maria an extra 25 percent of time, then she will use up that time, whether or not she really needs it.

But Vijay knows that Maria really does need that "extra" time even though she cannot precisely define what she will do with that time. For example, at the beginning of the project, Maria did not know that she was going to:

- Lose two workdays due to weather conditions
- Miss half a day due to a medical situation
- Give up a day to participate in peer inspections
- Lose half a day because she was asked to perform reviews of several documents
- Sacrifice a significant portion of several days to fill in for a vacationing project member.

The list of potential reasons vying for Maria's "extra" time goes on and on. In most cases, project members need the 25 percent contingency. In developing project plans, many organizations routinely build in contingency; for example, they may assume that only six hours of an eight-hour day are available—in effect, a 33 percent contingency.

There is another option to consider when deciding where to place the contingency. Instead of distributing the entire contingency across all of a project's activities, a portion can be held in reserve and placed at the end of the project plan. In Figure 24-1(d), 15 percent of the 25 percent contingency has been included in the project's activities. The remaining 10 percent has been placed at the end of the project and is called *management reserve*. As the project progresses and it is determined that we need to use up some of the management reserve, then the amount of reserve required is released and the portions of the project plan affected are updated.

Setting some contingency aside as management reserve can be a useful planning strategy.

How Should Contingency Be Used?

Contingency that is built into an activity is expected to be used up during the performance of that activity. Let's look again at the effect of Parkinson's Law in the example used earlier, where Maria needed four uninterrupted weeks to perform coding and was allowed five weeks. Whether or not Maria needs the full five weeks, the likelihood is high that she will use all that time. This is okay. It is the cost of working on complex, complicated projects in a challenging environment.

Estimating how long it takes to perform an activity is the most difficult task in constructing a project plan. Remember, however, that contingency is not intended to be viewed as a gift to project members; it is essential for managing a project and completing it in a reasonably predictable time. Contingency not only helps a project manager plan for the unexpected, but it also helps avoid burnout of project members by offering some breathing time to recover from aggressive spurts of work activity.

> *Contingency is an essential tool in consistently planning projects successfully.*

What if Maria does not use the extra week provided? What if she completes her coding activity in only four weeks? Can she give the contingency of one week back to a giant buffer in the project sky so that others might use it? Practically speaking, no. If you are thinking that she is able to deliver her activity output to someone one week earlier, thus allowing that person to use her unused one-week contingency, this almost always is not practical. Why? Because the project member she is handing off to is not prepared for the delivery a week early. The project member is still immersed in working on other planned activities that week.

What about the management reserve? How should that be managed? Chapter 22, Do Not Make Long-Term Project Commitments, presents a structured approach to re-evaluating, if needed, portions of a project plan. The re-evaluation is performed at the end of major milestones, which typically are one to two months apart. This means that a project plan can be rebaselined at the end of major milestones. This also is the best time to determine if any of the management reserve period should be released into the active portion of the project plan.

> *The release of management reserve can be decided at the end of major milestones, when the project plan is re-evaluated.*

Project plans need contingency. The unexpected *will* happen. It is not a matter of "if," but a matter of when and how often. Expect the unexpected and you will be far more effective in dealing with it.

Let's Talk: Questions & Answers

Q24.1 *What is the difference between contingency and buffer?*

A24.1   For purposes of this book, they are considered the same.

Q24.2   *It appears that you support the project manager rather than the project member applying the contingency. Have I interpreted you correctly?*

A24.2   Yes, only the project manager has the authority to apply contingency. The project member is charged with identifying how long it will take to perform an activity without including any contingency. The duration of time required to perform the activity should take into account any known, predictable interruptions. Then the project manager, working with the project member, applies the contingency. Although I have found a 25 percent contingency to work well in most cases, the judgment of the project manager—consulting with the project member—helps validate the contingency applied.

Q24.3   *If the PERT technique was used in estimating levels of effort for an activity, does that mean that contingency has been included in that activity's duration?*

A24.3   Let's first define PERT. Briefly, PERT (Program Evaluation and Review Technique) is a method of estimating the duration of an activity through the application of the formula $(O + P + 4L)/6$, where O is the optimistic estimate, P the pessimistic estimate, and L the most likely estimate. When the project manager asks a project member to estimate the duration of an activity, he or she is seeking the "most likely" estimate. The contingency will be added to this estimate. The PERT method does not yield the "most likely" estimate; it calculates a "weighted average." The weighted average likely will be larger than the "most likely" estimate. Therefore, one can deduce (arguably) that there is contingency in the PERT-derived estimate. Determining how much contingency requires comparing the "most likely" estimate to the "weighted average" estimate.

Q24.4   *Adding contingency to a project member's work activities likely means that it will be used up, whether or not it was really needed. Isn't that a bad thing?*

A24.4   As indicated, the contingency has been added to enable us to expect the unexpected. In most cases, the unexpected will occur. In those cases where the unexpected does not occur and the contingency portion is consumed anyway, so be it. We all need the load lightened from time to time. Estimating the duration of most activities is far more an art than a science. Because of the complexities involved, you won't hit the mark precisely every time.

Q24.5 *You say to add contingency to all activities. Do you mean just to activities on the critical path?*

A24.5 Contingency should be added to all activities identified in the project plan, regardless of whether or not they are on the critical path. Moreover, to leverage contingency, the owners of activities that are not on the critical path should strive to start those activities on their early start dates (versus their late start dates) and finish on their early finish dates (versus their late finish dates).

Q24.6 *Do you add contingency to an activity or add a separate related activity that is just for contingency?*

A24.6 Add the contingency to the activity. For example, if you have an activity called "Prepare document" with an identified duration of four days, then add another day to the four-day activity. This means the "Prepare document" activity now has a duration of five days.

Q24.7 *Figure 24-2(d) shows a 10 percent management reserve. Do you favor creating a management reserve or allocating the entire contingency across the activities?*

A24.7 In most cases, I favor allocating the entire contingency across the project's activities and not having a management reserve. I then would manage the project to major milestones, as discussed in Chapter 22, Do Not Make Long-Term Project Commitments. Also, this approach often is more palatable to a client who may express discomfort with seeing management reserve (a block of time, and therefore, funds) that is reserved for the unexpected, while no one can define precisely what the unexpected is. However, there are benefits to both approaches and the decision should be based on the project manager's and the project sponsor's business judgment.

Q24.8 *Does the project manager have the authority to release the management reserve?*

A24.8 Yes. The reserve is there for the project manager to use as he or she sees fit. It's the externally committed dates that the project manager does not have the authority to change without approval of the primary stakeholders of project sponsor or client.

Q24.9 *What is the relationship between scope creep and contingency?*

A24.9 Contingency is planning for the unexpected. One could argue that contingency also is used to help cover (1) additional scope that has not been accounted for, and (2) poor estimating of project plan activities. While contingency might be used to absorb a minimal amount of scope creep, it is generally not intended to cover the cost of scope creep. The change control process in place for the project is intended to deal with scope changes. Although contingency can help a bit for poor estimates, again, it is intended primarily for other unexpected occurrences.

Q24.10 *I have heard that overtime is a form of contingency and should not be planned for. Do you agree?*

A24.10 You have heard correctly. As a general rule, project plans should avoid including overtime. Overtime *is* a form of contingency. In many cases, overtime will be required from time to time throughout a project to smooth out periods of peak resource activity. If overtime was already scheduled in the project plan, then it no longer exists as a form of contingency. An exception to planning for overtime may be for projects that are only days or perhaps weeks long. Of course, business need will be a major factor in determining if overtime should be a requirement in a project plan.

Q24.11 *Are vacations and holidays also a form of contingency?*

A24.11 Vacations and holidays should not be viewed as contingency. However, in extreme business-need cases, they might be sacrificed.

CHAPTER 25

Scope Creep:
Runaway Train
or Good Business?

Scope is the sum of the products and services to be provided as a project (as defined by the Project Management Institute). Scope usually means the function elements (i.e., the features) of a project, but can also include schedules and costs. *Scope creep* is the change—typically the expansion—of the originally committed scope of a project.

As a project manager, you should always expect that the scope of the product you are building/enhancing or the scope of the service you are providing will change throughout the project cycle. Accordingly, an effective change control process must be defined, documented, and enforced on every project to deal with the scope changes that will inevitably be requested.

> *Change is constant; always expect scope changes.*

During the planning phase of a project, the scope and its associated elements are defined and baselined; that is, they are locked down and placed under change control. Although requests to change scope are usually associated with a client, any stakeholder, including the core project members, can request a change in scope. Common reasons for requests for scope change include:

- Government legislation/regulatory changes
- Competition
- Advancement in technology
- Interpretation/clarification of original scope
- Better understanding of client needs
- Business economy
- Change of stakeholders
- Poor planning of original scope
- Reducing costs and/or shortening schedules
- Change of mind.

You Are Running a Business

As you can see, there are many valid business reasons for requesting and allowing the scope to change. There also are reasons to not accept changes in scope. For example, do not agree to perform work that is unrealistic or not in the client's or your project's best interest. Furthermore, resist scope creep that goes beyond *meets minimum requirements*; that is, do not unreasonably increase the risk to the overall project by allowing a change to be approved that is not mission-critical or essential to the client's success. It often is bad business to satisfy the *wants* of the client at the sacrifice of satisfying the client's *needs*. Focus on what is critical, not on what is decorative. (See Chapter 21, Meet Minimum Requirements—Anything More Is Too Much.)

There are times when you estimate the cost to implement a scope change and the client accepts the cost, but you should not make the change—not in this release, anyway. In other words, don't always assume that because the client wants it and is willing to pay for it, it is the right business thing for *you* to do.

> *Scope creep can be the right thing to do; it also can be disastrous.*

Picture this:

> *Your business involves servicing many clients. You have deployed your resources across these multiple clients. When a project comes to an end, your resources are already committed to be rolled on to the next priority project. If you always allow your clients to have the last say in determining scope creep, then you can miss downstream commitments you have with other clients as you keep your resources tied down to a bulging project, or even worse, a runaway project.*
>
> *Your clients want you to manage your business. They do not want to be accountable for managing it for you. In almost all cases, your clients can live with an occasional "no," as long as they can take your commitments to the bank. They want you to be predictable and reliable. They do not want you to go out of business—which means everyone loses.*

Scope creep can be like a train out of control, gradually increasing in speed and momentum as it heads to a preset destination. The problem is that it has no or little chance of stopping once the destination (delivery date) comes into sight. Often the problem is not that unnecessary scope changes were allowed, but that the changes accepted were not sized adequately, if at all.

Enforce Change Control

All requests for scope change must be evaluated. To remain alert, always assume that every change request will have a significant impact on the project. The evaluation of the change request looks at the impact that the change will have on the product/service and the project overall. For example, will the change require additional costs, resources, time? Will the benefit from the change outweigh the negative impact to the project;

in other words, will an appropriate return on investment be realized?

All project stakeholders must follow the prescribed change control process before committing to or implementing any change. This mandate must be well understood and enforced across the project or the project can suffer grave harm—not just for the client, but also for all stakeholders.

Always assume that every request for scope change will have significant impact.

For very small projects, the change control process may be the project manager leading the evaluation process and determining the overall cost (e.g., dollars, schedule) for the change. Emails may be sufficient to both request and respond to a change. For larger projects, a change control board may perform this duty. Formal documentation, reviews, and a series of approvals may be required. It is important on projects of any size that the project manager be in the loop during the decision-making process, preferably as an approver. Of course, any potential changes to the project's external commitments must involve the project manager.

Every change request must go through the designated change control process.

The project manager must be involved in the change control process.

Changing the Baselined Project Plan

Typically the overall cost to implement a scope change is presented to the client; if the client is agreeable, then the baseline plan is appended accordingly. If the overall cost is too high, say, in terms of expense or schedule, then its implementation may be targeted in a later revision cycle or scrapped altogether.

If a change request can be accepted and absorbed into the existing plan, then consideration can be given to performing the work *gratis*; the goodwill can go a long way. However, if your good intentions backfire and you are unable to meet your expanded commitments, you also risk damaging your hard-earned relationship with the client. As a general rule, you should resist bearing the burden for any scope change that carries a noteworthy price in terms of cost or schedule.

The energy expended in evaluating and approving a change request often is insignificant compared to the great effort and coordination required to implement the change. If you are not careful, you can be a hero for a day by taking on the risk of accepting the change, and then be pond scum for weeks and months to come if the plan to implement the change was ill-conceived and falls apart. Do not underestimate the damage that can be caused by unconstrained or poorly planned scope creep.

It's one thing to size scope requests carefully; it's another to integrate the change into the project plan.

Let's Talk: Questions & Answers

Q25.1   *You imply that scope creep can include the reduction of scope. Is this really very likely?*

A25.1   While not as common as the expansion of scope, it often happens. For example, it is not unusual to cut back the scope to be delivered for a project that is at serious risk of missing its delivery date. We don't tend to think of the reduction of scope as "creep," but the fact that the scope has changed—increased or decreased—can be a challenge that the project manager and team must deal with. Scope can creep up or down.

Here's another example for reducing scope—a fairly common one, particularly when a company's cash flow is suffering. The client, citing financial challenges, may request that funding be slashed for a project already underway, yet still expect the delivery date to be met. Although we could brainstorm different approaches to handle this situation, a likely one is to reduce the scope delivered and, therefore, the overall cost to the client.

Q25.2   *You say that there may be times when you may choose* not *to allow scope creep, even though it was sized through a change control process and the client accepted the cost and schedule impact. I don't feel comfortable saying "no" to the client in this case.*

A25.2   Most times you will accommodate the client's requests; after all, it's good business to satisfy your client and to remain gainfully employed. Your job is to be as creative and resourceful as possible in securing new business and ensuring a satisfied client.

My point is that there may be times when "no" is the right business decision from your company's perspective (or your organization's perspective if the client is internal to your company). Be careful not to overcommit and spread your organization too thin, resulting in missing commitments both with your immediate client and with other clients waiting in the pipeline for your resources to be freed up and become available to them.

You are running a business. If you want it to be consistently successful, you must make decisions that, on balance, support both your business needs and your client's.

Q25.3   *You state that a scope change may not be in the client's best interest (versus your best interest). Why do you say that? It's what they requested.*

A25.3   A client may not always know the impact of what they are requesting. If you believe that their request will bring harm to them or the project, then your job is to bring it to their attention for resolution.

For example, in the scenario from Q25.1, let's say that the client asks for the project's costs to be reduced by 10 percent, yet they still want the delivery date met. Unrealistic you say? Happens all the time! What if the project is a data conversion where two companies have merged and they want their databases to be merged as well? There may be little or no scope to remove from the project plan on a data conversion project; however, because there are so many mock data conversion tests leading up to the real data conversion, the client may ask that you drop two or three of the 12 mock conversion tests planned.

If you believe that the quality of the final data conversion will be unacceptable if these tests are dropped, then the client needs to know that. This is an example of integrity on the part of the project manager—knowing right from wrong and doing the right thing.

> *Integrity must always be part of the change control process.*

Q25.4   *You say to focus on scope creep that is essential, not decorative. Are you saying never to provide a product/service or enhancement that is "decorative"?*

A25.4   It can be okay to provide less-essential function as long as it doesn't put at risk completing the essential function on time, within budget, and with the quality required.

Q25.5   *When should a project plan be rebaselined because of approved scope creep?*

A25.5   I suggest rebaselining at the end of major milestones. Major milestones should be placed every one to two months apart on projects of several months or longer. This means that there will be an opportunity to rebaseline a project plan every one to two months.

Rebaselining more frequently can be quite disturbing to the execution of a project plan. Moreover, project members can lose their focus in driving toward their original commitments

> **The best time to rebaseline a project plan is at the completion of the next major milestone.**

of schedule and costs. (See Chapter 22, Do Not Make Long-Term Project Commitments, for more on major milestones and rebaselining.) On projects of three-months duration or less, rebaselining is performed at the timing discretion of the project manager.

CHAPTER 26

The Project
Tracking Meeting

 *Obviously, a man's judgment cannot be better than the information on which he has based it."*

—Arthur Hays Sulzberger,
American newspaper publisher

The project tracking meeting and its derivative actions serve as the primary driving force behind the project. The project tracking meeting is an essential tool to ensure that the project plan and any approved scope changes that occur along the way are managed successfully.

What Is the Primary Purpose
of Project Tracking Meetings?

Project planning is about *getting in control*. But a plan is only as good as it was the day it was approved. It begins to fall apart from that moment forward. Project tracking is about *staying in control*. The No. 1 reason for project tracking meetings is to identify potential project problems before they occur. The No. 2 reason is to ensure that recovery plans are put in place before unrecoverable harm occurs. Project tracking is about being proactive, not reactive.

> *Project tracking is about staying in control—being proactive, not reactive.*

What Should Be Tracked?

Two general categories of information are tracked:

- Progress against plans
- Known problems (action items).

These categories encompass numerous specific topics addressed at project tracking meetings. Presenting the following specific topics—in the order shown—has proven to be especially effective:

- **Project high-priority areas.** The project manager presents the top three problems now plaguing the project, while their owners report any late-breaking news. These problems are currently impacting a major milestone or have the potential (called *risk*) to do so. The project manager tracks these high-priority problems *daily*, while all other project progress and problems typically are tracked weekly. (See Chapter 28, Manage to Your Top Three Problems, for more on dealing with a project's most important problems.)
- **Overview of project progress.** The project manager presents this information on a single chart that displays the project's major milestones. The chart is first presented as a high-level view of the project plan and is updated for each tracking meeting to illustrate the "big picture" of where the project's progress is in relation to where it was planned to be. This chart should give the project's sponsor and the client a reasonably good view of the forest without obstruction from all the trees. The chart likely will require updating by the end of the tracking meeting, after all participants have presented their status.

> *A chart that depicts a high-level view of the project plan offers a reasonably good view of the forest without obstruction from all the trees.*

- **Progress of project activities.** Each participant in a project tracking meeting presents status for his or her portion of the project plan. This status includes appropriate metrics to substantiate the progress made, identifies the top three problems and their corresponding status, and presents a 30-day outlook of what can be expected, including whether or not help is required.
- **Progress on action items.** An *action item* is a project problem that is logged, assigned to an owner to resolve, and then tracked until it is closed. The owners of action items present their progress. The project manager can decide to have the status of all action items presented at one time at this point in the project tracking meeting; alternatively, the owners of the action items can include this status in their report of progress on project activities.
- **Project outlook.** The project manager forecasts a 30-day outlook for the project. That is, 30 days from now, will the project be on schedule, will it be within cost, and what is the overall likelihood (high, medium, low) that the next major milestone will be achieved and the project will be completed as planned? Although this information initially should be prepared before the meeting, it is likely that it will need to be altered real-time based on the latest information collected at the meeting. (See Chapter 32, Declare Your Project's Risk Value, for a method of assigning a project's risk value.)
- **Work and escalation meetings.** The project manager ends the meeting declaring what project activities and action items require

special attention over the next day or so. If possible, these meetings should be scheduled now, preferably for the following day. These meetings typically become priorities within the project. (See Chapter 27, The Day After, for more on the benefit and implementation of these meetings.)

How Often Should a Project Be Tracked?

Project tracking meetings typically should occur once a week—same day, same time, same place. Meeting less often than each week can delay the discovery or discussion of serious problems, which can harm the successful outcome of the project. Meeting more frequently than weekly can be unproductive and waste scarce time, as it requires project members to spend time preparing for and attending meetings.

Most projects should be tracked weekly— most of the time.

For projects that are several weeks or less in duration, project tracking meetings could occur more frequently. When a project is approaching a major milestone, the end of a major phase, or the end of the project, more frequent tracking may be necessary to address problems and identify solutions more quickly.

On What Day of the Week Should the Meeting Be Conducted?

Routine project tracking meetings are very important to the health of a project and require participants to attend—on time and prepared. I suggest avoiding having meetings on Mondays or Fridays, which are often used as holidays or personal days for extended weekends. Furthermore, meeting participants use Mondays to catch up on progress that may have occurred over the weekend.

My preferred days for tracking meetings are Tuesdays and Wednesdays, because I like to reserve the day after the project tracking meeting for work and escalation meetings to address unresolved or new issues identified at the meeting. This means that Thursday would be used as the reserved day if the project tracking meeting were held on Wednesday. (See Chapter 27, The Day After, for more on reserving one day per week for work and escalation meetings.)

Project tracking meetings should be held on Tuesdays or Wednesdays.

It can be effective to have the team identify the day and time of the meetings. This approach can net a "subconscious commitment" from the team. The project manager can encourage certain days/times to help ensure that the best choices are made.

Who Should Attend?

For small projects of, say, 10 or fewer members, everyone might attend the project tracking meeting. For larger projects, a representative from each organization or team should attend. Managers (a.k.a. resource managers) typically do not own activities or tasks in the project plan and, therefore, are optional attendees. However, the most effective resource managers will attend as often as they can to support their employees who are assigned to the project and to stay abreast of the latest status. Other stakeholders may also attend from time to time.

Resource managers are optional attendees at project tracking meetings.

Meeting Ground Rules

The ground rules for the tracking meeting should be few, clear, and used to establish expectations for all project members. These could include:

- Come on time.
- Come prepared.
- If an activity may become late or is already late, then address:
  - Why it is late or potentially late
  - Areas of the project that will be impacted
  - Recovery plan
  - Whether you need help.
- Resolve time-consuming problems outside of the meeting.
- "Raise hands" if the meeting is perceived to be off track.

The participants should act like the professionals they are and arrive on time and prepared. Moreover, they should volunteer constructive information when they are behind on an activity instead of waiting for the project manager to drag it out of them.

Project tracking meetings should not be used as problem-solving (i.e., work) meetings. The project manager is searching for potential problems, recovery plans, and general status. Too much time can be wasted for too many attendees when the meeting is turned into a work meeting. A helpful aid can be for any meeting member to raise both hands when the meeting is perceived to be off its intended course. The project manager then decides to redirect the meeting or continue it along its current path.

How Should the Meeting Be Conducted?

The meeting agenda should be published and followed throughout the meeting. The project manager has the authority to declare that only a selected few of the participants will present their plan status, as well as which action items will be presented. This approach ensures that the most important areas of the project will be examined. It also helps keep the tracking meeting as short as possible. Any status not presented must still be submitted to the project manager at the end of the meeting. This allows the project manager to study the status without subjecting everyone to presentations on other than the currently most important areas of the project plan and action items.

Use an agenda to navigate the tracking meeting and stay the course for maximum results.

The meeting minutes should be distributed within two workdays of the meeting. These minutes contain two types of information. The first set of information provides data gathered/assessed from the project tracking meeting. From this information, project stakeholders can learn the overall status of the project. The second set of information is provided for use in the *next* project tracking meeting; examples include the agenda, updated areas of the project plan, and updated action items.

Distribute meeting minutes within two workdays.

The project manager must lead these meetings so that they run on schedule and are productive. A beneficial technique is for the project manager to assign a scribe to record the meeting notes so that the project manager is free to concentrate on running the meeting. How well this meeting is run and resulting actions are appropriately tracked to closure has a direct relationship to the discipline demonstrated throughout the project and therefore the overall health of the project.

As project tracking meetings go, so goes the project.

Let's Talk: Questions & Answers

Q26.1 *By saying that planning is* getting in control *and tracking is* staying in control, *are you implying that you need a project plan before you have routine project tracking meetings?*

A26.1 Bingo! If you don't have a reasonable plan from which to track a project, don't bother having project tracking meetings.

Q26.2 *You suggest conducting project tracking meetings on Tuesdays or Wednesdays. What if there are multiple ongoing projects across an organization, and project members find themselves assigned to more than one project? If all project tracking meet-*

ings were held on Tuesdays and Wednesdays, there would be too many meeting conflicts.

A26.2 Most organizations seldom experience this problem. However, in those cases where it does occur, the project managers need to meet and coordinate their project tracking meetings to avoid such conflicts.

Q26.3 *Why does the project manager track the top three project problems daily instead of weekly along with all other status?*

A26.3 The most important project problems are too critical to focus upon less than daily. (See Chapter 28, Manage to Your Top Three Problems, for more on this important topic.)

Q26.4 *You mention that recovery plans are required for activities that are late or have the potential to be late. Aren't recovery plans a bit too bureaucratic? Don't they involve too much overhead?*

A26.4 The No. 1 reason for tracking meetings is to discover potential problems before they have a chance to harm the project; in other words, to be proactive. What's the point of identifying these problems if nothing is done to mitigate them? Most recovery plans are not intricate or time-consuming. Their size or the time required to develop them is not the issue; having an effective recovery plan is.

Q26.5 *When an action item is logged, is there specific information that should be captured?*

A26.5 The minimum information typically recorded for an action item is:

- Name of the person opening the action item
- Date the action item was opened
- Brief title
- Required close date
- Suggested assigned person to own the action item
- Specific negative impact this action item may have on other scheduled activities
- Description of problem
- Tracking number or ID.

Of special significance, in light of the impact the action item can have on other areas of the project, are the "required close date" and the "specific negative impact this action item may have on other scheduled activities."

Q26.6 *Can other topics be discussed in project tracking meetings?*

A26.6 Yes, at the discretion of the project manager. For example, general information relevant to the project such as organizational changes, news/hot issues/requests from the client, client-related meetings, and marketing/product-related news could be included. However, it is important to stay focused on the core topics and purpose of the project tracking meeting.

Q26.7 *You said that project tracking meetings should not be used as problem-solving meetings. Are you saying that problems should never be solved in project tracking meetings?*

A26.7 Project tracking meetings can unravel if they also are used as problem-solving meetings. I favor a *two-minute rule*: If the project manager chooses to resolve a problem in the meeting and it can be done within two minutes, then that can be a very effective use of the meeting. After all, the required problem solvers often are present at the meeting.

The "two-minute rule" for solving a problem in a project tracking meeting can be quite effective.

If two minutes have elapsed during a tracking meeting and the problem is not resolved, then it should be deferred and discussed outside the meeting.

Another technique is to end the meeting 5–10 minutes early and conduct hyper-speed sidebar meetings to resolve as many problems as possible.

Q26.8 *You said that the project tracking meeting minutes could include updated areas of the project plan. Are you suggesting that the project plan is not baselined and that it is changed each week?*

A26.8 A project plan should be completed, approved, and then baselined. This means that the project plan is placed under change control and does not change unless approved scope changes or approved replanning of the project plan occurs. However, the minutes are expected to include the latest status against the baselined plan. (See Chapter 22, Do Not Make Long-Term Project Commitments, for a discussion of re-evaluating the project plan at the end of major milestones.)

Q26.9 *If a project tracking meeting has a scribe as you suggest, does the scribe write and distribute the meeting minutes? Or does the project manager?*

A26.9 That decision is up to the project manager. My experience is that if the scribe is the one who will author the minutes and distribute them, then the scribe will take far better notes throughout the meeting. However, if the scribe writes the minutes, they are distributed only after the project manager's approval.

Q26.10 *To whom should the project tracking meeting minutes be distributed?*

A26.10 Typically the distribution list includes the attendees of the project tracking meeting, their resource managers and selected other resource managers, and the project sponsor. The project manager can choose to copy other stakeholders such as senior management. The client should be updated weekly, but may receive an abbreviated version if the client is external to the company.

Q26.11 *Is it overkill for the project tracking meeting participants to meet briefly every day?*

A26.11 The weekly formal project tracking meeting is a must. However, an additional technique that can work surprisingly well is for the project manager to meet with participants of the project tracking team for 15–30 minutes at the start of each workday to ensure that the top-priority problems are receiving the attention they require. This mostly is an informal meeting that requires little preparation, if any, from the participants.

Q26.12 *As someone who has observed many, many project tracking meetings, have you found that these meetings reveal much about a project?*

A26.12 Absolutely yes! What these meetings reveal first to me is the discipline demonstrated by the project manager. The discipline shown in this meeting has a direct bearing on the discipline that can be expected throughout the project. If the project manager doesn't enforce members coming on time and coming prepared to the project tracking meeting, if members repeatedly are late on their deliverables yet have no recovery plans, if members are not forthcoming about their problems and whether they need help, then I see a project heading for failure. An experienced project manager type can sit through *one* project tracking meeting, study its exhibits and observe the actions of the members, and walk away with a reasonable

> *The project tracking meeting serves as a portal from which to sense the effectiveness of the leadership of a project.*

sense of whether the project is under control or is on the path of crash-and-burn.

Q26.13 *Other than the project tracking meeting, how can a project manager promote effective project-related communications among team members?*

A26.13 This broad question, in large part, is answered through the many best practices that are defined in this book. In short, ensuring that the following actions occur will go a long way toward effective project-related communications and good overall project management practices:

- *All roles and responsibilities are clearly defined for all project members.* (Part Two, Roles and Responsibilities, offers a good starting point by defining the roles and responsibilities of three power players: project manager, resource manager, and project sponsor.)
- *An effective process is defined and followed for building the product or performing the service that defines the project.* This process should include the use of reviews and inspections where appropriate. It also should designate the completion criteria for activities. All project documents should have designated approvers.
- *A project plan is created through the development of a work breakdown structure (WBS) that includes all project activities, their durations, dependencies, entry/exit criteria, owners, and other useful information.* The project plan becomes the road map of activities and is the keystone for project communications. (Details of creating and working with a WBS can be found in many basic project management textbooks.)
- *The project's top three priorities are tracked daily.* (See Chapter 28, Manage to Your Top Three Problems.)
- *Issues that are at an impasse for resolution are escalated within two workdays to drive their closure.* Every project member is taught that escalations are an effective business tool, as well as the proper process to follow when conducting escalations. (See Chapter 31, Escalate is Not a Dirty Word.)
- *The day after the project tracking meeting is reserved by the project manager to work off any items that are drifting and require work or escalation meetings among the project stakeholders.* (See Chapter 27, The Day After.)

- *Every project member is taught how to plan and conduct effective meetings.* (See Chapter 33, How to Run an Effective Meeting.)
- *A culture training class is conducted at the start of every project to ensure that everyone knows what is expected from them as part-owners of the project,* as well as the methods that will be employed during the project to ensure effective communications. (See Chapter 19, Create the Desired Culture for Your Project.)

Q26.14 *You have covered many topics related to project tracking. Is there a source you can identify that describes some of these topics in more detail?*

A26.14 Numerous books include project tracking information. One that I authored that addresses many of these topics in more detail is *Managing Software Development Projects: Formula for Success* (© 1995, Wiley Publishing, Inc.), specifically Chapter 5, Project Tracking: Staying in Control.

CHAPTER 27

The Day After

How does a project get behind schedule? "One day at a time," wrote Frederick Brooks in his classic, *The Mythical Man Month*.[1] Many of us have been associated with projects that completed late, or not at all. It is not unusual for projects to be days or weeks late, but some projects are—*yipes!*—months or years late.

Reflect on this for a moment: Based on how common it is for projects to finish late—not to mention over budget—the likelihood is high that you will experience—perhaps cause—one or more of your future projects to finish late. Not a comforting thought.

Obviously, there are many causes for late projects, such as incomplete/misunderstood requirements, poor planning/estimating, weak change control that allows unmitigated scope creep, ineffective project tracking and problem management, and weak project sponsorship. A big problem is that, despite our best efforts, a project can simply "get away from us."

A powerful tool to help keep your project on track is to reserve one day each week for work and escalation meetings. The day immediately following your project tracking meeting is best. All project members should be available on this day if called upon. By reserving the day after the project tracking meeting, project managers also buy a few more hours (between the tracking meeting and the scheduled work/escalation meeting) for the principals to resolve the problem. (Avoid scheduling Monday or Friday because these two days are common for project members to be away from work due to holidays and vacations.)

> *Reserve one day a week for work/ escalation meetings, preferably the day after the project tracking meeting.*

Let's see how this special day can benefit a project.

> Ross is a project manager. He has a weekly project tracking meeting every Wednesday morning. In this week's meeting he is obtaining status from Rachel, a test team leader. In last week's project tracking meeting Rachel said her team was two days behind schedule in developing the required test cases. However, she added that she expected her team to be on

---

[1] Frederick P. Brooks, Jr., *The Mythical Man-Month: Essays on Software Engineering*, 20th anniversary edition (2nd edition) (Boston: Addison Wesley, 1995). © 1995, Frederick Brooks.

schedule by this time next week and stated her plan to recover. Last week, it sounded like a reasonable plan to Ross. But in today's project tracking meeting, Rachel declares her team is now four days behind. Things appear to be getting worse. Ross writes Rachel's name on a small piece of paper and continues the meeting.

Joey, another project member, now has the attention of the meeting participants and is providing his status. In last week's meeting, Joey was late in obtaining the approvals required for a project document he had written. The document was scheduled to be approved the day before the project tracking meeting. Joey revealed his plan to obtain the remaining approvals within the next day or so and the plan appeared to be reasonable to Ross. However, in today's meeting, one week later, there is one approver, Phoebe, who still has not approved the document. Ross writes Joey's name under Rachel's on the small piece of paper and continues the meeting.

As the last action of the meeting, Ross reviews the small piece of paper and schedules two meetings for the next day. He declares that the first meeting will be scheduled for tomorrow morning, Thursday, in his office from 10:10 to 10:50 a.m. He invites Rachel and her resource manager. He says Rachel can bring anyone else she likes, such as a member from her team. Ross says he also plans to invite a couple of resource managers. He believes that Rachel needs more staff resources to help her get back on schedule and remain there.

Ross then declares that the next meeting will be in his office tomorrow from 11:10 to 11:50 a.m. Attendees are Joey and Phoebe and their resource managers. Ross says that if the issues holding up document approval cannot be resolved, then an escalation process will begin to help move the problem to closure.

What is happening here? Two members of Ross' project were late last week in meeting their commitments. In both cases, they appeared to have reasonable explanations and plans for recovering. However, in this week's project tracking meeting, they still had not recovered as committed. Ross has now become directly involved as a catalyst—a facilitator—to ensure that these problems are resolved appropriately and as soon as possible.

The project manager should not allow project-related problems to drift excessively.

The parties involved had the first crack at resolving the issues, but were ineffective in doing so. Ross is not upset with any of the parties. It's not personal; it's business. They may have performed the best they knew how. However, Ross has no intention of allowing these problems to drift any longer.

When a project manager reserves one day a week for closing out problems that are drifting, the project can reap major benefits. These include:

- Resolve problems that could eventually delay or sink a project
- Instill a sense of urgency for project stakeholders to deal with their problems
- Provide a support system to help stakeholders obtain the attention they need
- Demonstrate a level of discipline that project stakeholders expect and need from the project manager
- Improve productivity, saving time, expenses, and rework over the life of the project
- Foster communications among stakeholders
- Manage the difference between project success or failure.

Reserving one day each week to conduct work and escalation meetings does not mean allowing problems to drift until that day arrives. On the contrary, problems should always be resolved with the sense of urgency they require for project commitments to be met successfully. The one reserved day per week is a safety net to address the problems that escaped a quick resolution and may require special attention.

Brooks is right, of course, in saying that a project gets late one day at a time. But a project also remains strong or gains strength one day at a time. The reserved day can provide a gate for project stakeholders to open when problems require special attention. This gate can help project stakeholders diagnose and cure their problems before they fester and cause serious harm to the project.

> *Reserving one day each week for work and escalation meetings can significantly benefit a project.*

> *All project problems should be worked with the sense of urgency they require.*

> *How does a project remain focused and achieve its primary commitments? One reserved-day-per-week at a time.*

Let's Talk: Questions & Answers

Q27.1 *In the example, the project tracking meeting is Wednesday morning. Why wait until Thursday for the work and escalation meetings? Why not schedule them for Wednesday afternoon?*

A27.1 Wednesday afternoon provides the stakeholders who are the prime focus for the work and escalation meetings time to either resolve their problems or gather information that will be helpful in those meetings. Referring to the example, when Rachel attends the Thursday meeting, she will be prepared to discuss precisely her staffing needs (e.g., skills required, number of people, duration of help) so that the meeting can be more productive. The meeting with Joey and Phoebe may not even occur. Why? Because the scheduling of this meeting may be just the impetus needed to help them be more creative in resolving the problem between themselves or with a smaller audience.

Q27.2   *Referring again to the example, the project manager is scheduling the meetings for the next day. What if a project stakeholder is unable to attend at that time? I am especially thinking how hard it is for resource managers to be available on such short notice.*

A27.2   If a project manager adopts the concept of these meetings, then the project stakeholders are informed early in the project that the day after a project tracking meeting is "Ross' Day." This means that they are expected to drop what they are doing on this day if they are called upon to participate in a meeting. Obviously, some stakeholders will have a conflict, particularly those in management or outside the "control" of the project manager. If a stakeholder has a conflict, the project manager will do his or her best to reschedule a meeting to accommodate the attendees.

These meetings are important and they need to happen. Although, arguably, they could occur later on another day, I strongly recommend that they be held the day after the project tracking meeting, even if it means arriving at work early, moving lunch, or staying late.

Q27.3   *In the example, why do the meetings begin at 10 minutes after the hour?*

A27.3   The short answer is to make sure that people can arrive on time. Also note that the meeting is scheduled to end on or before 10 minutes before the hour ends so that attendees have time to get to their next meeting without leaving this meeting early. (The long answer can be found in Chapter 33, How to Run an Effective Meeting.)

Q27.4   *Looking again at the example, the project manager wrote the names of people on a small piece of paper and referred to the names at the end of the meeting. Isn't this a bit melodramatic? Why not just schedule the meetings as the problems are identified?*

A27.4   It may work fine to schedule the meetings as the problems arise, but I have found that the names-on-small-piece-of-paper approach works great. It gives the project manager an opportunity to determine how many problems could use special attention and to make sure that the most important problems are addressed first. Scheduling the meetings simultaneously also saves time and makes it easier to address schedule conflicts.

Q27.5 *When you say that the project manager should not allow problems to drift excessively, what do you mean by excessively? Is it ever okay to allow any problems to drift?*

A27.5 Among other things, projects are made up of people and activities, and the more a project has of either, the greater the likelihood for problems and conflict. We all experience problems within our domains of responsibility. We must be given some latitude to work these problems ourselves—to be held accountable. Of course there are exceptions, but, in general, a little drift of a problem typically does not pose a major obstacle for a project. To resort to micromanaging or performing the work of others can result in far greater harm to a project and its stakeholders.

Q27.6 *Do you expect that all projects will require a "day after" meeting every week?*

A27.6 The answer is highly dependent on many variables, including the number of people on the project and their proximity to one another, the complexity of the project, the skill/experience level of the project members, and the current phase of the project. For many projects, the "day after" meeting is not always needed each week. Moreover, if used, a substantial amount of the day is not required. However, this reserved day is extremely helpful if it is needed and is therefore a good habit to cultivate.

CHAPTER 28

Manage to Your Top Three Problems

Pop Quiz: What are your project's top three problems?

If you don't immediately know the answer, then you are not as effective a project manager as you should be and need to be. The No.1 reason projects run into trouble is that the project manager and other project members lose sight of the problems that need the most attention—the top three problems.

> *The No. 1 reason projects are in trouble is the failure of the project manager—and project members—to focus on their top three problems.*

I have observed many hundreds of projects, either as a project member or as an outsider. These projects ranged from less than a handful of project members to well over a thousand and from several weeks to several years. My experience has been that the top reason projects are in trouble is that the project's most important problems are not managed effectively, nor with the degree of urgency they require.

> *All project members should know—and actively be managing to—their top three problems.*

All project members—not just project managers—should manage to their top three problems to make the most effective use of their time. *The top problems become the top priorities.*

An effective approach for the project manager to follow in managing to the project's top three problems involves four steps:

1. ***Identify the top three problems.*** If you are not certain what they are, the following process can get you there. If you have a small project of a handful of members, then assemble the team. If you have a larger project, then assemble the project members that hold the lead positions. In either case, the assembled team will look similar to the members that make up the weekly project tracking team. Now the members of the assembled team brainstorm to identify the most important project problems. (The problems can include risks—areas where the project can be harmed, but no harm has yet occurred.) Now prioritize the list of problems and focus on the top three items in the list.

2. ***Assign an owner for each of the top problems.*** Preferably a different owner is assigned to each problem. Most times the owner will

be other than the project manager because most problems likely will be tied to a project member's domain of responsibility.

3. ***Each problem owner creates a plan to resolve the problem.*** Each plan identifies, at a minimum, the following items:
   - Who owns the problem
   - Activities to be performed to resolve the problem
   - Owner of each activity (if different from the owner of the problem to be resolved)
   - Dependencies that each of the activities have on other activities or on people/budget
   - Duration of each activity
   - Special items of note, if any, such as the likelihood of this problem occurring (if it is a risk)
   - Persons who must sign off on (approve) the plan; these are people with whom the plan has a dependency for it to be successful
   - How the plan can be tracked daily.

4. ***Track each plan daily.*** Each plan must be trackable on a *daily* basis, whereas all other project problems are tracked on a weekly basis. The owner of each of the top problems meets with the project manager at a designated time each day. For example, a problem owner meets in the project manager's office from 4:00 to 4:15 p.m. each day, another meets from 4:15 to 4:30 p.m., and so on. Meeting each day, even if only for five minutes, shows the sense of urgency that is placed on resolving the problems. Each problem should be resolved as soon as reasonably possible.

> *The top three problems must have measurable plans that are tracked daily and resolved as quickly as reasonably possible.*

It is expected that each owner of a top-three problem typically is spending most of his or her time each day on resolving the problem. If this is not the case, the person's time on the project is not being used effectively. Why track these problems daily, instead of weekly? Because these are the problems that can cause the project the most harm. The sense of urgency requires their daily focus to ensure they are getting the attention they require.

Most of the items on the top-problems list should be resolved within a week or two; they certainly should not remain on the list for more than several weeks. As the top problems are worked off the priority list, assign and then work off the next level of priority problems.

> *A problem must not remain on the top-problems list any longer than is reasonable.*

Because of the direct link between resolving the top three problems and a project's success, these problems must be identified, assigned, tracked, and resolved with the urgency they require. The project manager must exercise leadership, vision, creativity, and discipline to ensure that the most important problems are being addressed appropriately. If a problem remains on the top-problems list very long, then the owner of the problem as well as the project manager (if different) are not performing their duties effectively.

Let's Talk: Questions & Answers

Q28.1   *When you say to manage daily to your top three problems, are you also using the term "problems" to mean priorities, issues, and risks?*

A28.1   Yes, but I will clarify. I said earlier that the top problems become the top priorities; therefore, I use the terms *problems* and *priorities* interchangeably. I also said that problems can include those that are *risks*; that is, areas where the project can be harmed, but no harm has yet occurred. I use the term *issue* as another way of designating an important problem that can have a significant impact on a project.

Q28.2   *What if a project manager or project member cannot focus on his or her top problems each day because of so many other distractions? Is this acceptable?*

A28.2   There occasionally will be those days when the interruptions are so frequent and urgent that we will invest little or no time in resolving our top problems. However, if these days are the norm rather than the exception, then the problem is *you*. After all, you own your domain of responsibility. (See Chapter 1, Mind Your Own Business.) If you cannot effectively manage your domain, no one else will. You must find ways to make it happen, including asking for help if you need it. (See Chapter 3, Ask for Help—or Become Part of the Problem.)

Q28.3   *Can you provide any pointers that can help a project member remain focused on his or her top three problems?*

A28.3   When you begin each workday, create a to-do list of things to work on that day. For simplicity, say you begin the day with 10 items on your to-do list—your top three problems and another seven. When you drive home from work at the end of the workday and you have not worked on any of your top three, but you have crossed off your bottom seven, do *not* feel good about your accomplishments that day! You worked on the wrong items.

If, instead, when you drive home you have made significant headway in just one of your top three and have not touched any of your bottom seven, then you should feel good about your accomplishments. I am not saying not to work on your bottom seven, but I *am* saying not to work on the bottom seven at the sacrifice of your top three.

If you have five minutes between meetings, it may be enough time to cross off a bottom-seven item. However, if you have 30 minutes between meetings, do not use this time to cross off multiple bottom-seven items. Many people make the mistake of reserving 30 minutes or an hour each day to work off bottom-seven items. If you have this much time to reserve, work on a top-three item.

Why do so many of us work off our bottom seven at the sacrifice of completing a top-three? The bottom seven items tend to be easier or more fun. We get instant gratification. We rationalize that the collection of bottom-seven items is equivalent in importance to a top-three. *It isn't!*

One more point. Most of the project managers and management that I mentor visibly post on their office "white boards" their top three problems to work on each day. They do this as a reminder to help them maintain the discipline to stay focused on working the top three problems off the list.

Q28.4 *It seems that you are equating items on a to-do list with problems. I often put items on a to-do list that I do not view to be problems, but are actions that I choose to take. Your view?*

A28.4 Items are on a to-do list to either prevent them from becoming problems or because they are already problems and need to be mitigated. Therefore, I view a to-do list as being made up of problem-related items.

Q28.5 *If a project manager is managing multiple projects, should he know the top three problems on each project and manage to all of them each day?*

A28.5 The project manager should know the top three problems on each project. If he is managing, say, four projects at the same time, then that adds up to 12 top problems. However, 12 problems are far too many to manage with a sense of urgency each day. Instead, he needs to identify the top three problems from among the 12 and manage to those. The top three problems could all come from one project, three different projects, or somewhere in between.

Q28.6 *What method do you recommend for reducing a list of problems to its top three?*

A28.6 Once you have the list in front of you—say there are 15 items— assign an "H," "M," or "L" (high, medium, low) to each item by asking yourself, relative to all the items on the list, what priority this item should be assigned. After the first pass, the 15-item list may be reduced to eight top-priority items. Then repeat the process by focusing on the top eight. In a short time, you will be able to single out the top three problems.

Q28.7 *Do you have an approach for documenting the top three problems? That is, are they placed in a risk management plan or some other repository?*

A28.7 In most cases, I manage the top three problems (which may or may not include risks) in an "action item" database. They are recorded and tracked along with all the other open action items on the project. The main difference is that the top three problems are tracked daily, whereas all others typically are tracked weekly.

Q28.8 *Why track the project's top three problems daily? Isn't this micromanaging those who own the problems on the project?*

A28.8 Micromanaging is when a "leader" tells others what to do, how to do it, when to do it, where to do it. As a project manager, you are not doing any of these things. The person who owns a project's top problem creates her own plan and tracks to that plan. The project manager is only asking to review the plan and meet daily to ensure that it is being serviced as required.

Many project members, when tracked weekly, tend to "pour it on" just before a weekly project tracking meeting and then slow the pace somewhat just after the tracking meeting. However, when a person's plan is being tracked daily, she has almost no time to "slow down." She must be able to show measurable progress each day.

The top three problems are the problems that can hurt, or already are hurting, the project the most. It is good business to manage daily to the most important project problems. As a business person or the owner of a company, wouldn't you want it that way?

Q28.9 *Can you give a specific example of how not managing to the top three project problems harmed a project?*

A28.9 Any project in trouble is an example. Here's one.

> *I received a call in my office one day from a senior vice president of a large company. He described a project that he had inherited a few weeks earlier. The project was in deep trouble. It was originally expected to be 11 months in duration and peak at 60 members. However, three years had passed and no one knew when the project would complete. Moreover, there were now 500 people working full time on the project.*

While performing a two-day project review, I identified the top problems. Among them were these three:

- *There was no designated project manager, no focal point, no one to hold accountable.* The project was being run mostly by executives who either did not have the necessary project management skills or did not have the time to manage the project effectively.
- *The requirements were not complete.* Moreover, they were never approved, they were not placed under change control, and they were changing by the week.
- *No agreed-upon software development process had been defined and enforced.* There were about 10 development teams and they were all following very different processes and procedures. The quality being produced from each team varied from good to a total crapshoot.

At the time of the project review, approximately 1.5 million lines of code had already been delivered into a formal test, but there was no single formal product specifications document that defined the product to be tested. Had the project manager been managing to the top three problems daily, these major issues could have been resolved more than two and a half years earlier!

Q28.10 *This place can be a zoo. Some days I feel like I am losing it. I have a hard time keeping things in the right perspective. Any ideas?*

A.28.10 Welcome to the human race. I suggest finding a place where you can be uninterrupted for 10–15 minutes. Then do whatever works best to relax you. For some it may be a state of meditation, a relaxing position, or just closing your eyes and thinking calming thoughts. Another approach (while alone!) that can be effective is to ask yourself questions about how your day is going . . . and answer them honestly. This can bring a fresh perspective to your behavior and actions.

Yet another approach could be to seek a friend to help you clear your thinking.

In extreme cases—if the stress is especially overwhelming and this state is becoming the norm rather than the exception—you may want to consider professional help.

Make time to refocus and put your day or a certain event into its proper perspective.

In any case, I recommend you do something rather than nothing. You, your stress level, and your coworkers will be glad you did.

CHAPTER 29

Treat All Project Members Equally

What if a project is made up of client personnel, vendors, and contractors in addition to the company's personnel? How should the project manager relate to each of these diverse groups?

This is a common problem on many projects, yet the answer is simple. Once people are assigned to a project, regardless of where they hail from, they must all be treated the same. *No exceptions!*

> *All project members, regardless of where they come from or to whom they report, must be held accountable for their commitments.*

Figure 29-1 shows a project that consists of all these groups. For purposes of illustration, each team is led by a team leader and is made up of a different group of project members: client personnel, vendor personnel, contractors, and company personnel. The team leaders could be from the same or a different group as the team members. (Of course, although not depicted in this example, it is possible that a specific team can consist of a mixture of people from these different groups.) Also note that the project manager may or may not be an employee of the company.

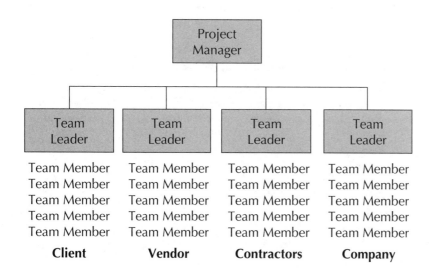

Figure 29-1   Project Comprising Diverse Groups

Once project members have been assigned to the project, the project manager should not focus on their origins. The focus must be on the project, the commitments from each team, and the corresponding actions that each project member performs toward achieving assigned activities. The project manager sees everyone as a project member and will work with each person and group as if they were personnel from the same project team . . . *because they are!*

Each team is expected to have plans, commit to those plans, and track according to those plans. If any team is in trouble, or headed that way, the project manager initiates the attention required to help the team get back on plan. Each team is held just as accountable for its commitments as any other team.

I commonly see project managers treat with kid gloves the client's personnel assigned to the project—quick to cut them slack at every turn. I often see vendors treated as if they are a "black box" that cannot be tampered with, their whims easily accepted as "cast in stone" with little or no chance of altering. I see contractors treated as second-class members of the team, where project information is often withheld from them—information that they need to function fully as members of the project. And I often see company employees treated harshly based on the view that they are the most accessible project members and, arguably, the easiest to lean on.

> *The project manager is responsible for ensuring that all project members are treated equally in being held accountable for their commitments.*

Consider this true scenario:

> *Project ABC consists of members from all four groups: client personnel, vendors, contractors, and company personnel. The project completes substantially late. This causes a great hardship to the client, who brings litigation action against the company that managed the project. After careful study, it is determined that the primary reason for the project's delay was poor performance by the project team that is made up of client personnel. The project manager had consistently cut the client team slack when their commitments were late or of low quality. The project manager's rationale was that the client was paying the bills and that it was good business not to bite the hand that feeds it.*

> *The "client" who initiated legal action is not anyone on the client team; it is the executive from the client company who signed the contract. The client executive said that had he known that the primary problems on the project were from his own organization, he would have worked swiftly to correct the problems. But no one routinely informed the executive. Therefore, the executive sued for breach of contract due to the missed commitments.*

This scenario is all too common. It is vital to remember that a project's success depends on the success of each and every project member. As the saying goes, "A chain is only as strong as its weakest link." Any one member or team can harm the project. An effective project manager recognizes this and works consistently, firmly, and unbiasedly across all members of a project to ensure that the project completes successfully, addressing weak links whenever and wherever they are identified.

> *A project suffers when preferential treatment is given to any group or person.*

Let's Talk: Questions & Answers

Q29.1 *You say there are "no exceptions" in terms of treating all project members the same. Are there really no exceptions?*

A29.1 In general, the project manager should have the mindset and operate as if there are no exceptions. Depending on the needs of the project members at any given point along the project's journey, the project manager will appear to be spending more time and energy with one group or project member than another. However, do not confuse this with preferential treatment. The project manager is behaving in the best interest of the overall project by nurturing "needy" points of the project along the way.

Could there ever be a scenario where one of these four groups (client personnel, vendor, contractors, and company personnel) should get special treatment over the other groups? Of course, we all can *imagine* a case where this could be; however, be careful! Don't lose sight of the fact that all project members are required to complete their commitments successfully for the project to succeed.

Q29.2 *What if one or more project members are executive types? Do you still say to treat everyone on the project the same?*

A29.2 Absolutely yes! In my view, it *should* be rare for an executive to be a member of a project. (In my model, even resource managers typically are not part of a project's core membership.) If this is the case, however, remember that it takes just one project member to miss his or her commitments for the project to suffer. Hold all project members accountable and treat them equally.

Q29.3 *If we treat contractors exactly like regular company employees, our legal organization will come down on us. What is your reasoning on this?*

A29.3   You should treat contractors the same as you would anyone else on the *project*—not the same as another *company employee*. This is an important distinction.

Contractors should be held just as accountable for their commitments as anyone else on a project. They should plan their activities the same, be tracked the same, and share in the project camaraderie the same. For example, if it is customary for the project members to go to lunch together each Friday, then contractors should be included.

However, things are very different from a *company* (versus *project*) perspective. If the company has a picnic for employees, contractors typically are not invited. If the company celebrates an event and everyone receives a T-shirt, contractors typically are not included. Consult with your legal staff before including contractors in company-related (versus project-related) events.

Q29.4   *What if a vendor is the root cause of a project in trouble? As a project manager, should I be as involved in the vendor's recovery planning and execution as I would for a company employee?*

A29.4   If a vendor's commitments are in jeopardy, the burden is on the project manager to do whatever is reasonably possible to help get the vendor back on track. If the vendor is performing outsourced work and resides in another country, then the project manager might best serve the project's objectives by traveling to the vendor location and participating in considering corrective-action options.

Obviously, there are limitations as to what a project manager can do, but the project manager should not assume that he or she is helpless in influencing the vendor's behavior. Remember, the project manager is accountable for the successful outcome of the project, no matter where that path may lead. Of course, consult with senior stakeholders such as the project sponsor if sensitive or costly actions are being considered.

Q29.5   *In the interest of treating all project members equally, should the project manager bypass team leaders and work directly with team members?*

A29.5   The project manager should work through the team leaders. However, if a team is at risk in meeting its commitments, then, if required, the project manager may work together with both the team leader and the team members.

CHAPTER 30

Inspect What You Expect

The phrase "inspect what you expect" has been around for a long time, but its message goes unheeded for many project managers. Who hasn't had a project where a team insists that things are fine, that the delivery will be on schedule and will meet the quality expected? But then the delivery date arrives, and it's not ready!

Case in point:

> I was asked to perform a review on a troubled project. The project originally was planned to run about eight months, but continued for nearly twice that without convincing data on when it would complete. After a project review and the resulting recommendations, the project was re-planned and estimated to complete in another six months.
>
> One month into the new six-month plan, I asked the project manager, Monica, what her top three priorities were. After some thought, she eventually identified her top three. Her top priority was to validate the long list of requirements with the client to ensure that both parties had the same interpretation. This was a new six-week activity that she had assigned to Chandler; he was just starting the fifth week.
>
> I asked if Chandler was on schedule. She said "yes." I asked how she knew that. Monica said that Chandler, a senior-level project member, repeatedly announced in the weekly project tracking meetings that he was on schedule. Because there were only two weeks left of the six-week activity, I asked Monica if Chandler and the client would work over the one remaining weekend available, if necessary, to protect their commitments to the schedule. Monica said that she had full trust and confidence in Chandler. After all, she said, "Chandler is a professional."
>
> Net result: Chandler was four weeks late in completing the activity and did not work any weekends. Moreover, Chandler said the activity "should be completed by next week" for the next four weeks.

If your clients or senior management micromanage your projects, it's for a reason: You likely invited it by your inactions. Most times, a person doesn't micromanage another for the sport of it. Rare is the person who actually enjoys or prefers to spend his or her limited time consumed in managing the affairs of another. Project managers are expected to manage their domains of responsibility. When they don't, others often must get involved to a level lower than anyone likes.

If you don't inspect the work of others as needed, your work will become the focus of inspection.

When a project member has made a commitment to you either directly or by way of the project plan, what are you doing to ensure that "I am on schedule" is true and meets your expectations? As the project manager, you are the commander of your ship. If a failure occurs, you are responsible and accountable—even if someone else misses a commitment—because the failure occurred under your command.

All eyes are watching you. These eyes belong to the other project members, the client, your boss, or some other project stakeholder. They are relying on your leadership, your integrity, your boldness to assert yourself when and where needed.

> *Consistently successful projects don't just happen; they are made to happen.*

Project members must know what they are being held accountable for; that is, what you expect from them. Furthermore, these expectations must be measurable. Project members must then routinely report progress against those measured expectations.

> *Progress must be measurable against a plan.*

As a general principle: Don't trust anyone. Question everything. Assume nothing. It's not personal. It's business. It's *good* business. How many times must a project manager get drawn into this trap? Requiring a trackable plan and routine progress reports demonstrates good leadership.

> *Don't trust anyone. Question everything. Assume nothing.*

When your instincts alert you that there is something suspect about a commitment, trust those instincts. We all have remarkably good instincts, but too many of us are too soft to act upon them. (See Chapter 8, Are You Too Soft?) Be fair, but firm. Inspect what you expect. Your projects will benefit greatly, as will your career.

> *You have great instincts. Listen to them . . . and then respond appropriately.*

Let's Talk: Questions & Answers

Q30.1 *In the opening scenario, didn't you describe a project manager who was "stupid" rather than too trusting? After all, look how poorly the project was managed.*

A30.1 I don't recall ever meeting a "stupid" project manager, but I frequently work with project managers who are ineffective for a variety of reasons: weak soft skills, weak hard skills, weak/no project sponsor. Ineffective project managers can be found just about everywhere. Most of us have performed ineffectively at some points in our careers or certainly have conducted ourselves in a manner that we have since improved upon.

My example may have struck you as being excessive because the project was so late. However, having seen hundreds of projects, I have come upon many project managers who have messed up big time, but were trainable and definitely "keepers." In the scenario, the project manager trusted the repeated assertions of a "professional" instead of requiring a plan that was trackable.

Q30.2 *Aren't you making it personal by saying that the project manager should not trust anyone on a project?*

A30.2 As I said earlier, it's not personal, it's good business. It's all about plan and controls. A project manager should not "trust" the assertions or statements of a project stakeholder without sufficient measurements to back up those assertions. It may well be that a project member has good intentions and even believes that the assertion of being, say, on schedule is true. Insisting on a measurable plan for measuring progress can greatly enhance the perspective, confidence, and credibility of the owner of that plan—as well as the project manager's understanding of actual progress.

Q30.3 *Are you saying never to trust anyone on a project?*

A30.3 I am not saying "never." Use good business judgment. If you have worked alongside someone for an appreciable amount of time and you observe that the person always can be relied upon to meet his or her commitments, then you can factor this into the level of detail/focus that you require of that person. However, if the person's reliability is unknown or unfavorable, then the project manager would be reckless in not insisting upon a trackable plan. In both cases, a plan that can be tracked is required; however, in the latter case, the plan may need to be more detailed and tracked more closely.

> *The best leaders demonstrate good business judgment in their day-to-day actions.*

CHAPTER 31

Escalate
Is Not
a Dirty Word

One of the most difficult but common situations we face in our jobs is how to resolve critical problems when we must depend on someone else—someone who chooses not to accommodate our needs.

I often have been asked to come into organizations and assess progress on troubled projects. *In every case*, the top problem I identify is that the most critical problems are not receiving adequate attention. I am talking about problems that, if not solved quickly, will cause significant harm, such as missed schedules, compromised quality, cost overruns, and lost customers. If inattention to these critical problems has such an impact on an organization's success, why aren't we better at wrestling them to closure?

A number of reasons come to mind:

- We are afraid of conflict.
- We are afraid we will "burn bridges" with our colleagues.
- We think we will lose on the matter anyway.
- We don't want to look bad.
- We don't want someone else to look bad.
- We aren't convinced our position is correct.
- We don't want to expend the time and energy.
- We don't know how to resolve the conflicts professionally.
- We aren't sure what is acceptable behavior in our organization.
- We don't deem the item critical (but it is).

What causes a problem to become critical, to become an *issue*? An *issue* results when two parties are unable to agree on the resolution of a problem that, if left unresolved, can have a significant impact on the project.

What do you do when an issue arises? *Escalate* the issue to closure. An *escalation* is the process of calling upon higher levels of project leadership or management to resolve an issue.

Escalations are good business.

When two parties are unable to agree on the resolution of an issue—after a sincere attempt to negotiate—an escalation is pursued to resolve the issue.

In most cases, neither party is "wrong." Both are correct from their own points of view and missions. Often a person with broader responsibility for the project is required to resolve the issue and weigh the options more objectively on behalf of the overall impact to the project.

Escalate is not a dirty word. If you owned a company and two parties within your company (or one inside and one outside your company) could not agree on the resolution of an issue, would you want them to raise the issue to higher levels of project leadership/management or allow the issue to drift? Of course, the former is the course of action you would expect.

> *An escalation does not mean that either party is wrong.*

Escalations are a healthy and essential part of business, largely because they:

- Provide a check-and-balance mechanism to help ensure that proper action is taken
- Resolve problems early
- Help reduce frustration among project members
- Improve overall productivity by reducing rework that can result from implementing the wrong plan
- Help prioritize work activities
- Encourage employee participation and ownership of problems.

There are different approaches to conducting an escalation. For example, some organizations insist that the next levels of management on *both* sides of an issue be present. Others allow the dissenter to take the issue up the other chain of management, with the optional presence of the dissenter's management. Be certain that you understand the approach followed in your organization.

Here are some guidelines for escalating an issue:

- ***Escalate only after a sincere attempt has been made to resolve the issue with the other party.*** Escalating is not an excuse to avoid confronting the other party. Moreover, it is important to attempt to negotiate a resolution sincerely before initiating an escalation. In most cases, the involved parties can reach an agreement and an escalation will not be necessary.
- ***The dissenter typically is responsible for escalating the issue.*** This means that if you are the one who needs the other party to come around, you must initiate the escalation. The exception is if the other party does *not* have approval rights on your work; in this case, the other party must initiate the escalation.
- ***Initiate the escalation within two workdays of knowing the problem is unresolvable at its current level.*** Usually the escalation meeting

can occur within two days. However, if you are escalating to high levels of management, you will find it more difficult to schedule immediate or near-immediate meetings. So *initiate* the escalation within two workdays to get your meeting on management's busy calendars.

- **Escalate the problem, not the person.** Don't make the disagreement personal. You are escalating because the issue is a business matter that must be resolved. Typically, neither party is wrong; each is championing a position from their perspective—as they should.

- *Always inform your management prior to initiating an escalation.* Your management must be aware of your intent because you will need their support. They may be able to help you in preparing your position, or they may wish to attend. Keep in mind that if they do not support your position, management might direct you to abstain. This step can also help you prepare and validate your point of view.

- *Always inform involved parties before beginning the escalation.* You want all parties prepared, to ensure that the escalation meeting is productive and focused on facts. Prepping the involved parties may also accelerate reaching a resolution.

- *While an escalation is underway, do not stop working the plan of record.* Even if some aspect of the plan is being escalated or might be affected by the outcome, don't wait for the issue to be resolved before continuing work on the plan. It would be disastrous for project members to sit idle or to work to an unapproved plan while the approved plan is being escalated. No one can know for certain the outcome of the escalation; therefore, it typically is best to keep everyone marching together until an official decision otherwise has been made.

After an issue is resolved, both parties should abide by the decision reached. Only if significant new information becomes available that could reverse the decision should the escalation be revisited. Otherwise, consider the issue closed.

Once an escalation has resolved a problem, it's time to accept the decision and move on.

Remember, issues are serious problems that, if left unattended, can bring a project to its knees. Issues deserve the highest priority attention within a project.

Let's Talk: Questions & Answers

Q31.1 *Are you placing too much emphasis on escalating before sufficient energies have been invested in attempting to resolve the issue?*

A31.1 As the first escalation guideline states, escalate only after a sincere attempt has been made to resolve the issue with the other party. By far, most issues can be resolved without having to engage in an escalation. However, my experience shows that most people in most organizations delay too long in initiating an escalation. Instead, after they attempt to work with the other party but are at an impasse to resolve the issue, they allow the issue to drift. As the third escalation guideline states, they should initiate the escalation within two workdays of knowing the problem is not resolvable at its current level.

Q31.2 *How does a person know how far up the management chain to take an escalation?*

A31.2 You should continue escalating an issue until one of four conditions occurs:

- You obtain a resolution that is acceptable to you.
- A decision is made by the person who is the head of the organizations of both dissenting parties.
- A decision is made by the project sponsor.
- Your resource manager or a manager directly up your management chain tells you to stop escalating.

Q31.3 *Are there specific steps that should be followed when escalating?*

A31.3 An organization should have an escalation process defined for all projects and all employees to follow. This process should clearly document the steps to be taken. A sample process is described in Chapter 16, The Escalation Process, in *The EnterPrize Organization: Organizing Software Projects for Accountability and Success* (© 2000, Project Management Institute, Inc.).

Q31.4 *As a project manager, must I always inform my resource manager before initiating an escalation?*

A31.4 You should follow whatever is proper protocol within your organization. If you are uncertain about the escalation process, then confer with your resource manager or project sponsor. Many resource managers and project sponsors will want to be informed, at the least, but also possibly involved to ensure the appropriate and timely closure of the issue.

Q31.5 *What role does a project manager have in ensuring that stakeholders understand the escalation process to be followed on the project?*

A31.5 The project manager has full responsibility for ensuring that every stakeholder understands the importance of the escalation process and how to use it. At a minimum, a document should be developed and distributed to all stakeholders addressing this topic. However, it is more useful to call a meeting of all stakeholders to discuss, with real-life scenarios, the application of the escalation process. The preferred approach is to teach the escalation process near the start of the project by way of the culture-training class. (See Chapter 19, Create the Desired Culture for Your Project.)

Q31.6 *What should I do if I am unable to resolve an issue with another party—an issue that if left to drift will have a harmful effect on my commitments and my project—and I work in an organization or on a project that views escalations as personal rather than good business?*

A31.6 Again, you should follow the escalation process in place for your organization or project. If one is not in place, then seek guidance from your resource manager or project sponsor.

  If you worked for me (and I was either your resource manager or project sponsor), I would hold you accountable for ensuring the proper resolution of all issues related to your assignments and commitments. Using the excuse that you did not escalate an issue to closure because you feared it would be considered personal by someone else would not get you off the hook in terms of your accountability.

  Remember, an escalation does not mean that either party is wrong; rather, they are coming at the problem from two different perspectives. Remember also, if you owned the company, would you want your employee to drive to resolve the issue or to allow the issue to drift unresolved and harm the outcome of the project? Precisely! Escalate! It's good business.

Q31.7 *When conducting an escalation, which approach do you prefer: (1) the next levels of management on both sides of an issue are* present, or (2) the dissenter takes the issue up the other chain of management, with the optional presence of the dissenter's management?

A31.7 The approach is a choice that your escalation process should define. However, my preference is almost always option 2. I prefer to teach self-reliance and personal accountability whenever reasonable. In cases where the person who must initiate the escalation is a new employee or is uncertain of himself or herself, then I would like to be there to assist.

Q31.8 *It's not clear to me when I must be the party to initiate the escalation of an issue or when the other party has the duty to initiate the escalation. Can you help me here?*

A31.8 Let's first talk about what it means to be an *approver* versus a *reviewer*.

An *approver* is a person who must personally give his or her approval on an item (for example, a document, plan, or action) before that item can be considered approved. Approvers frequently have a dependency on the item to perform their work and meet their commitments.

A *reviewer* is a person who has an interest in an item (for example, a document, plan, or action), but the item does not necessarily impact his or her own work or commitments. The item should be made available for review to reviewers but can be considered approved without their agreement.

Let's look at the likely permutations:

- If you are unable to obtain agreement (sign-off) from an approver, then you must initiate the escalation.
- If you are unable to obtain agreement (sign-off) from a reviewer, you "don't care" because you do not need the reviewer's agreement. Of course, you want to be professionally considerate; after all, the reviewer may have some information worthy of consideration that can be of benefit.
- If you are the approver and do not give your approval, then the other party must initiate the escalation to obtain your approval (sign-off).
- If you are the reviewer and are unable to obtain agreement from the other party, then you must initiate the escalation because the other party doesn't require your agreement and, therefore, is not motivated to spend time negotiating your agreement.

Q31.9 *Should escalations funnel through the project manager or bypass the project manager and proceed up through management?*

A31.9 The project manager should always be kept informed of issues that require escalation. Working with the involved parties, the project manager may be able to help resolve some of the issues. Here again, the extent of participation and authority of the project manager to resolve project issues with little or no management involvement varies across organizations. Consult with your resource manager and project sponsor for the process to be followed on your project and in your organization.

Interestingly, I have found that many, if not most, escalations involve the availability of people resources and the prioritization of those resources. For example, it is common for a project member to be working across multiple projects and an escalation is required in an attempt to shift the priority of that person's efforts from one project to another.

Q31.10 *After an escalation has been resolved, should the result be documented?*

A31.10 It is good practice to document the outcome of an escalation. The document can be used to communicate the agreement to all interested parties. It also can be referenced during post-project reviews to reflect on decisions made during the project. The document should be professionally written—accurate, complete, and without bias or emotion.

CHAPTER 32

Declare
Your Project's
Risk Value

Assigning a *risk value* is a means of gauging the likelihood of a project achieving a designated key commitment. The commitment could be, for example, the next major milestone or the delivery date for the product being built or the service being offered.

Defining Levels of Risk Value

Risk values that can be assigned to a project vary widely in practice. Some examples are:

- Low, medium, high
- Green, yellow, red
- One, two, three
- Up arrow, down arrow, sideways arrow.

The risk value reveals the current state of the project through the assignment of a relatively simple measurement mechanism; in most cases, three levels of risk are sufficient.

Figure 32-1 presents an example of definitions that could be applied to three levels of risk (low, medium, high), along with sample actions that complement each level of risk.

You may choose to have other than three levels of risk defined for your projects. Moreover, you may choose to modify the definitions listed here. What is important is that an acceptable set of definitions is defined and standardized for use by all projects across an organization. If every project adopted a different set of definitions for their risk values, then assigning a risk value for your projects would lose its meaning across an organization.

> *A standard set of risk values should be defined for all projects within an organization.*

When and Where to Use Risk Value

After a project tracking meeting has been conducted, minutes of the meeting should be prepared and distributed within two workdays of the meeting. (See Chapter 26, The Project Tracking Meeting, for more on these highly essential meetings.) On the top left corner of the top page, post a simple phrase denoting the overall health of the project.

Risk:	**Low**
Definition:	The project *likely will meet* its significant commitments.
Action:	Perform normal monitoring and control.

Risk:	**Medium**
Definition:	The project *may not meet* its significant commitments.
Actions:	• Closely scrutinize all contributing factors.
	• Control significant contributing factors.
	• Establish a recovery plan.
	• Consider developing a contingency plan.

Risk:	**High**
Definition:	The project *likely will not meet* its significant commitments.
Actions:	• Closely control all contributing factors.
	• Establish a recovery plan.
	• Develop a contingency plan and identify the factors that will trigger its implementation.

Figure 32-1   Levels of Risk and Corresponding Actions

> *All projects should routinely be assigned the appropriate risk value.*

> *Of greatest benefit is to assign two risk values: one related to achieving the next major milestone and the other directed to achieving the final product/service delivery date.*

For example: RISK=HIGH. This posting alerts all project stakeholders that it is unlikely that the project will meet its significant commitments.

The posting might read with more specificity, for example: RISK=HIGH for achieving the next major milestone; or RISK=MEDIUM for achieving the product delivery date.

Assigning a project risk value helps the project manager get out from under the day-to-day fires and take stock of where the project is heading from a big-picture perspective. It is helpful to assign a risk value for achieving both the next major milestone and the project completion date. While the project completion date is the most crucial date to focus on, we arrive there one major milestone at a time. (See Chapter 22, Do Not Make Long-Term Project Commitments.)

Benefits of Disclosing a Project's Risk Value Each Week

The primary reasons for assigning a risk value are:

- *Posting a call for help.* Assigning a risk value can be a method of communicating, "I need help." For example, assigning a

RISK=HIGH value can trigger the needed attention for help or support regarding project members who are underperforming. Maybe the project manager needs help with a client, the project sponsor, senior management, a vendor, a sister organization, or some other key stakeholder. Assigning a risk value communicates with the people who can help the most.

- *Alerting stakeholders.* The risk value helps give stakeholders a "heads up" that the project plan is proceeding just fine or is in great jeopardy—or something in between. For example, many stakeholders have dependencies on deliverables from other stakeholders. Any early warning that a deliverable will be late or that their deliverable is no longer required as early as the plan shows is important information. For example, a client does not want to be surprised at the last minute that the delivery of the long-awaited product will be weeks or months late. If the client has information that strongly points to a delay in product delivery, then the client is in a better position to make the proper business decision, such as adjusting the planned rollout of the new product.
- *Focusing on the big-picture perspective.* Projects are often in trouble a little here and a little there. Until the impact of the trouble spots is collectively weighed against the overall project, stakeholders may not realize the full impact. Assigning a risk value to the project helps create a big-picture perspective that allows all stakeholders to make more informed and educated decisions.
- *Helping senior stakeholders manage their time.* Assigning a risk value to a project also helps senior stakeholders manage their time. Consider the following scenario:

> You own a company of about 200 employees, with over a dozen projects underway at any point in time. You receive a project status report for each project each week. These reports designate a risk value as the most prominent item on the top page.
>
> What do you do if you come across a report that says RISK=LOW? You probably will note the project's name and the project manager in charge and move on to another piece of mail. You deduce that this project does not need any special attention.
>
> What do you do if the next report you come across says RISK=HIGH? You likely will scan through the report and afterwards meet with the project manager. You feel the need to better understand the risk and determine if you need to become involved.

In this example, designating a risk value helps senior stakeholders (in this case, senior management) better manage their time.

They will not spend much of their limited time on projects assessed as low risk. However, high-risk projects and, to a lesser degree, projects of medium risk will grab their attention, especially if those projects carry special weight in the future success of the organization or company.

- **Encouraging the project manager to react appropriately.** Labeling a project with a risk value can have an important personal impact on the project manager. Many people, both inside and outside the project, will view a project that consistently is tagged RISK=HIGH as being run by a project manager who is ineffective. Even though the risk value of a project and the effectiveness of the project manager do not always correlate directly, a negative stigma can develop for the project manager.

> *A project designated as RISK=HIGH can have the effect of motivating the project manager to work harder and smarter to manage the project to a lower risk designation.*

As project managers, we typically do not feel good about assigning *our* project RISK=HIGH. Therefore, we tend to work harder and smarter to mitigate the risk to medium or low. That's good. Everyone wins: project manager, project members, client, management, and, of course, our company's bottom line.

What Level of Risk Is Best?

There is really no "best" level of risk to achieve. A risk of low, medium, or high could all be the right level of risk for a project, depending on the project and its parameters—or it could be inappropriate. For example, a project labeled high risk may be quite appropriate for a project that the company has a lot at stake in being finished as soon as possible. If this project was planned with any level of risk other than high, then the team might not work as diligently as required.

On the other extreme, a project labeled low risk may send the message that the project members are coasting and not working as proficiently as they could. Perhaps the project members are not assuming enough risk to maintain competitiveness. Perhaps there will be a tendency for members of this project to be raided by a high-risk project.

One thing is certain, a RISK=HIGH label will always sound an alarm. If that is your intent, then you got your wish. If it isn't, you'd better get busy strategizing to reduce the risk. All projects are different, but here's

> *Assigning a project a risk value of HIGH will gain attention.*

something to consider: Typically, a project manager—and project—are best served if the risk mostly hovers between RISK=MEDIUM and RISK=LOW. Why? Because this condition tends to broadcast that stakeholders are all being squeezed to work both efficiently and effectively, yet the delivery date is within reach and, with continued due diligence, can be met.

A note of caution: If a project consistently hovers around the RISK=HIGH and RISK=MEDIUM levels, the quality of the delivered product or service could suffer. Moreover, the project members could experience a stressful environment where gradual burnout of its members is occurring. Even though a major milestone or the final delivery date is achieved, that does not mean that all is well.

> *Just because a major commitment is achieved does not mean that everything is rosy.*

Let's Talk: Questions & Answers

Q32.1   *You say that assigning a risk value to a project can be a call for help. Is this all you expect a project manager to do to get the attention of senior stakeholders?*

A32.1   A project manager absolutely must do more to resolve a major project problem than simply record the project's risk value each week and distribute the message. Assigning a risk value can send a message, but doing so does not in itself resolve anything. Even worse, it could be that no one is reading the message. Other actions must also be implemented, such as pursuing work and escalation meetings.

> *The act of assigning a risk value to a project does not in itself resolve anything.*

Q32.2   *Why does the risk value have to appear in the top left corner of the top page of the project tracking meeting minutes (a.k.a. project status report)? Why not in some other area of the top page?*

A32.2   Posting the risk value in the top left corner means that it will likely be spotted first. This is the objective. Another location is fine (say, the top right corner), as long as the risk value is prominent and immediately noticeable.

Q32.3   *Why do you say that quality can suffer for a project that consistently hovers at RISK=HIGH and RISK=MEDIUM?*

A32.3   These risk levels reveal a project that may be treading water feverishly to achieve its commitments. When project members fall behind or are at risk of missing their commitments, there is a strong tendency to take shortcuts to help get to the completion date. Shortcuts almost always negatively affect quality.

Q32.4   *Some project managers assess the risk value of several of a project's parameters, such as staffing, schedules, budgets, complexity, and project management. Do you favor assigning a risk value to so many parameters or just to the overall project?*

A32.4   The bottom line is that the overall project should have a risk value assigned. In determining that risk value, many project parameters can be taken into account. Moreover, each project member (for small projects) or each team leader (for larger projects) can declare a risk value for their portion of the project plan. All these factors can be taken into account in determining a project's overall risk value.

Q32.5   *Wouldn't it be better to communicate a project's risk value as a percentage? For example, say that the likelihood of the project completing on schedule is 91 percent instead of saying that the project is low- to medium-risk?*

A32.5   Caution! Such numbers are often misinterpreted or even abused. Assigning a specific value implies that risk analysis is a science and is as reliable as the numbers presented. Stakeholders tend to believe the math, yet the reality is that the numbers are only as good as the data available—and the interpretation of that data. It can be very misleading to trust the numbers at face value.

CHAPTER 33

How to Run an Effective Meeting

"Meetings, meetings, and more meetings. Aren't we ever going to get some real work done around this place?"

How many times have you heard this? Perhaps you've said it yourself a time or two. It has been my experience that most meetings are poorly planned and conducted and, frankly, waste a significant amount of time.

Local Meetings

Let's look at a short list of guidelines for local meetings (where all participants are physically present in a single room) that can correct this common, but pervasive problem:

- *Plan the meeting.* Make sure that the attendees critical to the meeting's success are properly informed and have committed to attend. Reschedule the meeting if the required attendees cannot participate. Inform attendees of the meeting objectives so that they can come to the meeting with the proper mindset and preparation. Of course, inform them of the meeting date, time, and location. If needed, send a copy of the meeting guidelines to all participants so they know what is expected of them. Plan the meeting so that it best accommodates the needs of the participants. For example, resist starting meetings very early in the day because of difficulties it can create with car pooling, day care, and even traffic.

If a required participant cannot attend the meeting, then consider canceling the meeting rather than conducting two meetings.

- *Start on time.* Always begin meetings on time. Don't review progress for latecomers during the meeting, but do make sure that they are briefed after the meeting on topics on which they must be informed. Consider scheduling meetings to start precisely 10 minutes after the hour so that attendees can arrive on time from prior meetings. This is referred to as the "10-minute meeting transition rule."

Start meetings precisely at 10 minutes after the hour.

> **The meeting leader is accountable for the meeting's success.**

> **When meeting members know what is expected of them, they are far more likely to comply.**

> **An agenda helps maintain the meeting focus.**

> **Problems—not people—are attacked.**

- *Identify the meeting leader.* All attendees need to know who is in charge of the meeting. Everyone looks toward this person to demonstrate the needed leadership throughout the meeting.
  - *Set the meeting ground rules.* Inform meeting members of your expectations of them. The ground rules can include items such as: make every reasonable effort to remain present throughout the meeting; participation is encouraged from everyone; differing views are healthy; "discussion tangents" are discouraged; start-ups after breaks will be timely; set PDAs to "silent"; be constructive and make the meeting a positive experience for everyone.
  - *State the meeting objectives.* Clarifying the objectives of the meeting at the start will help the attendees remain focused and productive. If more than one topic will be addressed, then a meeting agenda should be presented to help keep the meeting on track.
  - *Assign a person to take minutes.* For other than the briefest meetings, the meeting leader must *not* take the minutes. The meeting leader needs to be fully engaged in driving the meeting. It also negatively affects the progress and pace of the meeting. If possible, the minute taker should be someone who is not otherwise an essential participant.
- *Keep the meeting on track.* The meeting leader ensures that the meeting begins and remains on track to achieving its objectives. Overly lengthy discussions, tangential topics, and scope creep are discouraged, and appropriate actions are taken to refocus the meeting attendees.
- *Enforce common respect for all participants.* The meeting leader creates and enforces a productive and respectful meeting environment. The meeting's success is dependent on the free flow of information and ideas, as well as the full participation of the attendees.
- *Summarize meeting achievements.* When the meeting objectives have been met, the key results and assignments are briefly summarized. This action helps the attendees be clear on the meeting outcomes and allows them to immediately begin taking the appropriate actions while the meeting minutes are being prepared.
- *End the meeting on or before its scheduled end time.* The meeting ends on time to accommodate other commitments of the attendees. Consider ending the meeting 10 minutes early to accommodate attendees leaving so that they can arrive to their next meeting on time.

(This technique also falls under the "10-minute meeting transition rule.") If the meeting requires more time than was scheduled and cannot be continued immediately, then give attendees a heads-up as to its likely rescheduled date and time.

> *End meetings ten minutes before the hour . . . or sooner.*

- **Distribute meeting minutes within one workday.** Either the minutes taker or the meeting leader prepares and distributes the minutes within one workday of the meeting. In either case, the meeting leader is ultimately responsible for the content of the minutes and ensuring timely distribution. The exception to the "one-workday rule" is for project tracking meetings. Project tracking meeting minutes can require a considerable level of effort to produce and the meeting leader (typically the project manager) is given an additional day for their distribution.

Remote Meetings

The meeting guidelines for local meetings also apply to remote meetings. However, a few additional guidelines apply:

- **Accommodate time zone differences.** Strive to have meetings occur during prime hours for each meeting participant. If this is not possible, then work with the participants before the meeting is scheduled to find the most workable solution. If the meeting is routinely scheduled, consider changing the time each week or month to accommodate participants equally.

> *Whenever possible, rotate the inconvenience experienced by the meeting participants.*

- **Accommodate cultural differences.** It is the responsibility of the meeting leader to learn if there are relevant cultural factors for the different participants and how best to accommodate them. For example, some cultures resist having meetings during lunch or rest periods or after normal working hours.
- **Perform roll call at the start of the meeting.** As participants arrive for the meeting, have them announce their presence to everyone. The goal is to have all participants available at the start of the meeting. If participants arrive late, they should declare their presence as well. Although latecomers cause a distraction, everyone should be aware of who is present.
- **Actively seek the participation of all attendees.** Participants should be giving their undivided attention to the meeting. A method to ensure that this is occurring is to occasionally and randomly solicit input from individual participants.

- ***Define a method for allowing interruptions.*** Depending on the method of linking remote participants (e.g., teleconference, video-conference, messaging) and the products that are used to provide the linkage, interrupting the current speaker can be challenging. Devise a method that makes it easy for attendees to participate in the discussions. For example, the meeting leader can poll participants every few minutes for questions and comments. Moreover, before a topic is considered closed, the meeting leader can query the participants to ensure that all pertinent information has been considered.

> *Participants should announce when they arrive and if they must leave early.*

- ***Require that participants leaving early sign out.*** Although no one should leave early, there will be justifiable reasons for occasional early exits. When this happens, the person leaving should inform the meeting participants.

Enforcement

Attendees rightfully look to the meeting leader to run effective meetings. There is a direct relationship between effectively run meetings and the overall effectiveness of the project, team, and organization.

These meeting guidelines can form the basis of the guidelines that are adopted in your project or organization. Add, delete, and modify these guidelines so they best serve your needs.

> *Posting meeting guidelines in all meeting rooms can help educate and remind meeting participants what they should expect—and demand—when they give up so much of their limited time to meetings.*

The meeting leader is responsible for following the meeting guidelines as well as ensuring compliance. In most cases, the meeting leader is driving the pre-meeting events, the actual meeting, and the post-meeting events. The areas where the meeting leader does not have direct control relate to the tardiness, absenteeism, and unpreparedness of the participants. In these cases the meeting leader should confront the offender professionally and work to help him or her correct the problem. If this is not effective, then the meeting leader must escalate the issue to the proper level of management to resolve the problem.

An often-useful technique to help curb tardiness and absenteeism is to identify as the first point in the meeting minutes:

- Who was at the meeting
- Who was excused from the meeting
- Who was absent unexcused
- Who was tardy.

Almost no one wants to be viewed as a non-team player.

Let's Talk: Questions & Answers

Q33.1 *What is proper behavior for reacting to a meeting request?*

A33.1 If your calendar is open and you perceive "meeting value"— that is, you either will gain value from the meeting or will provide value to the meeting participants—then you should attend. If you perceive that there is no "meeting value," then channel your time and energy in more productive directions. But be careful here. You may perceive no value to you and that you bring no value to others in the meeting, but it is possible that your perceptions are false. If you sense any chance that you could be incorrect in your assumptions, then contact the meeting leader for clarification; don't operate in a vacuum.

If your calendar is not open, yet you view there to be "meeting value," then weigh the importance of the meeting against your current commitment and choose where you must focus your time. Out of professional courtesy (and professional maturity), inform the meeting leader of your conflict.

> *Attend a meeting based on its "meeting value."*

Q33.2 *You say to consider canceling a meeting if a required participant does not attend. Isn't this overkill?*

A33.2 No meeting leader has time to conduct two meetings when one will do. The emphasis must be on conducting only one meeting. Of course, the meeting leader must use good judgment. If the leader determines that conducting the first meeting with only a partial set of required participants can make sufficient progress, then that's what happens. The final call will be about what's the best business decision.

> *There is no substitute for applying good judgment. No rule fits all occasions.*

Q33.3 *Does the "10-minute meeting transition rule" really make a difference in meetings starting on time?*

A33.3 A significant difference! If you start your meeting 10 minutes after the hour, then you significantly increase the likelihood that participants can show up on time to your meeting. The extra 10 minutes can allow attendees to get from their last meeting to your meeting on time. Moreover, they give attendees a moment to reconnect with their day by checking voice mail, returning a call, or taking a restroom break—all this on their own time, not your meeting's time.

Starting a meeting 10 minutes after the hour can also allow the prior meeting that is finishing late to clear out before your meeting begins. Ending a meeting 10 minutes before the hour has many of the same benefits as starting 10 minutes after the hour. It can be quite disruptive to a meeting for participants to leave your meeting early so that they can arrive on time to their next meeting, which starts exactly on the hour.

> *The 10-minute meeting transition rule sets people up for success, not failure.*

Q33.4 *You say to brief meeting latecomers after the meeting on what they missed. Isn't this behavior only going to encourage them to be repeat late offenders?*

A33.4 Meeting latecomers must be briefed after the meeting on relevant topics. Although these outside debriefings are extra work for the meeting leader (and possibly others that may need to be involved), they are essential for the team's success—and your own. Not only must each team member stay abreast of relevant information, but team members must be solicited for feedback so that communication is flowing two ways. In many cases, the latecomers will have legitimate reasons for being late. If there is not a valid reason, then they must be encouraged to be effective team players. As stated earlier, the problem must be addressed immediately.

Q33.5 *What should the meeting leader do when someone attempts to take the meeting off on a tangent?*

A33.5 Pull it back on track and follow the agenda. Extraneous items can be "parked" by opening action items that are addressed outside of the meeting. Of course, the meeting leader should carefully examine new items and use good business judgment to determine if they should be included for discussion in the meeting.

CHAPTER 34

The
S-Shape Curve
50/70 Rule

Various models are used to predict an activity's percent complete based upon time expended. Two common, but typically ineffective, models are the linear 50/50 rule and the S-shape curve 50/50 rule (depicted in Figure 34-1), both used for equivalently weighted tasks (i.e., tasks of approximately the same level of effort). Have you ever noticed that both the linear and S-shape curve 50/50 rules do not seem to work well on your projects?

The *50/50 rule* states that an activity should be 50 percent completed when half the allotted time has elapsed and should be 100 percent completed when the other half of the allotted time has expired. The *linear 50/50 rule* is an instance of the 50/50 rule depicted as a straight line representing expected accomplishment; that is, a linear progression. The *S-shape curve 50/50 rule* is a variation of the 50/50 rule depicted as a curved line representing expected accomplishment in the shape typically of a symmetrical S.

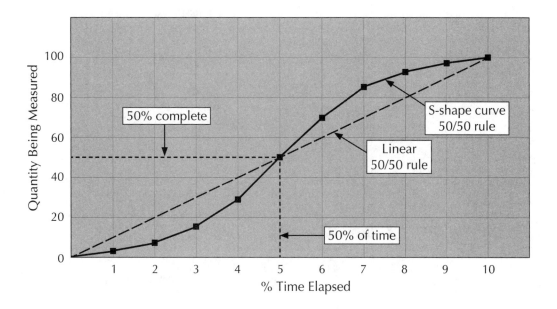

Figure 34-1 The 50/50 Rule

> **The "50/50 rule" typically is not a reliable predictor of progress for an activity made up of equivalently weighted tasks.**

In most cases, the linear 50/50 rule and the S-shape curve 50/50 rule are poor models to follow. A major problem with both these models is that just because 50 percent of the work has been completed in 50 percent of the allotted time does not mean that the remaining 50 percent of work is likely to be completed in the remaining 50 percent of the allotted time. Often, if the activity in question is only half complete when half the time has elapsed, the likelihood is high that the activity will not be completed on schedule.

So, what can we do differently? When planning an activity that spans multiple weeks and is made up of many equivalently weighted tasks, do not use any variation of the 50/50 rule; instead, use the "S-shape curve 50/70 rule" (as depicted in Figure 34-2).

The *S-shape curve 50/70 rule* states that an activity should be 70 percent completed when half the allotted time has elapsed, and the remaining 30 percent of the work should be completed in the remaining 50 percent of the time.

The S-shape curve 50/70 rule is commonly used for planning many types of endeavors. It suggests that progress usually is slow at the start

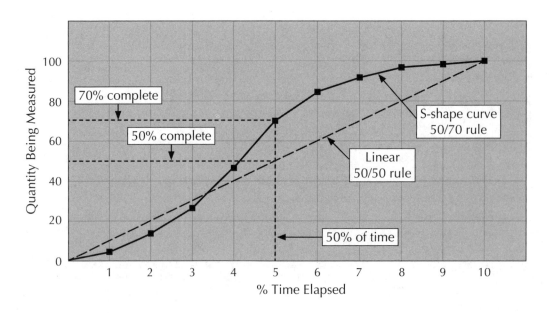

Figure 34-2   The S-shape Curve 50/70 Rule

of an activity, builds to a peak when productivity is at its very best, and then slows again during the more difficult phase of completing the activity. Figure 34-2 shows the contrast between the S-shape curve 50/70 rule and the linear 50/50 rule. Notice that the S-shape curve 50/70 rule is not symmetrical; for the S-shape curve 50/70 rule, the progress made at the end of the activity is considerably slower than the slow progress made at the start of the activity.

Almost every activity you take on in life tends to play out this way. This is why many of us say we are on schedule midway into an activity, and believe we are, yet we often are late in completing the activity.

The S-shape curve mimics how many of life's activities play out.

Let's look at an example. Figure 34-3 shows the application of the S-shape curve 50/70 rule to writing 100 pages of product documentation over a 30-day period. When we begin to write the documentation, we start out slowly for potentially many reasons. Perhaps we need to decide on the writing standards of format and style we want to follow; the processes to follow to ensure the document content is consistent, complete, and accurate; and the naming convention for the computer file(s) in which the document pages will reside. Moreover, we may start out slowly because we are determining the content and presentation

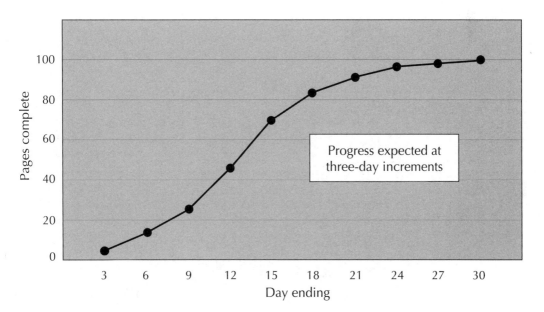

Figure 34-3   Application of the S-shape Curve 50/70 Rule to Writing a Document

sequence of that content, as well as our choice of wording as we get up to speed in transferring our thoughts into words.

Eventually we find ourselves cruising productively through page after page until we have completed most (about 70 percent) of the document. But as we come down the home stretch, we find that we have saved many of the document's more difficult and tedious pages for last. These pages may require more research, they may be labor-intensive with data and graphs, and they may require greater thought as conclusions are drawn. Moreover, we may find that we have to go back and review all 100 pages to make sure that our presentation style and terminology are consistent throughout.

It is important to keep in mind that the tasks that make up the activity must be relatively equivalently weighted. For example, the 100 pages depicted in Figure 34-3 can be considered equivalently weighted; that is, at first look, it takes about the same time to write each page.

Figure 34-4 shows another example of the importance of the tasks that make up the activity being equivalently weighted. The graph depicts the plan for a development team to code 100 modules in 10 weeks. For the S-shape curve 50/70 rule to be applicable, the modules must be similarly weighted—for example, each module's size might be between 100 and 200 lines of code. If some modules are 100 lines of code and others are

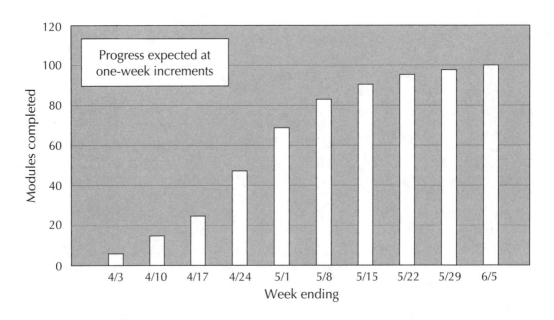

Figure 34-4   Application of the S-shape Curve 50/70 Rule to Coding Modules

5,000 or more lines of code, then the S-shape curve 50/70 rule is not directly applicable. It would not be reliable to compare modules that are weighted so differently.

The next time you are creating a plan for yourself, or are working with your team or project members in creating a plan, make sure that your plan takes into account the realities of the S-shape curve 50/70 rule when planning activities that span multiple weeks and are made up of equivalently weighted tasks. Furthermore, when the progress of these activities is being tracked, show the planned progress depicted as following the S-shape curve 50/70 rule where the vertical axis depicts the quantity being measured, such as the number of pages to be written, modules to be coded, or test scripts to be run. Then report your actual progress against the S-shape plan.

> *Use the S-shape curve 50/70 rule for planning and tracking activities that span multiple weeks and are made up of equivalently weighted tasks.*

Using the S-shape curve 50/70 rule in planning and tracking activities that are suited to this curve can significantly improve the reliability of plans and assessments.

Let's Talk: Questions and Answers

Q34.1   *Although Figures 34-3 and 34-4 both show an application of the S-shape curve 50/70 rule, the graphs look different. Is one style better than the other?*

A34.1   Figure 34-3 is often called a *line chart* and Figure 34-4 is called a *bar chart*. One style is not necessarily any better than the other. The choice is yours.

Q34.2   *Figure 34-4 shows the plan to code 100 modules. Do you really expect a development team leader (or developer) to routinely update this chart to show progress against the plan for each project tracking meeting?*

A34.2   I certainly do. If your team leader (or developer) says that he doesn't have time to create and maintain these so called "works of art" charts—that he could have coded another module during the time required to keep this chart updated—inform your team leader that he is not creating this graph for you—it's for him and his team. The team leader claimed that his team could code 100 modules in 10 weeks. All you are asking is to see the graph that the team leader had to develop to know that this was possible and how best to pace his team so they finish on schedule. Moreover, unless the team leader updates the chart for each project tracking meeting, how will he know his progress against the plan?

Q34.3   *You gave two examples of activities of applying the S-shape curve 50/70 rule—writing pages of documentation and coding modules—each with equivalently weighted tasks. Can you give some more examples?*

A34.3   The examples abound from any industry. Here are a few more:

- *Clearing for roads for a new commercial development.* Clearing involves removing trees, rocks, and other obstacles. There are 10,000 linear feet (3,048 meters) of roadway to clear and the plan is to complete the clearing activity in 50 days. The S-shape curve 50/70 rule means that 70 percent—7,000 feet (2133.6 meters)—needs to be cleared in 50 percent of the time—25 days. We can plot the planned progress for each of the 50 days. The clearing begins relatively slowly as the equipment and workers assemble and the terrain is studied and worked. A pattern and pace of work slowly develop where everyone is synchronized in terms of dozing trees, chain sawing, loading trucks for tree/debris removal, etc. In the final days, productivity slows because some of the more difficult obstacles were left for last, such as downing and removing the larger trees; excavating and removing large rock formations; and overcoming the difficulty of the steeper sloped terrain as well as the pockets of swampy terrain. Special equipment and uniquely skilled individuals may be employed near the end.

- *Building home backyard decks in a new housing area.* Each of 30 homes scattered across a diverse landscape requires an attached back deck. Although the decks all will be relatively the same size and architecture, some will be more difficult than others to build because of sloping terrain, difficulty in delivering building materials, obstacles to remove where concrete pads must be built, and electrical access problems. The plan is to build all the decks in 120 days. That means that 70 percent—21 decks—must be completed in 60 days. The work begins somewhat slowly as the workers, equipment/tools, and building materials are gathered and a pattern and pace begin to emerge. It is likely that the easier-to-build decks will be constructed first so that those homes can be sold and occupied as soon as possible. The last decks to be built will be those that pose the most challenge, and therefore, take the most time.

- *Acquiring suppliers for a new product.* Your company has built a new product and now needs to find suppliers to carry and sell the product. The plan is to contract 50 suppliers over a 100-workday period. This means that 35 suppliers need to be signed up within the first 50 workdays. Some suppliers will be eager to carry the product and others will be reluctant. The easy pickings are often secured first. The last suppliers committed may be those that require special terms and conditions where your legal staff has to be involved. Some of the last suppliers are the more difficult and time-consuming in terms of returning your calls or making themselves available.

Q34.4 *I was taught that activities should be reduced to one-week duration or less. Why are you showing activities that span multiple weeks?*

A34.4 I agree that, whenever possible, activities should be one-week duration or less. In this chapter, I refer to activities that are made up of equivalently weighted tasks. These *tasks* are of one-week duration or less. So I am referring to the smallest-sized activities as tasks.

Q34.5 *You give an example of code modules being in the range of 100–200 lines of code. Is this really reasonable? In my company we commonly have modules of 5,000 or more lines of code.*

A34.5 This book is not about design standards for modules; however, I will address the question to avoid confusion by some readers who may be puzzled by the notion that modules can be viewed as equivalently weighted tasks. There are a number of good business reasons why modules should be on the order of 100–200 lines of code. This assertion has been around for over 30 years. Benefits of developing small modules include (1) better unit (module) testing, (2) less time required to isolate and correct design/code defects, (3) higher quality delivered to the client, and (4) easier to maintain modules by other than the author. Object-oriented design and coding techniques also favor smaller modules.

Q34.6   *It seems too aggressive to expect 70 percent of work to be done in the first 50 percent of the time for activities that span multiple weeks and are made up of equivalently weighted tasks. Why so aggressive?*

A34.6   I am not saying how long it should take to complete such an activity. You decide the duration. What I am saying is that experience reveals repeatedly that progress on activities tends to be slow at their beginning and even slower as they are approaching completion. Analysis shows that when we think we are midway time-wise in performing an activity, we are not. Instead, the midway mark is typically when 70 percent of the work has completed. Although this concept may not be intuitive for many, understanding it can help you be a better project manager, leader, and teacher.

Q34.7   *Based on the assertions in this chapter, can one conclude that—across a project—70 percent of the activities must be completed when only half the project time has elapsed?*

A34.7   No. The S-shape curve 50/70 rule applies to tasks that make up an activity, not to activities that make up a project. To apply the S-shape curve 50/70 rule, the tasks that make up an activity must be relatively equivalently weighted. The activities that make up a project are not typically relatively equivalently weighted. Therefore, it should not be expected that 70 percent of the work of a project will be completed when half the project's time has elapsed.

Project
Closeout

CHAPTER 35

Conducting a Post-Project Review

A *post-project review* is the review of a completed project by a selected group of project members who represent all the major organizations that participated in the project. The group identifies those things that went right, areas for improvement, and, optionally, recommendations for improvement. The objective is to learn from project experiences so that future projects can benefit.

In Chapter 19, Create the Desired Culture for Your Project, we discussed an effective method of applying lessons learned from past projects. In this chapter we focus on a simple, straightforward approach to conducting post-project reviews that will identify those lessons.

The six steps to follow in conducting a post-project review are:

1. Declare intent.
2. Select participants.
3. Prepare for review.
4. Conduct review.
5. Present findings.
6. Prepare report; develop and adopt recommendations.

Step 1: Declare Intent

Conducting the post-project review should be the last activity—or one of the last activities—identified in your project plan. Preferably, the post-project review should be conducted within one week after the project completion date. This review should be mandatory for projects of at least several members and at least two to three months duration. The project members selected to participate are required do so and should be made aware of the importance of these reviews to the future health of the organization and company.

> *Post-project reviews should be mandatory for all projects meeting the criteria of at least several members and a duration of at least two to three months.*

Step 2: Select Participants

On small projects, everyone should participate in the post-project review. On larger projects, only a subset of the project members might attend. If only some of the project's members attend, then the best candidates are those members who routinely participated in the project tracking meetings. These members represent virtually all of the project's members and have the greatest breadth and depth of experience on the project.

Allow as many project members as reasonably can be facilitated to participate in the review—up to 30 may be workable.

If unusually sensitive information will be discussed, then some groups (e.g., vendors, contractors, clients) can participate in reviews that are more narrowly focused. For example, if a major problem on the project was related to the client, then it may be wise to address the lessons learned with the client separately in a special setting where more diplomacy can be exercised.

The facilitator of the review should be someone from outside the project—preferably someone with a project management background, such as a peer project manager who is a trained facilitator. The facilitator should not be the project manager because this person's closeness to the project may cause a bias that could present an obstacle in conducting a fair review. Resource managers should not participate in the review because their presence may inhibit others from fully expressing their views.

A person outside of the project should be selected to conduct the post-project review; no resource managers should participate.

Step 3: Prepare for Review

Only one person prepares for the post-project review: the facilitator. This frees the project members to focus on their new assignments as they are rolled onto new projects.

Only the facilitator should perform prep work before the review.

As an option, each participant can be asked to come prepared for the review with "lessons learned" about their activities, processes, and the project in general. However, experience shows that it is acceptable for the review participants to perform no preparation. A primary objective of a post-project review is to identify the top three to five areas for improvement and the top three to five areas of praise; experience suggests these will be identified whether or not participants perform homework beforehand.

The facilitator prepares three charts:

Chart 1. Post-project review meeting guidelines
Chart 2. High-level overview of the major activities/processes to be discussed (for improvement as well as for praise)
Chart 3. Ticklers (i.e., general topics for discussion when reviewing the major activities/processes that make up the project).

Guidelines (listed on Chart 1) that can be used for conducting the post-project review meeting include:

- Selected members make every reasonable effort to be present throughout the review meeting.
- Criticism of the project and its processes is encouraged.
- Criticism of people is not permitted.
- Participation is encouraged from everyone; differing views are healthy.
- "Discussion tangents" are discouraged.
- Start-ups from breaks will be timely.
- PDAs are set to "silent."
- Participants should be constructive and make the meeting a positive experience for learning and growing.

Of course, these guidelines can be altered to conform to your needs. A post-project review should be as much *fun* as possible—a business get-together that people look forward to and see as an important investment by the organization. Consider having lunch included as part of the experience. Moreover, the constructive and objective attitude demonstrated by the facilitator can have a profound impact on the willingness of the participants to open up and share their lessons and views.

The post-project review should be a positive event for both the participants and the organization.

The second chart (Chart 2) prepared by the facilitator depicts the project's major activities/processes (see Figure 35-1). This chart

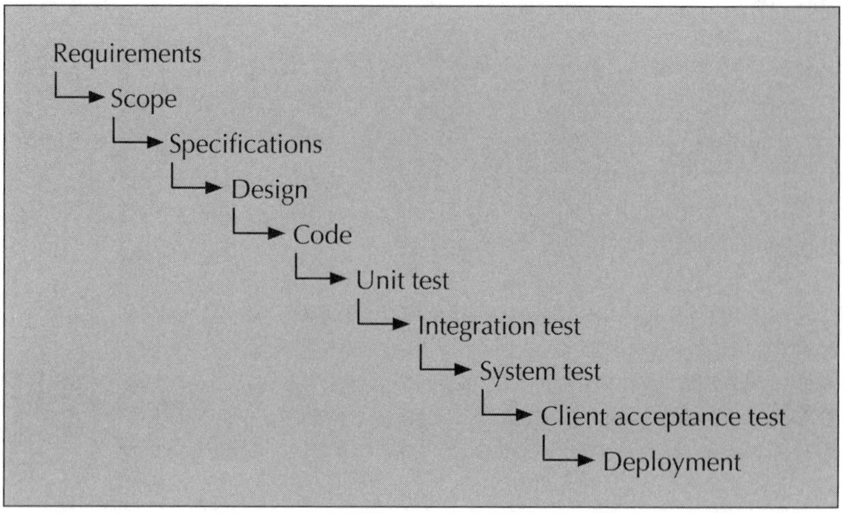

Figure 35-1   Chart 2: Sample Life Cycle for a Software Development Project

is a high-level view—from left to right—of the overall development/ service process that was followed. When the review is conducted, this chart is used to drive the discussion/brainstorming. The activities/ processes should be discussed in the implementation sequence that they were intended to be executed during the project. (Figure 35-1 is a sample life cycle chart of a software development project, but it could have been a life cycle chart for construction or pharmaceuticals or any other industry.)

As an aid in identifying problems, as well as areas for praise, the third chart (Chart 3) is a tickler list prepared by the facilitator, showing general topics to consider as each major activity/process is being evaluated. Sample items include:

- Staffing and skills
- Client involvement
- Education and training
- Schedules and milestones
- Change control and scope creep
- Approvals
- Productivity
- Quality
- Tools
- Budget assessment, if applicable
- Noteworthy accomplishments
- Problems.

Let's look at an example of how Charts 2 and 3 can be used together. Early in the review, the participants are focusing on Chart 2, which displays the major activities/processes that were intended to be followed on the project. The first activity presented on Chart 2 is *Requirements*. The facilitator asks the participants what they can say noteworthy (praise) about the requirements, as well as what they can say was a problem. The group can use the items listed in Chart 3 as ticklers to help them recall useful information. For example, a participant might say that the client's involvement was weak and this caused development of the requirements document to be delayed. Another participant might note that the requirements were never approved or placed under change control.

Step 4: Conduct Review

For most projects, conducting the post-project review can take anywhere from two hours to one day. The duration of the review can depend on a number of factors, such as the size, duration, and complexity of the project, but should rarely take more than a day.

Here's an effective approach for conducting the review meeting. The facilitator begins the review meeting with two flipchart stands loaded with flipchart paper. One flipchart will be dedicated to creating a list of "areas of praise"; the other flipchart will be dedicated to "areas for improvement." The facilitator then displays the chart (Chart 2) that shows the high-level view of the major activities/processes intended to be followed. Moving from left to right on the major activities/processes chart, the facilitator takes the participants down memory lane. As members identify areas of praise or areas for improvement associated with each of the activities or processes, the information is captured on the flipcharts. Once a flipchart sheet has been filled, it is posted on a meeting room wall for future reference.

> *A primary objective of the review is to identify the top three to five areas of praise and the top three to five areas for improvement.*

At the end of the review, the items on the wall charts are prioritized as *high*, *medium*, and *low*. The objective is to identify the top three to five items (*high*) in each of the two lists.

Step 5: Present Findings

After the review, the facilitator builds two sets of presentation charts: "areas of praise" and "areas for improvement," each identifying the top three to five items. Informally, the facilitator first presents to the project manager. This is done primarily out of professional courtesy; after all, the project being reviewed was the project manager's "baby." The project manager has a professional right to see the filtered presentation before anyone else. However, there should be no unexpected news for the project manager because the project manager participated in the review meeting where the information was derived.

The facilitator then presents to management: the project sponsor, resource managers, senior management, and, if appropriate, the client. (Depending on the sensitivity of the review data, the client meeting may be separate.) The presentation should address the top three to five lessons learned from each of the two lists, always presenting the good news first. Any lessons learned beyond the top three to five from each list should not be presented, as they might overshadow the key lessons.

> *Always present "good news" lessons first.*

Lastly, the facilitator calls a meeting that is optional to attend. The invited guests are other project managers, team leaders, and team members who were not members of the project being reviewed. This meeting is offered so that non-project personnel can learn from this project and possibly apply the lessons learned to their ongoing projects. The lessons learned beyond the top three to five items from each list may be presented because this group may benefit from the increased detail.

> *A great benefit of post-project reviews is sharing the findings with members of other projects so that the lessons might be applied to ongoing projects.*

Step 6: Prepare Report; Develop and Adopt Recommendations

The facilitator prepares a post-project review report, which is distributed to all project members and others as appropriate. The report is archived for future reference as new projects are started.

The post-project review report should include general information about the project, such as project name, level of effort, participants' names, and key project dates. This could be Chapter 1. The presentation charts become part of the report: Chapter 2 can list the top three to five areas of praise, and Chapter 3 can list the top three to five areas for improvement. All other items from the two lists that were not considered among the top three to five should be included in the report in a separate section or as an appendix so as not to deflect focus from the most important lessons. For example, Appendix A can list the remaining areas of praise and Appendix B can list the remaining areas for improvement.

> *Don't overlook the most important outcome of a post-project review: a means to institutionalize the lessons learned so that new projects will benefit.*

Members from across the organization should be assigned to address the top three to five items from each list so that the lessons learned can be constructively addressed and institutionalized within the organization. Although recommendations could be developed during the review (Step 4), my experience is that the group is not as motivated nor is it as productive to both identify and solve problems in the same meeting.

Let's Talk: Questions & Answers

Q35.1 *Why are you such a fan of post-project reviews?*

A35.1 There may be no better mechanism than post-project reviews to expose a project's strengths and weaknesses. If these lessons are applied to future projects, a great tool is now in motion for continuous improvement of all that an organization does that affects the success of projects.

Those who cannot remember the past are condemned to repeat it."

—George Santayana, American poet and philosopher

Q35.2   *Why not make post-project reviews recommended rather than mandatory? Don't you think that professionals are mature enough to voluntarily conduct them and then apply their lessons on new projects?*

A35.2   Making post-project reviews mandatory is one way of ensuring that management recognizes their value and supports the beneficial investment of their employees in conducting the reviews. Companies are littered with projects that end without the slightest review, yet they are made up of "professionals."

The best leaders sometimes make decisions that may not always be popular, but create a more effective work culture.

Q35.3   *Should mandatory post-project reviews apply to all projects?*

A35.3   No. The head of an organization should have a strategy of mandatory post-project reviews for selected projects. The selected projects may need to meet some criteria such as cost, duration, or level of effort, or represent a special case for an organization. Projects smaller than two to three people and two to three months in duration typically do not merit routine reviews, based on the low return on investment of time and resources in conducting and documenting the reviews. However, you may choose to perform post-project reviews on small projects occasionally to decide for yourself if they are beneficial for your organization.

Q35.4   *Should an organization bother to conduct post-project reviews for projects that are canceled?*

A35.4   Absolutely! Canceled projects are often the most important to review because of the "sunk costs" that have been lost. An organization must strive to reduce or eliminate the occurrence of canceled projects as well as projects that exhibit traits of failing, such as budget overruns, missed major milestones, and low quality.

Q35.5   *Is there a time when you should not conduct a post-project review with a client?*

A35.5 Yes, there are situations where a post-project review may do more harm than good. An example would be with an external client who is considering litigation against your company because of the project. In this case, performing a post-project review would give the client plenty of fuel to be used during the litigation process.

A more common example is working with an external client that performed poorly on a project. A full-session post-project review may appear to the client like everyone is out to get them. In this case, a smaller, more discreet post-project review may be preferable. If you have a good working relationship with an external client and expect to conduct many more projects with them, then I favor including them in full-session reviews, but always consult your legal counsel before proceeding. If your client is internal to your company, it is almost always preferable to include the client in the full-session reviews.

> *If you have project members from outside your company, consult your legal counsel before including them in a post-project review.*

Q35.6 *What is a good method to use to reduce the areas-of-praise and the areas-of-improvement lists to the top three to five items?*

A35.6 Near the end of the post-project review meeting, after all the items of note have been recorded, the facilitator can individually point to each item on both lists and propose to the meeting participants a relative weight of importance of, say, *high*, *medium*, or *low*. If most participants disagree with the proposed weighting factor, then it can be decided by a group poll. After all items in both lists have been weighted, the objective is to have only three to five items from each list be weighted *high*. If there are too many items weighted *high*, then revisit only the *high*-weighted items and again propose their weights relative to each other. After the second or third pass, you probably will have reduced the *highs* lists to the top three to five items.

Q35.7 *Should an objective of the post-project review meeting be to identify the recommendations for improvement that need to be institutionalized across the organization?*

A35.7 I do not recommend that the post-project review meeting also be used to solve the problems identified. Doing so can take a significant amount of time and many participants will not be motivated to spend the quality time required. Instead, after the post-project review results have been compiled and presented, members of the organization should be identified to own the top three to five items from each list.

Preferably a different person in an organization would be assigned to own each item. Those assigned people should then assemble the players, if appropriate, to help in identifying and institutionalizing the necessary improvements.

Q35.8   *How can you keep people from clamming up during a post-project review? In my organization, post-project reviews are viewed as destructive, demoralizing, and fraught with finger-pointing.*

A35.8   The facilitator has a lot of influence in creating a positive, productive environment where members both behave and participate as mature professionals. For example, the facilitator should never allow people to be attacked, whether those people are present in the meeting or not.

A trained facilitator can help a group get past any negative perceptions the members might have of post-project reviews.

Q35.9   *What do you think about anonymously collecting lessons learned from project members as a technique to encourage some members to open up more and feel less threatened by potential confrontation from their peers?*

A35.9   Bad idea. If project members can say anything without having to defend it or participate in a follow-on discussion, then some of the anonymously obtained responses may be misleading, destructive, or even vindictive. We should encourage professional responsibility and maturity. This means we should discuss lessons learned openly, honestly, and constructively. Allowing project members to be secretive and avoid confronting issues among themselves only perpetuates distrust, weak accountability, and professional immaturity.

Performing post-project reviews anonymously can breed distrust and endorse professional immaturity.

Q35.10 *In choosing a facilitator to conduct the post-project review who is not also the project manager, are you saying that the project manager is too biased to facilitate a post-project review effectively?*

A35.10 It is preferred that the post-project review be conducted by someone who was not on the project, such as another project manager or a trained facilitator. The project manager often is too close to the project and can become defensive as problems are discovered. After all, most problems, either directly or indirectly, can be seen as being a reflection of the leadership demonstrated by the project manager. However, the project manager should attend the post-project review and may actually be the most valuable contributor. Why? Because the project manager is the only project member whose job it is to have a whole-project perspective, not just the perspective of smaller aspects of the project. Having said all this, it is possible that some project managers have the wherewithal to facilitate a post-project review effectively, although this is not the preferred approach.

Q35.11 *When the results of the post-project review are being presented, why do you say to present "good news" first?*

A35.11 If "bad news" (areas for improvement) is presented first, you may never get to the "good news" (areas of praise). If you do manage to present the good news, a lot of the audience may still be focusing on the areas for improvement. The areas of praise are important and should not be taken lightly. Present the good news first, when you have everyone's undivided attention.

Q35.12 *Should the project manager attend the meetings where the facilitator is presenting the post-project review results to management, as well as the optional meeting that is open to all?*

A35.12 Absolutely yes! The facilitator does not know the project anywhere near as well as the project manager. The project manager must be available to address the questions that come up.

Q35.13 *What if my project is of long duration? Should I still wait until the completion of the project to perform the post-project review or should I perform "post-project reviews" at strategic points along the way?*

A35.13 If a project is of long duration, consider performing a "post-phase review" at least every six months or so. Of course, when you wait much longer the project members may have difficulty remembering events. But the most important reason for performing post-phase reviews along the project life cycle is that you can learn lessons and apply many of them immediately to the next phase of the project.

> *Long-duration projects require "reviews" along the way.*

Chapter 22, Do Not Make Long-Term Project Commitments, discusses re-evaluating the project plan (or portions thereof) at the end of each major milestone (which are one to two months apart). This timing also can accommodate performing "post-milestone reviews" as part of the re-evaluation process of the project plan.

Q35.14 *How are a post-phase review and a post-milestone review different from a post-project review?*

A35.14 A post-phase review follows essentially the same process as a post-project review, with two key differences. The first is that the post-phase review occurs while a project is still underway. The second difference is that a post-phase review does not address the project from start to finish, but instead focuses on a relatively small snapshot of the project.

A post-milestone review is less formal and may require less time than a post-project review. It can be as informal as the project manager visiting each project team (for larger projects) or project member (for smaller projects) and having them declare their top three to five lessons learned. The lessons that can apply to an upcoming milestone are discussed and assigned for action, as applicable. Lastly, the whole team (for smaller projects) or a representative subset (for larger projects) gathers to identify the top lessons learned across the project and what action should be taken, if any.

Q35.15 *What would you say about an organization that is great at ensuring that post-project reviews are conducted, but has a poor track record for applying lessons learned to new projects?*

A35.15 What's the point of conducting post-project reviews if lessons are not learned and applied? I have found that the morale in an organization often is improved after post-project reviews are conducted—assuming that they are conducted properly. However, in organizations that do not apply the lessons learned to new projects, the morale often sinks lower than it was before the post-project reviews were conducted. This phenomenon is caused largely by high expectations of people believing and hoping that the lessons learned will allow the organization to improve on a multitude of fronts, such as higher quality, improved client relationships, increased productivity, lowered costs, and better schedule performance. If the lessons are not carried forward to new projects, then no one will care about participating in post-project reviews. (See Chapter 18, Are You Learning from Project to Project? for ideas on applying lessons learned to new projects.)

Post-project reviews have minimal value unless the lessons are applied at the start of new projects.

Q35.16 *What if there is never time to perform post-project reviews?*

A35.16 Nice try! The more one argues that there is not time to learn from our past mistakes, the more convinced I am that you cannot afford to bypass performing this critical activity. Only naïve or weak leadership would hold on to such a lame excuse for consistently ignoring learning from the past and applying those lessons going forward.

> *The most consistently successful organizations apply past lessons to future endeavors.*

 You will never find time for anything. If you want time you must make it."

—Charles Buxton, English author

PART SEVEN

Promoting the Advancement of Project Management beyond Your Projects

Up to this point, we have focused on how project managers can be more effective in their day-to-day activities. We now turn to what project managers can do outside of their primary domains of responsibility to promote the advancement of project management across their organizations and companies. These areas are essentially *extra credit* for project managers. If you don't feel ready to lead in implementing these tools and techniques, you can nevertheless choose to promote and support their adoption. *These ideas can help both you and your organizations look great!*

Project Review Mentoring Workshops

Institutionalizing project management best practices across an organization is a work in progress. It never ends. A great tool that you can initiate and champion across your organization is the project review mentoring workshop.

A *project review mentoring workshop* is a technique for mentoring project managers—and their stakeholders—from across an organization in the proper application of project management best practices. The delivery medium is conducting project reviews in a classroom setting. *Project reviews* are a technique for examining active projects to assess their overall health, identifying areas of both praise and improvement.

A project review mentoring workshop typically runs two workdays; any longer and it can be too exhausting for the participants. Three to four projects are selected, and their project managers and up to four members of each project are invited to attend. The audience should total about 20, no more than 30. The attendees also can include lead people from across the organization, including management.

The facilitator/instructor of the workshop should be an experienced, successful project manager with a strong working knowledge of project management best practices. The facilitator should also have strong soft skills to be able to teach others professionally and constructively. Although this person could be contracted from outside your company, it is best to develop these skills from within your company.

Each project manager and his or her team are instructed to prepare a set of slides describing the state of their project. Topics addressed on the slides can include:

- Overview of customer requirements, product scope/specifications
- Organization of project; roles and responsibilities
- Staffing and skills
- Overview of actual vs. baselined schedules and milestones
- Lessons learned from other projects that apply to the project being reviewed
- Project management practices followed
- Development process (or equivalent) followed
- Change control and scope creep
- Quality perspective

- Customer relationship; customer expectations
- Support from external groups
- Support from senior management
- Project morale
- Accountability issues
- Project budget assessment
- Business and legal issues
- Top three areas noteworthy of praise and top three problems
- Forecast of project outlook in terms of risk (high, medium, low) of meeting the next major milestone and the final delivery date
- What needs to be done differently from this point forward for this project to complete "successfully."

At the start of the workshop, guidelines are presented so that everyone understands the behavior expected. For example, attacking problems is encouraged and welcomed, but attacking people is out of bounds.

The facilitator must role-model—and enforce—an open, positive, and constructive workshop atmosphere.

As the slides are presented, the workshop facilitator probes with questions aimed at assessing the true health of the project. The other attendees are encouraged to ask questions as well.

Two sets of flipcharts are available in the workshop. One set is labeled "Praise" and the other "Problems." When the facilitator determines that a noteworthy item of praise has been identified, he or she records it on the Praise flipchart for all to see. A problem item is recorded on the Problem flipchart. When a flipchart sheet is filled, the facilitator removes and posts it on a wall in the meeting room for easy reference.

When a project review is nearly complete, the facilitator asks each attendee (or a selected subset) to assess the risk (e.g., high, medium, low) of the project achieving its delivery date and to explain that assessment. The facilitator openly reviews each of the problems recorded and weights them according to their impact on achieving the delivery date. The facilitator then provides a bottom-line assessment of the overall health of the project.

The next project review then starts, following the same sequence. Most project reviews are allotted a half-day or so for their review. The members of the projects that have completed their reviews are expected to participate actively during the remaining project reviews.

After the workshop, a brief report is prepared outlining the findings from each project review. The report captures the items that were listed as praise and problems for each project as well as the risk assessments made by the facilitator and participants. The project managers whose

> *After the project review mentoring workshop is complete, the project managers develop action plans to address the most important problems identified.*

> *All workshop attendees can learn and grow from the problems, praise, and discussions that result from their workshop participation.*

> *The project review mentoring workshop is a character-building, skill-development opportunity for the participants that will not soon be forgotten.*

> *The project review mentoring workshop is one of those tools that transition an organization from good to great.*

projects were reviewed can then develop action plans to address the most important problems identified for their projects.

The project review mentoring workshop benefits all those who participate. The project managers who have their projects reviewed learn a great deal about how well they and their teams are performing and walk away with specific items to address. All participants learn from the other projects presented and take back new ideas and thinking for current and future projects.

The project review mentoring workshop is not only a great teaching tool for skill development; it also is a character-building experience for the members of the projects being reviewed, especially for the project managers. It can be difficult to hear others publicly call your baby "ugly," no matter how constructive the analysis comes across. The lessons learned will not soon be forgotten. Furthermore, often just preparing the presentation will force a project team to think through and solve many of their problems before publicly exposing the state of the project.

For maximum benefit, project review mentoring workshops should be conducted every four to six months. The goal is to focus on the major projects across an organization, as well as to provide follow-up reviews on longer-running projects to ensure that they are making the necessary progress.

The project review mentoring workshop can transition an organization from good to great, and is therefore of enormous value to executives. There is no better method than mentoring to develop effective project managers and teams. But the workshops don't just focus on helping projects across the whole organization achieve success. Project review mentoring workshops push the envelope on *continuous* positive change across an organization that benefits all stakeholders. As a project manager, championing change never felt so good!

Let's Talk: Questions & Answers

Q36.1   *You say that lead people and management from across the organization can also attend. Can you provide some examples?*

A36.1 Many other groups will have an interest in attending these workshops. The project sponsor may attend from time to time. If the clients are internal to the organization, some of them will likely attend. The resource managers of some of the review participants may choose to attend to stay abreast of the progress of these projects as well as the performance of their people assigned to these projects. Other project managers as well as project management office, quality assurance, and process-interested people may also attend.

Q36.2 *Should external clients be invited to attend?*
A36.2 This can be a sensitive issue. In a perfect world, I would prefer open communications between external clients and other project stakeholders. However, if sensitive information may be exposed that could fuel litigation or other negative actions, then you should refrain from including external clients. I suggest consulting with the project sponsor or perhaps legal counsel before including external clients.

Q36.3 *You discourage hiring a contractor to be the workshop facilitator. What if the skills are not available in-house?*
A36.3 I prefer not using outside contractors only because I want an organization to work at developing and honing these skills in-house. However, if the skills are not available in-house or a contractor has exceptional skills to perform as the facilitator, I favor hiring the contractor. In the case of a contractor with exceptional skills, a treasure chest of ideas and techniques can be learned.

Q36.4 *What else is said to the attendees at the start of the workshop?*
A36.4 Most importantly, the workshop is all about the mentoring experience—helping the project teams and each other learn and grow from the experience. The facilitator is expected to keep the meeting on a positive footing. Everyone should be encouraged to participate constructively; openness and candidness are essential.

There should be an acknowledgement that the presenters may feel discomfort and uneasiness from the constructive criticism and probing questions. However, without frankness and digging beneath the surface, the workshop would lose much of its value. Presenters are urged to volunteer areas of praise as well as improvement. (Don't forget to set the workshop times each day as well as the break and lunch times.)

Q36.5 *Why is it good for the project team, when preparing for the presentation, to fix problems before the review? Don't you want the problems exposed during the review to reveal the actions of the project team as well as alert everyone attending to the problems?*

A36.5 A major benefit of performing a project review is that the project and its stakeholders being reviewed will correct many of their problems before they are publicly revealed. Let's not penalize people for finding and resolving their own problems. Personally, I want the project team to look great in a review. The more problems they correct prior to the review, the more we all win.

Q36.6 *What medium should the presenters use to address the prepared topics?*

A36.6 This is strictly up to the facilitator. I most commonly have the prepared topics presented from a laptop through an LCD projection system. However, the medium used is less important than the substance and completeness of the prepared presentation.

Q36.7 *When a project review is nearly complete, the facilitator asks each attendee or a selected subset to assess the risk of the project achieving its delivery. What do you mean by "selected subset"?*

A36.7 If there is time, I may ask all the attendees to assess the risk of the project. This forces attendees to think for themselves and to remain alert. If time is limited or the assessment appears relatively straightforward, then I will ask only the project managers.

Q36.8 *Can a review of a project take a day or longer?*

A36.8 Depending on the size of the project in terms of people, complexity, and duration, a review could easily consume more than a day—*but it shouldn't!* You are not looking to identify every actual and potential problem on a project. Instead, you want to make sure that the top three problem areas as well as the top three areas of praise are revealed. My experience has shown that the top three areas are almost certain to be apparent in four to six hours.

Q36.9 *How useful do you see the workshops from a senior management or executive perspective?*

A36.9 Extremely useful. Senior managers and executives witness continual improvement in the application of project management best practices across the organization. They see the results in the form of lower costs, increased productivity, and improved schedule and budget commitments—all leading to improved client relationships.

Q36.10 *Do I need the sponsorship of a senior manager or executive to make the workshops happen?*

A36.10 Do you need the sponsorship? No. Do you want the sponsorship? *Yes!* The senior manager or executive of an organization is in the best position to sponsor and rally the organization behind this great mentoring tool. Their sponsorship can make your job far easier.

But be careful here. Don't think that you cannot make significant headway without their direct support or involvement. Effective leaders find a way to make things happen despite what is going on around them.

One more thought: Don't dump and run. That is, don't dump this workshop idea on the senior manager or executive and then run from being central to its implementation. Be willing to lead its institutionalization across the organization.

Q36.11 *I want to champion the practice of project review mentoring workshops in my organization, but I am uncomfortable with being the facilitator. Is it important that I participate as the facilitator?*

A36.11 Bringing this state-of-the-art mentoring technique to your organization is a definite feather in your cap, not to mention all the other benefits that the organization will realize. However, your value to the organization becomes even more apparent when you facilitate the workshops—or at least the first few workshops.

If you are uncomfortable with facilitating because your project management or communications/soft skills are weak, then by all means, strive to find a more suitable facilitator. But if you hesitate because you are uncomfortable in the limelight,

I suggest you work to overcome this fear. If you don't, it will continue to haunt your career.

Q36.12 *As a facilitator, I want to focus fully on running the reviews. Any special tips here?*

A36.12 I recommend enlisting an assistant—a scribe. This person can be a project manager-assistant type assigned to work under your direction. The person's primary job is to list on the flipcharts the problem and praise items that you and the attendees identify. This allows you to remain seated and fully engaged. By the way, no item should appear on a flipchart without your approval. This means that the scribe will wait for your direction before logging an item on a flipchart.

Another tip: Request that presenters give you a copy of their presentations a day or two before the workshop. The extra time can be useful in getting up to speed on the projects.

Q36.13 *Who writes the project review mentoring workshop report?*

A36.13 The most likely candidate is the facilitator. However, in cases where the assistant/scribe has the skills, that person can prepare the initial draft of the report, or possibly write and distribute the full report.

Q36.14 *Who follows up after the workshop to ensure that the project managers have developed action plans for the most important problems identified for their projects?*

A36.14 The responsibility for follow-up can rest with any of a number of players, including the facilitator, a program manager, the resource managers of the project managers reviewed, or a quality assurance person. Ideally it should be one person, such as the facilitator. The follow-up is not just to ensure that action plans are developed; it's also to ensure that the action plans are implemented.

CHAPTER 37

The Project Manager/ Resource Manager Leadership Workshop

*P*roject managers direct the planning and execution of a project and are held personally accountable for the success of the project. Simply stated, they *nurture the project* to meet its objectives.

Resource managers hire, fire, make job assignments, coach, counsel, evaluate, award, promote, and secure future work opportunities for direct reports. In other words, they *nurture people* to meet their commitments on projects and to reach their individual potential. Everyone in an organization works for a resource manager.

Project managers nurture projects; resource managers nurture people.

The project manager champions the project. The resource manager champions people. These are oversimplified definitions, but the distinction in the roles and responsibilities of these two critical leadership positions is important. They need to work together for the mutual good of the enterprise.

Employees cannot perform at their best if they are uncertain of their duties. When employees specifically understand what is expected of them, my experience is that they will rise to meet those expectations. In almost all cases, problems inhibiting the success of an organization can be traced to those who hold the critical positions of project manager or resource manager.

Most major problems inhibiting the success of an organization can be traced to the leadership skills exhibited by the project managers and the resource managers.

So what must be done to ensure that these leadership positions are being developed? To begin with, the roles and responsibilities of the project managers and resource managers must be defined clearly. Then the people placed in these positions must be trained, mentored, and evaluated on a routine basis so that they are continually improving. The success of an organization is largely in the hands of the people who hold these two vital positions.

A best-practice tool for developing the leadership skills of people in these key positions is the project manager/resource manager leadership workshop. Here's how it works.

A best-practice tool that can develop effective leadership skills among the project managers and the resource managers is the project manager/ resource manager leadership workshop.

The attendees are a mix of project managers and resource managers, up to 20 participants. A week or two before the workshop begins, attendees are required to identify the top three work-related scenarios that they would like addressed in the workshop. These are compiled into a single list with duplications removed.

At the start of the workshop—usually of one-day duration—a description (or brief refresher) of the roles and responsibilities of both the project manager and the resource manager is presented. Then the list of scenarios drives the remainder of the workshop.

Here are some examples of scenarios that are commonly played out:

- *Coaching and counseling employees.* Should the resource manager stay abreast of his employees' performance against their project plans or is that the exclusive territory of the project manager?
- *History repeats.* New projects consistently suffer from the same problems encountered on previous projects. Where's the problem? Who's primarily accountable?
- *Test plan.* A project has no test plan. Who's primarily accountable? The project manager? The test team leader? The test team leader's resource manager? The project manager's resource manager? Someone else?
- *Missed commitments.* A project member consistently misses commitments. Who's not doing their job? The project member? The project manager? The resource manager? Someone else?
- *Escalation.* When two parties are unable to resolve a conflict related to a project, what role should the project manager play in resolving the conflict? What role should the resource manager play?
- *Management style.* Which is worse: *over*managing or *under*managing?

During the workshop, everyone is called upon to provide the "correct" answer to one or more scenarios. First-time participants likely will be surprised at the number of scenarios they answer incorrectly. Coming into the workshop, many attendees assume they know what is expected in their job. However, many will leave the workshop with a renewed understanding of their roles and responsibilities as they relate to projects, people, and the overall organization. These workshops teach leadership behavior and reinforce effective leadership behavior already in play.

> *All workshop attendees are included in the interactive discussions.*

At the end of the workshop, the scenarios and their correct answers can be documented and distributed for reference and reinforcement. In relatively new, inexperienced, or weakly run organizations, the workshop should be conducted monthly. As the experience of the project managers and resource managers improves, the workshops can be scheduled quarterly.

For senior managers and executives struggling with the issue of whether leadership can be taught, *this works!* As a project manager, being the catalyst to adopt these workshops across an organization is a great demonstration of *your* leadership. You have the opportunity to be in the middle of a movement to define the critical role clarification between the two highly influential positions of project manager and resource manager. This workshop is another great tool that you can sponsor to assert yourself and broaden your domain of responsibility from your immediate projects to improving effectiveness across your organization.

Let's Talk: Questions & Answers

Q37.1   *Why is the workshop usually only one day?*

A37.1   The workshop is rather intensive and the scenario discussions can move relatively quickly. This means that there is a lot to absorb. Because we learn best by doing, it is important that the attendees take a bite during the workshop and then be given sufficient time to chew and swallow it back on the job.

   If the first workshop includes a full presentation on the roles and responsibilities of project managers and resource managers, then one and a half days may be optimum. Any succeeding workshops can begin with a brief refresher of the roles and responsibilities and last only one day.

Q37.2   *Can the workshops ever be phased out?*

A37.2   Yes. However, I suggest they go from monthly to quarterly until the project managers and resource managers are routinely demonstrating the appropriate behavior. Until the lessons are "sticking" and are practiced routinely, don't stop the workshops. By the way, you will likely find that people look forward to attending the workshops. They can be fun and a chance to enhance the bonds among workshop participants.

Q37.3   *Do I need sponsorship of the senior manager or executive head of the organization before making this workshop happen?*

A37.3   Yes. You may also need to include a representative from your organization's human resources department. This workshop is aimed at defining the roles and responsibilities of two of the most critical positions in the organization. You will need to make sure that all appropriate senior management is supportive. Some issues may come up in the workshop that need to be settled by the head of the organization, who should be included in the early workshops.

By the way, don't fear that the workshop may bring up some thorny issues of roles and responsibilities between project managers and resource managers. That's exactly why the workshop is so important—to face these issues so they can be resolved instead of continuing to be obstacles.

Q37.4 *If the correct answers are documented and distributed after the workshop, who takes on this duty?*

A37.4 A scribe should be assigned to attend the workshop and record the proper responses to each scenario discussed. The scribe can then create a draft of the document for review and approval by the workshop facilitator as well as designated participants. Once approved, either the scribe or the facilitator can distribute the document.

Q37.5 *Is it the workshop facilitator who determines the "correct answers" that are documented?*

A37.5 Yes, in part, but I need to clarify. I often conduct these workshops and have already defined the roles and responsibilities of both the project managers and the resource managers. (A brief list of these duties is presented in Chapters 14 and 15, respectively.) With the support of senior management, these roles are discussed with the participants at the start of the workshop. Some of these defined duties may need to be tweaked based on the inputs of senior management.

From that point on, we discuss the many scenarios that the participants submitted before the workshop. After each scenario is discussed, I offer the "correct" answer based on (1) the foundational work that I have performed (see *The EnterPrize Organization*, © 2000, Project Management Institute, Inc.), and (2) the tweaking that occurs to support the desired organizational culture. As facilitator, I am in a good position to participate in approval of the document that lists the problem scenarios and their corresponding "correct answers." Of course, senior management also approves the answers.

Having said all this, you do not, of course, need me to facilitate the workshop. A senior manager or senior project manager who has a vision of the duties of these two critical positions—project manager and resource manager—can study the information in this chapter and other information sources and conduct the workshop.

Q37.6 *These workshops appear to be a great idea, but I am not sure I am up to facilitating them. The players in my organization are pretty tough to work with. Any ideas?*

A37.6 As with the project review mentoring workshops discussed in Chapter 36, if you feel unprepared and way over your head, then don't volunteer to facilitate. Nominate someone you believe will do well as the facilitator. However, you can still be the main champion and promoter of the workshop for your organization.

If you have a clear understanding of the roles and responsibilities of the project managers and resource managers, and you feel you have developed the level of communication/soft skills required to facilitate, then go for it. We are never at our best the first time, but we get better. That is how leaders are developed.

CHAPTER 38

How to Institutionalize Improvements in Your Organization

Every organization is due for change. Most organizations have giant steps to take, while a small minority are passionately striving to push the state of the art. This means that as a project manager, you have a wide range of opportunity to move beyond the domain of your projects and become a catalyst for change across your organization . . . and even beyond.

This chapter presents a highly effective approach that I frequently use with clients to help them improve the performance of their organizations and the projects within those organizations. However, you do not need an outside consultant to make this happen. You can initiate and champion this approach for yourself.

My approach involves seven steps:

- *Step 1. Invite people to a brainstorming session.* The participants come from across the organization and should be the power players—the leaders. These are people who typically have the most knowledge about and experience with the processes, tools, and products. Strive to have a large percentage of the participants be other than managers.

- *Step 2. Conduct the brainstorming session.* The objective is for the participants to brainstorm, identifying the most important problems facing the organization that, if properly addressed, could have a positive, measurable impact on the overall performance of the organization. Depending on the size of the organization, this session might include from five to 20 persons and take from one to three hours.

- *Step 3. Identify the top three to five problems to solve.* After a reasonably exhaustive list of key problems has been brainstormed, select the top three to five problems. An effective approach is to list all the brainstormed problems on flipcharts and post these charts on the meeting room walls. Then, with everyone participating, assign a weight to each problem such as *high*, *medium*, and *low*. Anywhere from 10 to 50 problems may be identified, but only a relatively small number will be judged *high*. Identify the top three to five problems from this short list.

- **Step 4. Assign owners to these problems.** A different person should be assigned to champion the solution to each problem. These owners have the responsibility to drive the problems to closure and will be evaluated on their results (not effort) to institutionalize the solutions across the organization.
- **Step 5. Create a project plan for addressing each problem.** Deriving the solution for each problem and institutionalizing that solution becomes a project plan. The assigned owners now become project managers and each project manager will plan, execute, and track his or her project through to its completion. The plan will show that many people will play a role on each project, even if the role is only to review and approve appropriate deliverables.
- **Step 6. Track each project plan weekly.** A senior project manager (SPM) is assigned to review the progress of each plan weekly. The SPM works, one-on-one, with each project manager. This step is essential as a check-and-balance to ensure that these plans are progressing as needed. In effect, the SPM is serving as a *program manager* over all the projects.
- **Step 7. Repeat steps 1-6 every six months.** After the top three to five problems have been addressed, identify the next layer of top three to five problems and work them off in the same fashion.

This seven-step process may seem remarkably simple, but it can be highly effective. There are three keys to its success:

- The commitment by someone (you?) to champion and drive its implementation
- The assignment of a senior project manager to look over all the plans and ensure that they are being managed effectively
- The duty of the resource managers of the project managers (and the SPM) to include in their performance evaluations a line item that addresses the effectiveness of the project managers in completing their assigned projects successfully.

The seven-step approach is remarkably simple, but highly effective.

Problems that are frequently identified as needing to be resolved to improve the organization include:

- Clearly defined roles and responsibilities for project stakeholders (e.g., project manager, project sponsor, resource manager, team leader, business architect)

- A consistent project management methodology defined, documented, followed, and routinely improved as required
- An effective portfolio project management process to nominate and prioritize projects
- Dedicated project managers and resource managers, especially where these roles are not intermixed
- A development process that is defined, documented, followed, and routinely improved as required
- An employee development program that includes a focus on training and certifications
- A defined and communicated awards program.

A project plan for, say, the first item—clearly defined roles and responsibilities for project stakeholders—might include milestones such as:

- Define and obtain agreement on the scope of the problem.
- Draft a high-level solution to the problem and have it reviewed by a short list of peers.
- Draft the solution and have it approved by the appropriate organization's members.
- Train the members of the organization so that they understand the roles and responsibilities.
- Enforce compliance as new projects are started.

Here again, the approach may seem disarmingly simple. It is. But it only works if the three keys to its success are managed appropriately. As a project manager looking to expand your influence beyond your immediate projects, you can champion this approach. That will satisfy the first of the three keys to its success. You also may be qualified to provide the second key: Perform as the senior project manager approving all the plans and tracking the project managers of those plans to ensure their effective implementation.

Rather than just talk about the improvements you want, why not plan and execute them?

My experience shows that almost all problems can be solved and institutionalized within three to six months. This means that after about a year of implementing this approach, your organization will look and behave remarkably different because it will be remarkably more effective. Every member of the organization will not only see and experience the changes, but many also will have participated on those projects that caused the changes. As a project manager, you are in a great position to assert yourself and offer your skills to work for a greater good. You can be the catalyst for change.

Almost all problems can be solved and institutionalized within three to six months.

Let's Talk: Questions & Answers

Q38.1   *In Step 1, why do you say to strive for a large percentage of the participants to be nonmanagers?*

A38.1   You need management participation and support. However, nonmanagers need to participate in the brainstorming session because they are on the ground floor across the organization—they understand many of the problems firsthand and often better than the managers. Moreover, it is important to obtain the ownership of the nonmanagers in defining and implementing change. Participation by the nonmanagers also offers an excellent opportunity for them to assert themselves and to continue to develop their leadership skills.

Q38.2   *In Step 2, you say the brainstorming session could take one to three hours. This is a lot of time to sequester these power players. Need it be that long?*

A38.2   It's not about time; it's about progress, improvement, competitiveness . . . even survival. The time invested in this meeting is minimal compared to the time invested in all the projects that will come out of the meeting. Most important, however, is the positive impact that can result for the organization in the form of improved productivity, reduced costs and time to market, improved quality and reduced rework, improved client satisfaction . . . and all those other great side benefits that can accrue from institutionalizing positive change. I would argue that an organization cannot afford *not to do this*.

> *The investment an organization makes today can pay handsomely tomorrow.*

Q38.3   *In Step 3, you say to select the top three to five problems to resolve. What if seven, eight, or more are selected? Is this a big deal?*

A38.3   Yes, it is a big deal. Resist! The more problems that are committed to be worked, the greater the hardship for an organization to find the resources, money, and time to implement. You don't want these institutionalizing projects to be viewed as a negative burden on the organization, which will undoubtedly increase the likelihood that they will be canceled. It is far better to select the top three problems and work them to a successful completion than to tackle many more and have no success stories.

Q38.4 *Three to six months to institutionalize major problems seems too short a time, especially for larger organizations.*

A38.4 My experience has shown that three months is sufficient for institutionalizing the resolution to *most* problems. Do the math and sketch out a project plan with achievable dates and you will see what I mean. Moreover, these projects are not usually full-time endeavors for most of their project members. I suggest taking up to three months longer (i.e., six months) because of the aggressive commitments the organization already has booked. We all know, when push comes to shove, these institutionalizing projects will take a back seat to commitments made to clients. I want these institutionalizing projects to have every chance to run their course and be successful.

> *Consistent incremental improvement can be the least disruptive approach, yet the most productive and successful long term.*

Q38.5 *Do I need the sponsorship of the head of the organization?*

A38.5 You conceivably could make headway without serious support from the senior manager or executive, but moving forward without that support may become a major obstacle down the road. Why? Because you likely will run into demands for the people you are trying to have work part-time on the institutionalizing projects. Thus, I strongly urge you to obtain the support from high up. Be prepared to play a lead role in making this approach work. As stated with regard to project review mentoring workshops, don't "dump and run."

Q38.6 *As a project manager, am I better off volunteering to work outside my domain of responsibility (i.e., my committed projects) and occasionally perform poorly on my projects, but do well for the organizational improvements?*

A38.6 You should never sacrifice your primary duties and commitments within your domain of responsibility. Your duties and loyalties are first to your core commitments. (See Chapter 1, Mind Your Own Business.) However, once you volunteer to move outside your domain of responsibility, you should also strive to meet your new commitments . . . because they now become part of your domain of responsibility. But be careful not to overcommit. If you do, you may be remembered more for failing than for volunteering to go beyond your domain.

Despite that warning, I applaud you for caring enough to expand your horizons and to strive to be in the minority that pushes an organization forward, rather than in the majority that maintains it at its current momentum.

PART EIGHT

Some Final Thoughts

The most successful leaders have learned to believe in their ability to make things happen—to follow their dreams and transform those dreams into reality. They draw from an inner strength that they have chosen to acknowledge is there to work for them—an inner strength that no one can take away, unless they allow it. You must believe in yourself if you expect to become and remain a consistently successful leader, and if you expect others to believe in you. In fact, belief in your own capabilities magnifies the contribution of all other attributes that make an effective and admired project leader.

 *Always bear in mind that your own resolution to succeed is more important than any one thing."*

—Abraham Lincoln, 16th President of the United States

You deserve to be what you choose to be *and* work at becoming—regardless of your age, race, sex, religion, wealth, whatever. You are what you perceive yourself to be. Your vision of yourself becomes your reality. As a leader, you must believe in your ability to get the job done, to achieve results. If people took on only those jobs where they knew all the answers and had no chance for conflict or failure, there would be little need for leaders. A successful leader knows that no one person holds the answer to every problem, but with the proper balance of time, energy, and talent, no problem escapes unsolved.

> *You are what you perceive yourself to be. Your vision of yourself becomes your reality.*

 *Do the one thing you think you cannot do. Fail at it. Try again. Do better the second time. The only people who never tumble are those who never mount the high wire. This is your moment. Own it."*

—Oprah Winfrey, American entrepreneur, philanthropist, and popular talk show host

It's almost always true that *we*, ourselves, are our own greatest obstacle to becoming what we truly want to be. If it is truly important to you, then never, never, never give up. As Henry David Thoreau, American writer, philosopher, and naturalist, said: "If one advances confidently in the direction of his dreams and endeavors to live the life he has imagined, he will meet with a success unexpected in common hours."

I believe that everyone has the capacity to be a consistently successful project manager. Everyone! Although some may be more effective than others, or rise to greater heights, this does not diminish the great opportunities for turning your vision into reality. All the attributes of a successful project manager can be learned and practiced if you choose to do so. Believe you can make a difference . . . and you will!

Now, go make a difference!

Glossary

Note: Bold terms within a definition are also defined in this glossary.

50/50 rule. The principle that an activity should be 50 percent completed when half the allotted time has elapsed, and 100 percent completed when the other half of the allotted time has expired.

accountable. Being answerable for the results of one's own acts and commitments.

action item. A project problem that is logged, assigned to an owner to resolve, and then tracked until it is closed.

approver. A person who must personally give his or her approval on an item (e.g., document, plan, action) before that item can be considered *approved*. Approvers frequently have a dependency on the item to perform their work and meet their commitments. See **reviewer**.

benevolent dictator. A leader who actively solicits information and opinions from project members and others: listens, then demonstrates the **leadership**, courage, and **boldness** to personally make the right decision, and stands **accountable** for that decision.

boldness. Demonstrated behavior that may be viewed as daring by some, but is essential to address the issue at hand effectively; doing whatever is necessary to achieve the objective, provided it is legal and ethical.

buffer. See **contingency buffer**.

client. The person, organization, or company that typically pays for and uses the product or service being developed or deployed.

complaining. Behavior of talking *at* a problem rather than constructively working to correct the problem.

completed staff work. See **due diligence**.

contingency. See **contingency buffer**.

contingency buffer. A designated period that is built into a plan to serve as extra time to help absorb delays that might occur unexpectedly; also referred to as **contingency** and **buffer**.

culture training. The formal training of all project members in key hard skills, soft skills, and processes that are essential in helping ensure a successful project; provides all project members with a common understanding of how the project will be run and the role that each team member is expected to play.

customer. See **client**.

dictator. See **benevolent dictator**.

difficult person. A person who routinely exhibits one or more of the following behaviors: hard to work with or manage; doesn't want to play by conventional social or organizational rules; is disruptive and disturbing to others.

domain of responsibility. All responsibilities and commitments that fall within the scope of a person's assignment.

due diligence. The thoughtful analysis of a problem or situation before initiating an action.

empowerment. Understanding your job, taking ownership of your job, and doing whatever is necessary (within legal and ethical parameters) to accomplish that job.

equivalently weighted tasks. Tasks requiring approximately the same level of effort.

escalation. The act of calling upon higher levels of project **leadership** or management to resolve an issue. When two affected parties are unable to agree on the resolution of an issue after a sincere attempt to negotiate a resolution has occurred, an escalation is pursued to resolve the issue.

issue. A situation that results when two parties are unable to agree on the resolution of a problem that, if left unresolved, can have a significant impact on the project.

John Wayne mentality. The mistaken belief that asking for help is a sign of weakness, but going it alone is a sign of strength and virtue.

leadership. The art of getting things done through people.

lessons learned. See **post-project review**, **post-phase review**, and **post-milestone review**.

linear 50/50 rule. An instance of the 50/50 rule depicted as a straight line representing expected accomplishment; i.e., a linear progression.

management reserve. Typically, **contingency** added to a project's schedule and/or budget to help plan for the unexpected; usually used at the discretion of the **project manager**.

meets minimum requirements. Providing the **client** with a product or service that satisfies essential, mission-critical requirements.

mentee. A person being **mentored**.

mentor. A trusted counselor whose primary objective is to help a **mentee** be more effective in a specific area of interest by helping develop the mentee's potential.

passion. An intense inner drive or feeling that compels a person to achieve a specific objective; steadfast enthusiasm and eagerness a person demonstrates in the pursuit of a cause; spirited embrace of a mission.

personal risk. Doing something that goes beyond a person's normal routine.

PERT. Formally referred to as Program Evaluation and Review Technique, a method of estimating the duration of an activity through the application of the formula $(O + P + 4L)/6$, where O is the optimistic estimate, P the pessimistic estimate, and L the most likely estimate. The formula yields a "weighted average" duration estimate.

post-milestone review. Similar to a **post-project review**, but performed at the end of major milestones that are typically spaced one to two months apart. Usually requires less time and formality than a **post-project review**.

post-phase review. Similar to a **post-project review**, but performed at the end of phases of an ongoing project. Typically performed every six months or less.

post-project review. The review of a completed project by all or a selected group of project members who represent all the major organizations that participated in the project. The group identifies what went right, what went wrong, and, optionally, where improvement can be made on future projects. The objective is to learn from past project experiences so that future projects can benefit.

professional immaturity. Behavior that is disruptive, destructive, or otherwise void of benefit in a business environment. It often manifests itself through weak personal initiative, weak **accountability**, self-absorption, and low awareness of the impact of one's own behavior.

Program Evaluation and Review Technique. See **PERT**.

project manager. The person who directs the planning and execution of a project and is held personally **accountable** for the success of the project.

project manager/resource manager leadership workshop. A technique to teach roles and responsibilities to the people holding two critical **leadership** positions within an organization: **project managers** and **resource managers**. Through the use of scenarios and role-playing in a classroom setting, project managers and resource managers learn leadership skills and how to work together for the mutual good of the organization.

project review. An independent review that is performed at specified intervals in a project to assess the health of the project. Actions are then recommended to address immediately any significant problems that are identified.

project review mentoring workshop. A technique to mentor **project managers**—and their stakeholders—from across an organization in the proper application of project management best practices. The delivery medium is conducting **project reviews** in a classroom setting where the overall health of the projects is assessed and areas of both praise and improvement are identified.

project sponsor. The person who champions the project from a business perspective and helps remove obstacles that might impede its overall success.

resource manager. The person who hires, fires, makes job assignments, coaches, counsels, evaluates, awards, promotes, and secures future work opportunities for direct reports; also called the *boss*.

review board. Typically, a board made up of three **project managers** that serves to review the actions that the project manager of a new project has taken—or plans to take—to ensure that the relevant lessons learned from the most recent **post-project reviews** have been applied appropriately to the new project.

reviewer. A person who has an interest in an item (e.g., document, plan, action) that does not necessarily impact his or her own work or commitments. The item should be made available to reviewers but can be considered *approved* without the agreement of the reviewers. See **approver**.

risk, personal. See **personal risk**.

risk value. A means of gauging the likelihood of a project achieving a designated key commitment, such as the next major milestone or the delivery date for the product being built or the service being offered. Examples of risk values are low, medium, high; green, yellow, red; and one, two, three.

S-shape curve 50/50 rule. An instance of the **50/50 rule** depicted as a curved line representing expected accomplishment, typically in the shape of a symmetrical S.

S-shape curve 50/70 rule. States that an activity should be 70 percent completed when half the allotted time has elapsed, and the remaining 30 percent of the work should be completed in the remaining 50 percent of time. The S-shape curve 50/70 rule is depicted as a curved line representing expected accomplishment in the shape of a nonsymmetrical S.

scope. The sum of the products and services to be provided as a project.[1] Scope can include elements of function (also called features), schedule, and costs; however, when reference is made to scope, it usually means the function portion of the definition.

scope creep. The change, typically expansion, of the originally committed **scope** of a project.

sufficient. In reference to **technical**, represents the level needed to yield an effective and successful outcome.

---

[1]*A Guide to the Project Management Body of Knowledge (PMBOK® Guide), 2000 Edition* (Newtown Square, PA: Project Management Institute, 2000). © 2000, Project Management Institute.

technical. The capability of a **project manager** to understand **sufficiently** the terminology, technology, and processes relevant to the product being built or the service being performed.

too soft. Behavior that results in consistently being less effective than what is otherwise possible—and needed—in carrying out responsibilities.

Index